INDIC PERSPECTIVE ON INTERNATIONAL RELATIONS

INDIC PERSPECTIVE ON INTERNATIONAL RELATIONS

Edited by

Vivek Kumar Mishra

Foreword by

Sunil Ambekar

Akhil Bharatiya Prachar Pramukh, RSS

PENTAGON PRESS LLP

First published in 2023 by

PENTAGON PRESS LLP
206, Peacock Lane, Shahpur Jat
New Delhi-110049, India
Contact: 011-64706243

Typeset in Palatino, 11 Point
Printed by Aegean Offset Printers, Greater Noida, U.P.

ISBN: 978-93-90095-56-8 (HB)

www.pentagonpress.in

Contents

Foreword

It is observed that few scholars have attempted to write on International Relations (IR) discipline from the Indic perspective or contribute to the academic discourse based on the Indic School of thought. Even the mainstream academic institutions and think tanks have made no significant efforts to evolve an indic perspective on International Relations and Strategic Studies. We do not have a clear-cut roadmap about inculcating the *Bhartiya* thought in our academia. It is a fact that when you are in a state of a free mind, you will take an independent decision. We were not free and did not enjoy autonomy in the arena of International Relations due to Western dominance. The colonial mindset in International Relations has blocked India to leave a mark on the global pitch. Western values have been predominant in the teaching and research of International Relations. After Indian independence, the Western mindset influenced the first generation leadership in India. Even our relations with other countries were guided by the same paradigm. We have not given preference to develop a sacrosanct *Bhartiya* narrative in International Relations.

It is now a challenge for us to address the undue influence of Western values in the field of International Relations and to establish an Indic perspective. Benoy Kumar Sarkar wrote an article titled *Hindu Theory of International Relations* in the *American Political Science Journal* in 1919. After that, no serious efforts were undertaken in the field of International Relations to take the discourse forward. Benoy Ji Sarkar has deliberated upon the teachings of Kautilya and Kamandaka's *Nitisara* into a re-calibration of the doctrine of *Mandala,* which he described as the "Hindu idea of Balance of Power." I have had the pleasure of reading the book titled "Nationalism" penned by Rabindranath Tagore, which elucidates that Western countries are interested in controlling larger part of the world. Gurudev Tagore has aptly articulated the lack of human values and the political role of the nation-state in the East and the West in this book. He discusses the revival of the East and its challenge to Western domination calling for a future based on tolerance, a future where tradition and modernity are balanced. Tagore's analysis of Nationalism holds much relevance in today's environment of violence and intolerance.

Many contemporary scholars have also taken up initiatives in this regard. Professor Umesh Ashok Kadam, in his work, *French-Maratha Relations: Indian in the 17 Century,* has described the relations between the French and the Marathas that were the striking features at that time and has tried to relate them with the Hindu theory of International Relations in the 17th century. Shivaji Maharaj had initiated the concept of a "naval wing of the Maratha military" for the first time in India, but these issues were never incorporated in the academic discourse. Hindu rulers such as Krishna Dev Raya of the Vijaynagar Empire, and Prataparudra Dev (Rudradev II), the last ruler of the Kakatiya dynasty of India, charted a new trajectory of bilateral relations with other empires in those hallowed ages to serve as the primary premise of the Indic perspective. Presently, we are enjoying the fruits of their efforts in International Relations specially with reference to the Act East policy and the Indo-Pacific narrative.

The rich heritage of India, one of the world's oldest civilisation, is an all-embracing confluence of religions, traditions and customs. The foundation of our secular philosophy rooted in Art, Music, Literature, Classical dance etc is not much talked about. Therefore, our cultural relations can play an important role in exploring the potential in International Relations. The Indian subcontinent, rich in culture, holds enormous potential to leverage, culture as a foreign policy tool to strengthen its relations with the South-East Asia. Through cultural diplomacy, we can foster the relationship among countries of India's interest by emphasising more upon weaving the common threads of culture. We can bolster foreign relations and community engagement to lay strong foundations of International Relations based on the idea of inclusivity, cultural exchange, and confidence-building. Ramayana is as deeply embedded in South-East Asia as it is in India. Ramayana can act as a thread connecting the two regions deep into mutual and inclusive relations, which can benefit both the region and its people to engage with each other better. People-to-people ties in terms of shared beliefs, values, and philosophy of life learnt from the epic make the firm foundation for India's look and Act East policy. India is currently reinforcing cultural diplomacy as a medium with South-East and East Asia, which shares a common belief in Buddhism and Ramayana, as evident from various architectural and cultural traditions existing in South-East and East Asia. Our cultural and civilisational relations are our Unique Selling Proposition (USP), so we have to contextualise the same while exploring our relations with other countries. If we have relations based on ancient values and civilisation, they can be more stable and enduring. For instance, India-China cultural exchanges dates back to many centuries. Evidence shows that cultural and linguistic exchanges existed between the Shang-Zhou civilisation and ancient Vedic civilisation in 1500-1000 B.C. During the first, second and third centuries A.D., several Buddhist pilgrims and scholars travelled to China through the historic "silk route". Kashyapa Matanga and Dharmaratna made the White Horse monastery at Luoyang their abode. Ancient Indian monk-scholars such as Kumarajiva, Bodhidharma and Dharmakshema contributed to the spread of Buddhism in China.

Similarly, Chinese pilgrims also undertook journeys to India, the most famous being Fa-Hien and Xuanzang. Former Prime Minister Atal Bihari Vajpayee visited Luoyang Cave in Henan Province, China, in 2003 and renovated these Buddhist sites. Luoyang is a place where Indian monks first introduced Buddhism to China.

In 2011, I also got an opportunity to visit Luoyang Cave. During my visit to the site, one Chinese family was willing to have a snap with me on a boat ride. When I asked the family members why they wanted a photograph with me, they replied that "you are from Bharat, the land of Lord Buddha, so you are important for us". In history, the India-Han Dynasty relations were based on our cultural and civilisation exchanges for many centuries. The civilisational ties would be more beneficial for designing our International Relations and security doctrine. From the geostrategic perspective, India shares 3,488 km of border with China along the states of Jammu and Kashmir, Himachal Pradesh, Sikkim, Uttarakhand etc. In addition, the border of Tibet also touches India. There are some disagreement on borders between the two countries. If we initiate a rapprochement on a cultural keel, we can avoid a military engagement with China. The same cultural bonhomie is true with other South Asian and Southeast Asian states. We have to amalgamate the soft power-related themes of the neighbours for regional peace and stability. For instance, the Yoga day celebration across the world has placed India in the limelight. The Buddhist philosophy of peace and Yogic tradition of Sadhana are central to our engagement with the world. Our cultural heritage saves us from secular hypocrisy, so we need to establish and strengthen our cultural doctrine in the context of International Relations.

In his memoir, *Dreams from My Father* (1995), US President Barrack Obama wrote about his bi-racial identity by tracing the lives of his deceased father and extended family in Kenya. He travelled to Kenya and highlighted his cultural roots in memory of his father. This only underscores the growing importance of indigeneous culture at the global level.

The Arabic numerals in China are called Indian Arabic numerals, which speak volumes about the diversity and tradition of acceptance of Bharat. Musical instruments like the *Tabla* and the *Sitar* are emblematic of Central Asia's cultural lore. To make India a *Vishva Guru*, Indians have to play on the cultural pitch.

The Indian Diaspora has played an important role in promoting India's interests abroad and acting as its unofficial civilisational ambassadors. This is more so in the fields of culture, education, economic development, health and arts etc. Above all, the Diaspora has played an important role by investing in the Indian industry and infrastructure to encourage its economic growth. In addition, the NRIs/ PIOs have enormously supported India in the form of "Resurgent India Bonds" during the economic sanctions imposed by the United States of America and other Western states just after the Pokhran nuclear test in 1998.

Our graduates from IIT, IIM, and other centres of excellence institute who are working abroad must know our culture and rich heritage. These graduates may face questions about our culture in foreign lands. How Sanskrit symbols be incorproated intellectually and recontextualise Indian civilisational heritage in Artificial Intelligence? what are the similarities between AI techniques and Sanskrit grammar? As NASA claims that Sanskrit - the ancient Hindu language - is the most suitable language to develop computer programming for their Artificial Intelligence program, these are the natural queries for people of Indian origin. Therefore, we have to teach Indic values to our youths and prepare them to learn the fundamentals of our culture and rich heritage. We must remember the facets that delve into the notion of cultural artefacts. Due to the general public's increasing concern about ethical issues in business, many organisations have tried to address problems problems by institutionalising ethics. Family and cultural values play an important role in business activities, even in the appointment of CEOs in the corporate world.

India has started applying its strategic theoretical principles in International Relations. An example was the Doklam crisis of 2017 when China applied the Sun Tzu strategy based on *The Art of War*. According to SunTzu doctrine, "the clever combatant looks to the effect of combined shi...the shi (or energy) developed by good fighting men is as the momentum of a round stone rolled down a mountain thousands of feet in height." Therefore, the best scenario for China was winning without fighting in Doklam. This strategy is based on the assumption that a war can be won without actually going into battle, and we have also developed our counter-strategy and applied it. That is why we gave the best response to China in Doklam - with a tit for tat approach.

I firmly believe that we have started to incorporate Indic values in the field of International Relations, and this book will be a milestone in providing a non-Western paradigm to the academic discipline. India's foreign policy is developing upon the idiom rooted in our civilisational values which needs to be cherished and nurtured.

Sunil Ambekar
Akhil Bharatiya Prachar Pramukh, RSS

Preface

Emerged as a distinct academic discipline in the aftermath of the World War II, International Relations (IR) remains a Western-dominated enterprise. Whether it is the foundational narratives or the philosophical and normative underpinnings or the theories and concepts developed to study world politics—all of this reveals that the discipline is profoundly Western-centric. The growing discontent with its exclusion of non-western experiences, ideas, values and agency has led many critical scholars to call for de-centering the West and broadening the discipline so as to make it a truly global field of study. While the process of building an inclusive post-Western IR has seen the introduction of diverse perspectives and approaches put forward by scholars from China, Japan, Turkey, Islamic world and Latin America, Indian vision of 'international' is markedly absent. Reflective of this, scholarly efforts in the recent years have been focused on integrating Indian voice into either Global South perspective or a re-defined Global IR, thereby denying autonomous space to an indigenous Indian alternative.

The absence of a systematic and cohesive Indian IR comparable to the English School or the Chinese School is generally attributed to the lack of interest in theory-oriented studies as majority of the Indian scholars prefer empirically rich and policy-relevant descriptive analysis. But those who engage IR theories, concepts and methods show little interest in exploring alternative optics for theorization drawing on the philosophical ideas and intellectual tradition unique to the geo-cultural space, historically known as *indikē* or Indic. They, on the contrary, maintain a theoretical position, which is dismissive of the very idea of creating an Indian or Indic School of IR on the grounds that any such project carries with it the risk of 'lapsing into uncritical nativism or seeking some essentialist "Indian" vision.'[1] Besides, many of them are also skeptical about the academic value of ancient Indian texts including the *Vedas*, the *Upanishads*, the *Ramayana*, the *Mahabharata*, the *Bhagavad Gita* and other related literature, which, according to them, do not fall under the category of 'canonical texts.' They seem unaware of the fact that several of such canonical texts shaping the IR discipline are either the product of the imperial encounters or interstate rivalries of Europe.

Take, for example, the path-breaking work of Hugo Grotius, a Dutch jurist on freedom of the seas and the norms of just war, which continue to inform theories of international legal order, emerged in the historical context of the Dutch struggles against the Spanish and the Portuguese over their share of colonial trade in Africa and Asia during the 17th century Europe. As pointed out by an analyst, 'During the early phase of Dutch hegemony, Grotius built on the right of booty, unilateral appropriation, self-defense, and retribution to develop specific rules that protected Dutch interests and encouraged Christians to engage in mutually beneficial relationships. In his writings, he demonstrated his inclination for inter-European accommodation and dialogue, which would benefit the Netherlands as an emerging power.'[2] Similarly, the notion of anarchy, which Kenneth Waltz uses to describe the state system in his canonical work on the nature of world politics, according to postcolonial critics, has been appropriated from 'European accounts of encounters with indigenous peoples.' The ancient Indian texts, in contrast, defy space and time, and its meaning and message is meant for the humankind in its entirety, not confined to any particular community, sect or nation. It is, therefore, academically prudent not to pre-judge these iconic works and that too by Western standards, which endorse or condone the violent exclusion of the other.

Unfortunately, it is because of their training in Western educational institutions that the sceptics have difficulty in appreciating the ancient Indic traditions, its autochthonic philosophical systems and above all, the vast Sanskrit literature from the *Vedas* to the *Mahabharata*, Buddhist and Jain literature and the *Puranas* as a valuable source of IR knowledge. In the words of a critic, they are 'social science socialised products of American graduate schools that cannot be anything other than what they have been taught.'[3] This, arguably, explains why they continue to rely on the theoretical wisdom flowing from a 'British-American intellectual condominium' based on which they treat the Indic geo-cultural space like any other in the Global South regardless of its distinctive ways of seeing and knowing the world. Underlying this standpoint is the proclivity to deny a distinct non-Western Indian perspective to emerge, which the sceptics view as a nativist enterprise and monolithic conception of IR. Locating the Indian variant in a broader framework of post-Western IR, however, entails the risk of compromising its originality, notably its philosophical base drawn on the principle of *Ekam Sat, Viprah Bahuda Vadanti* (Truth is one, but sages speak of it by many names), its cosmopolitan vision as reflected in *Sarve Bhavantu Sukhinah Sarve Santu Nairaamaya* (May all be happy, all be free from disease) and above all, historicity of a 'civilizational state'.

Underlining how the Indic is 'differently different' (different from the West and within the non-West), Benoy Kumar Sarkar, one of India's early leading political theorists in his book titled *The Beginning of Hindu Culture as World Power*, which was published in 1916, argues, 'Hindustan had never been shunted off from the main-track of universal culture. To come to India in the age of Guptas was to imbibe the internationalism of the atmosphere.' In a similar vein, he has brought to the focus the 'longstanding tradition of Hindu speculation on the subject of international relations' in his 1919 article titled 'Hindu Theory of International Relations' in the *American Political Science Review*. Commenting on his contributions to the IR discipline, a reviewer writes, 'Sarkar's work was rich with references to the 'western' canon — ideas that he encountered in his time in the United States and Europe. But his scholarship was far from a simple process of emulation. Through the global intellectual encounters that his travels fostered he offered an 'epistemic' challenge to 'western' knowledge of international affairs.'[4]

While Sarkar in his pioneering work has highlighted what he calls the 'world-sense' of ancient Indian rulers and thinkers, Amitav Acharya of American University among the contemporary IR scholars has underlined the need for utilising India's spiritual knowledge and ancient texts including Hindu epic *Mahabharata* as the rewarding source of IR concepts and theories. Likewise, Amrita Narliker and Aruna Narliker in a fascinating study titled *Bargaining with a Rising India: Lessons from the Mahabharata* have traced the cultural roots of Indian negotiating strategy to the anecdotes from the *Mahabharata*, whereas Deepsikha Shahi and Gennaro Ascione in a scholarly article have evoked the concept of *Advaita*, an ancient Indian philosophy as an epistemological-methodological tool to formulate post-Western IR theory.[5] Several such studies in the past years have reinforced the belief that the Indic perspective has the potential for auto-developing into a viable alternative to the Western Westphalian IR. Implicit in this is also the rejection of a syncretic Global IR approach, which is premised on the specious argument that 'Eurocentrism is indispensable but inadequate.'

Even though the Global IR project remains stuck in the critique-stage, the 'social science socialised' Indian IR scholars persist with their efforts towards fashioning a post-Western IR while discouraging academic engagement in the development of an indigenous Indic perspective to understand and explain world politics. Their disproportionate influence in the Indian IR community has predictably undermined the process of scholarly exploration for the Indian ways of knowing the 'international' despite the analytical spaces of enquiry created by the disciplinary crisis of the IR and more so, by the ascendant power status of India. Against this backdrop, the book represents an attempt to reinvigorate the Indian vision of world politics under the rubric of Indic perspective on IR by bringing in a variety of theoretical ideas drawn on its philosophical insights, interpretation of ancient texts, historical experiences and rich spiritual heritage.

The introduction chapter of the book presents an overview of the disciplinary crisis of the IR since the latter half of the 1980s over the epistemological and methodological issues, which has resulted in its fragmentation without a 'theoretical centre, or even a core problematique.' The crisis has its origins in the postpositivist challenge to the dominant mainstream IR theory, realism, liberalism and their neo-neo synthesis. Comprising a diverse range of theoretical perspectives and approaches, including critical theory, poststructuralism, postmodernism and feminism, postpositivism rejected the value-neutral and empirically validated scientific knowledge claims of the mainstream IR. In the face of the de-constructivist challenge to positivist epistemological consensus, the latter dismissed the postpositivist work as irrelevant to the discipline.

The divided discipline with two theoretical camps has led some critics to wonder if this marks the end of International Relations theory or the IR itself.

Although non-western voices do not figure in an essentially Western-centric IR debate, the disciplinary crisis has created intellectual thinking space for the Indian IR community to reflect over the possibilities of developing alternative perspective on world politics, drawing on the country's unique philosophical traditions, spiritual knowledge and cultural practices. Accordingly, the concluding section of the chapter provides the layout of the proposed Indic School of IR comprising three inter-related components: historical, philosophical and axiological. While the historical component represents the 'resource base' of the Indic School in terms of identifying and collecting related literature including ancient texts, its philosophical underpinnings define the analytical framework designed to understand and explain the global political puzzle, and finally, its knowledge claims guided by the idea of 'One Self is in all beings; every *Jivatma* (creature) is a portion, or reflection, of the One Self' underline the normative dimension of the research programme.

In the first chapter, Praveen Kumar attempts to explain the concept of power in India's strategic culture, which consists of physical and spiritual dimensions. The power in its spiritual dimension operates in the realm of 'reality that requires transcending sensual perceptions.' This enables humans to attain higher values and capabilities than what can be achieved in the temporal world through physical means. The physical and spiritual dimensions of power are related and interdependent. However, in either respect, the Indian conception of power is not directed against 'fellow humans' to forcefully dominate 'the other' and depriving the latter of their ability to act. On the contrary, power is more of an enabler of an act than a 'restrainer'. The power in this sense would also mean that it is something that is permanent and universal. The manifestation of power is in the form of an action, which is more concerned with the performance of duties than with the enjoyment of power for power's sake. Power in its physical dimension operates in the lower realm but is eventually absorbed and undertaken by the higher form, its spiritual dimension. Thus, power is more a means than an end in itself, and its manifestation can be realised in what makes other nations/cultures gravitate towards it than to be fearfully submissive before physical strength alone.

The second chapter begins by highlighting the general lack of interest among Indian IR scholars in analysing and exploring the Indic world's strategic dimensions. Then it goes on to explain the contemporary relevance of the strategic culture and grand strategy in Valmiki Ramayana. While Kautilya's *Arthashastra* has emerged as the focal point in the theorisation of an Indic perspective on strategic issues, the strategic dimension of *Valmiki Ramayana* has not drawn much scholarly attention. In this chapter, Anoop Kumar Gupta argues that strategic reading of the Ramayana could be another landmark in the evolution of an Indic perspective on strategic cultures and international relations. His analysis reveals two paradigms of strategic culture in Ramayana: strategic culture of Rama and strategic culture of Ravana. The kaleidoscopic view of strategic thought and strategic preferences of Rama and Ravana demonstrate a different world view regarding the core values, the concept of the adversary, nature of power and above all, the war strategy. The fundamental difference between Rama and that of Ravana in terms of their respective strategic vision and strategic preference resides in their different core values. Whereas Rama's core value, for instance, lies in spiritual non-dualistic ideas, the core values of Ravana are materialistic. The fascinating study of strategic culture in Ramayana, doubtless, would provide useful insights into building an Indic perspective on strategic thinking as well as the theorisation of contemporary world politics.

In the third chapter, Vivek Kumar Mishra analyses how the Indic Values of Shanti and Shakti are embedded in Modi's Pakistan Policy. Prime Minister Modi has made a difference to India's traditional Pakistan policy with his activism, effective operational diplomacy and visualisation of a strong state and border policy. Modi's Pakistan policy can be best described as a unique combination of the *Shanti* (Peace) and *Shakti* (Power) paradigm drawn on Indian cultural values. Put differently, the analysis is premised the basic proposition that "peace with Pakistan could only be achieved by demonstrating strength (power) in the changing security environment." Chapter four examines Modi Doctrine and Public Diplomacy in the context of what Manan Dwivedi calls 'Singularity of the India-United States Bilaterals.' The kernel of Dwivedi's argument is that the context of media-generated hype and the much-needed constructs of nationalism and patriotic themes do not militate against the conjoined theme of public diplomacy with the USA. The chapter brings to the focus the efficacy of a distinct style of public diplomacy of Prime Minister Modi in terms of resolving bilateral issues and maximizing the country's influence abroad.

In the following chapter Abhishek Srivastava highlights the cultural continuum in India's policy under Prime Minister Modi with countries located in different regions. As argued by Srivastava and rightly so, the foreign policy of India does not exist in a cultural vacuum, it is a continuation of certain values and philosophical traditions that India has imbibed over the centuries, in the form of works such as the *Dharmashastras*, *Vedanta*, the Mahabharata, Ramayana, the Arthashastra and the syncretic tradition of India and religious values implicit in Buddhism, Jainism and Hinduism. All this constitutes the country's enduring cultural capital, which Prime Minister Modi has so effectively utilized in projecting India's image abroad as *Vishwa Guru*.

In the chapter six, Shounak Set reviews international relations in ancient India based on Kautilya's thinking, which dates back to nearly 2,500 years ago. His *magnum opus*, the Arthashastra, praised by many for its breadth, examines a wide array of topics ranging from fiscal policy at one end of the spectrum to public administration at the other and even deals with gender relations. In view of the space constraints, this chapter is exclusively devoted to an analysis of Kautilya's ideas about International Relations and its contemporary relevance. Works from classical antiquity like the *Arthashastra* merit scrutiny not merely for their profound philosophical insights transcending the confines of space and time but also because they can provide a cognitive tool for analysing the present and anticipating the future. Thus, the commentary aims to clarify his extraordinary originality and transcendental universality and distil its potential significance in terms of contemporary applicability.

Chapter seven explains liberal-idealist tradition in the non-Western World based on the case study of *Ubuntu* (Africa). Ideational inadequacy and connected operational inefficacy of the West-dominated world order has evoked renewed interest in ancient cultural ethos originating in the non-Western regions. The pre-colonial idea of *Ubuntu* carries a revealing legacy in the pursuit of humanism in Africa, which has been subjected to the century-long process of domination and brutality unleashed by external forces, more specifically the Western powers. Resurging Africa has started re-engaging with the external world, opening up the scope for stressing its cultural connectivity with other non-Western civilisational entities for their active engagement in the idea-shaping exercises of global affairs on humane terms. In this chapter, Sandipani Dash examines liberal idealism as an analytical construct emanating from the Western world and seeks to contextualize the liberal idealist tradition in the regions beyond the West.

In chapter eight, Jajati K. Pattnaik discusses the Bangladesh-China-India-Myanmar (BCIM) sub-regional cooperation and strategies for India's northeast. Growth and development in neighbouring countries based on shared partnership constitute the basic thrust of a sub-regional cooperation. The borders that were earlier treated as barriers for cross-country development became catalysts for cross-country collaboration/ cooperation models. It became a new mode of interaction that entailed de-territorialised economic cooperation and free trade architecture, thus making the spatial domain of territory secondary in the contemporary political economy of international relations. Aware of the region's tremendous potentialities and the geo-economic importance of Northeast India, decision-makers in New Delhi view the latter as an important link between the East and South East Asia in an era of increasing regional and global cooperation. Against this backdrop, the Look East Policy (LEP) has envisioned Northeast India not as the periphery, but the centre of a blooming and inclusive economic space that can link two vibrant regions with multiple networks interweaving the entire region.

Closely related to Pattnaik's analysis of BCIM is Sourabh Jyoti Sharma's attempt to assess the role of soft power in India's 'Look East' policy in chapter nine. As pointed out by Sharma, Southeast Asia and India are civilisational natural allies, and their cultural links date back thousands of years, perhaps even well into the prehistoric period. However, ideological differences precluded close political ties from developing after India's independence from the British in 1947 and throughout most of the Cold War period. The chapter concludes by underlining the need for utilizing India's ancient cultural heritage to translate her foreign policy's 'core objectives' into realities, notably effective containment of an 'aggrandising' China based on a 'countering without confronting' strategy in Southeast Asia. While Sharma's analysis is more of prescriptive, meaning what Indian needs to do in terms of its soft power deployment in Southeast Asia, the following chapter by Chau Khahn Tam is evaluative, focusing on the efficacy of India's soft power diplomacy globally and Vietnam in particular.

Vietnam, a country in South East Asia, has been influenced by India's soft power as ties between the two countries go back to the ancient Cham civilisation when people from Odisa travelled to Vietnam and spread the language, culture and ethos to this country. Moreover, Indian soft power imprints are visible in Vietnam in cultural terms following the spread of Buddhism across the country with Mahayana's dominance in the north and Theravada schools in Vietnam-Cambodia border. All the same, what is important to remember is that the basis of soft power is the logic of appropriateness, which defines the acceptable criteria for assessing the impact of the power-holder on the targeted country. The discussion in the last two chapters by Arvind Kumar Singh and Amit Kumar respectively is focused on Buddhist Heritage as the tool of India's soft power diplomacy in the projection of her image as a *Vishwa Guru* to guide the world and in reinforcing the identity of Buryats in Russia. While Arvind Kumar's chapter explains the instrumental function of Buddhism in preserving the distinct identity of the Buryats, Amit Kumar brings to the fore the significance of Buddhist traits of humility, gentleness, justice, and charity in international relations.

In all, barring a few chapters on India's foreign policy practices and projection of the country's image as a non-coercive, benign global power, the rest of this edited volume is about developing the Indic narrative on international relations. Some of the chapters related to the broad theme are descriptive while others, analytical and interpretative but together they represent a work in progress.

Dr. Vivek Kumar Mishra
Prof. Aswini K. Mohapatra

NOTES

1. Kanti Bajpai (2005), "International Relations in India: Bringing Theory (back) Home" in Kanti Bajpai and Siddharth Mallavarapu, eds., *International Relations in India: Brining Theory Back Home*, New Delhi: Orient Longman, p. 31.
2. Siba Grovogui (1996), *Sovereigns, Quasi-Sovereigns, and Africans: Race and Self-Determination in International* Law, Minneapolis: University of Minnesota Press, p. 61.
3. Donald Puchala (1998), "Third World thinking and contemporary International Relations", in S. G. Neuman, ed., *International Relations Theory and the Third World*, London: Macmillan, p. 139.
4. Martin J. Bayly (November 2017), 'The Forgotten History of Indian International Relations', *ORF Issue Brief*, Issue No, 210, p. 3.
5. Deepsikha Shahi and Gennaro Ascione (2016), 'Rethinking the Absence of Post-Western International Relations Theory in India: 'Advaitic Monism' as an Alternative Epistemological Resources', *European Journal of International Relations*, vol. 22, no, 2, pp. 313-334.

Notes on Contributors

Prof. Aswini K. Mohapatra is Professor and former Dean of the School of International Studies (SIS), JNU, New Delhi.

Dr. Vivek Kumar Mishra is PhD from JNU, New Delhi and Assistant Professor and former Head of the Department, Political Science and International Relations, Gautam Buddha University, Greater Noida, UP.

Dr. Praveen Kumar is PhD from JNU and Associate Professor, Department of Political Studies, Central University of South Bihar, Gaya, Bihar.

Dr. Anoop Kumar Gupta is PhD from JNU and visiting researcher at the Hebrew University of Jerusalem, Israel. He is a prolific writer on India's Foreign Policy and National Security.

Dr. Manan Dwivedi is PhD from JNU, and Assistant Professor (International Relations and American Affairs), Indian Institute of Public Administration, New Delhi.

Dr. Abhishek Srivastava is PhD from JNU, New Delhi and Assistant Professor, Diplomacy and Disarmament Division, School of International Studies, Jawaharlal Nehru University, New Delhi.

Shounak Set is a Marie Sklodowska-Curie Global India Research Fellow at King's College London, specialising in Foreign Policy Analysis and Strategic Studies.

Dr. Sandipani Dash is PhD from JNU and Assistant Professor, Department of African Studies, Faculty of Social Sciences, University of Delhi.

Dr. Jajati K. Pattnaik is an Associate Professor at the Centre for West Asian Studies, School of International Studies, Jawaharlal Nehru University, New Delhi.

Dr. Arvind Kumar Singh is Director, International Affairs & Assistant Professor at the School of Buddhist Studies and Civilization, Gautam Buddha University, Greater Noida, UP India.

Mr. Sourabh Jyoti Sharma is an Assistant Professor, Department of Political Science, D K, College, Guwahati University, Assam.

Mr. Chau Khahn Tam is a Lecturer, University of Social Sciences and Humanities, Vietnam National University, Ho Chi Minh City, Vietnam. He studied Indology at the University of Social Sciences and Humanities, Ho Chi Minh City, Vietnam.

Dr Amit Kumar is PhD from the Centre for Russian and Central Asian Studies, SIS, Jawaharlal Nehru University, New Delhi.

Acknowledgements

This book is the outcome of the two-day National Seminar on *Indic Perspective on International Relations*, which was organised by the Centre for the Studies of International Relations (CSIR) in February 2019 at Gautam Buddha University, Greater Noida. My heartfelt appreciation goes to the dedicated CSIR team of IR scholars for the successful Seminar and their valuable contributions to this volume. I am deeply indebted to Sri Sunil Ji Ambekar, social activist & All India Prachar Pramukh, RSS, who is the perennial source of inspiration for me. I am grateful to him for his insightful foreword to the volume. I am thankful to Mr. Anand Srivastava, Joint Zonal Organisation Secretary (ABVP), North Zone, for his unstinted support. I express my deep gratitude to Sri Prafulla Ketkar, editor of the Organiser Weekly and Prof. V.K. Malhotra, Member Secretary, ICSSR, New Delhi, for their constant encouragement and support.

I would like to extend my special note of appreciation to Prof. Aswini K. Mohapatra, SIS JNU, Dr. Rajiv Nayan, Senior Research Associate at Manohar Parrikar Institute for Defence Studies and Analyses (MP-IDSA), New Delhi, for their valuable and constructive suggestions during the planning and development of this work. In addition, I take this opportunity to express my sincere thanks to Dr. Uttam Sinha, Prof. Satish Kumar, Dr. Himansu Bosh, Dr. Nalin Kumar Mohapatra, Dr. Amit Kumar, Dr. Manan Dwivedi, Dr. Abhishek Srivastava, Dr. Charu Ratna Dubey, Mrs. Aayushi Ketkar, Sri Nitin Sharma, for their academic and moral support.

I also express my sincere thanks to Mr Rajan Arya of the Pentagon Press LLP for his patience and support.

Above all my parents and my wife Jyoti Mishra and son Aarav & Anay is beyond my expression of gratitude.

Vivek Kumar Mishra

Introduction

Disciplinary Crisis of IR and Indic School Alternative

Aswini K Mohapatra

International Relations (IR) emerged as a separate academic discipline in the aftermath of the World War II[1] and ever since, it has been dominated by the West in terms of its genealogy, methodology, epistemology as well as axiology. So much so that the discipline was peddled as 'an American Social Science'[2] until the recent shift in the gravity of global politics away from the West to the non-western ascendant powers. However, just as the hegemonic decline of the U.S. and plurality of actors vying for geopolitical primacy have spawned a spell of uncertainty and fluidity that characterizes the contemporary world politics, so the diversity of theories, approaches and alternatives have landed the IR discipline in a state of disarray. While some scholars talk of 'de-centering the West' and 'post-Western IR' by introducing non-western perspectives into the discipline, others argue for the Global-South perspective, and still few others opt for the 'Global IR'.

The roots of the current disciplinary crisis lie in what is described in IR literature as the 'third debate' in the 1980s between positivist/ rationalist orthodoxy and postpositivist reflexivity.[3] The former represents the foundational epistemology of the mainstream IR theories, namely realism and liberalism, which view International Relations as a social science discipline to be modeled on physical sciences. What flows from this viewpoint is a belief that 'the social world is amenable to the same kinds of analysis as those applicable to the natural world.'[4] Hence, methodologies applied in the natural sciences can be used in IR to provide scientific credentials to its knowledge claims about complex global politics.[5] Postpositivism encompassing a diverse range of theoretical perspectives and approaches, including critical theory, poststructuralism, post-modernism and feminism, have not only rejected this simplistic philosophy of science but also called into question the mainstream theorists' role as gatekeepers by using their parameters to prevent alternative knowledge claims from being examined.

Post-Positivist Challenge

In a standard IR textbook, the 'third debate' is presented as an 'inter-paradigm debate' involving realism, pluralism/liberalism and Marxism/structuralism over three competing paradigms: state-centric, multi-centric and global-centric.[6] While the traditional IR scholars have portrayed the 'inter-paradigm debate' as a way-forward in terms of discipline defining as compared to the two previous debates -idealism versus realism and realism versus behaviouralism-, critics find it an 'artificially constructed debate, mainly invented for specific presentational purposes.'[7] What subsequently weakened this inter–paradigm debate was the merger of the two supposedly 'incommensurable paradigms',[8] realism and liberalism, into a 'dominant neo-neo synthesis'.[9] As neo-realism and neo-liberalism joined together in the latter half of the 1980s to represent what Robert Keohane labels the 'rationalistic research programme',[10] the focus of 'third debate' shifted to the question of epistemology and methodology between rationalists and reflectivists.[11] The term 'reflective' was used by Keohane in reference to those scholars opposing the mainstream IR research programme characterized by positivist methodology and empiricist epistemology. The label 'reflectivist' used by Keohane was later changed to 'reflexivist' because reflexivity is intimately related to meta-theory (questions about the theory of theory and the mode of theorising), the central thrust of the postpositivist challenge.

It is, however, worth mentioning that post-positivism in itself does not constitute a theory in the academic field. It indicates the philosophical/theoretical or methodological position of a diverse group of scholars, including those either inspired by the Frankfurt School, most notably Jurgen Habermas or French postmodernism or those linked to social constructivism and feminism. Frankfurt School Critical Theory, for example, aims to recast rather than abandon the 18th century Enlightenment Project of rationality and science.[12] While post-modernism rejects the Enlightenment legacy, poststructuralism is neither directed against nor in support of it. The latter, instead, considers the Enlightenment version of modernity as an ongoing project open to scrutiny and contestation.[13] Likewise, postmodernism rejects any unified, integrated theory and believes in 'everything is permitted' and 'anything goes', whereas post-structuralism describes itself as an 'approach' that sees theory as practice, and underlines the importance of representation.[14]

Feminism questions the masculine assumptions of the emancipatory project of the Frankfurt School Critical Theory even though both of them are part of the Enlightenment tradition. So does social constructivism, which represents the 'middle ground' between positivism and post-positivism as it retains state-centric assumptions of realism and fact/value distinction while attaching importance to norms, ideas and inter-subjective meanings.[15] Despite the differences over nuances and truth claims what the variants of critical theory have in common is a rejection of the positivistic scholarship in the mainstream IR theory. As aptly put by Smith, "they are not united by what they agree on but by what they oppose."[16]

The core of the debate is the value-neutral and empirically validated scientific knowledge claims of the dominant IR theories, which the postpositivists, especially Frankfurt School Critical Theorists, have categorised as 'problem-solving theories.' Problem-solving theory, according to them, has system maintenance biases as it 'takes the world as it finds it and investigates only to manipulate it in order to achieve their pre-given ends.'[17] In other words, knowledge derived from problem-solving theory cannot be value-neutral because it 'does not question the present order, but has the effect of legitimizing and reifying it.'[18] The fact that theory is shaped by power relations has led Robert Cox to conclude, "theory is always for someone, and for some purpose."[19] Further, problem-solving theory employs positivist methods to explain international politics in terms of continuities of war and great-power rivalry while ignoring transformative possibilities in the name of parsimony. In challenging the positivist mainstream IR, the Frankfurt School Critical Theorists, notably Mark Hoffman and Andrew Linklater, have argued for the normatively oriented transformation of global politics so as to achieve a higher level of human freedom. Inspired by Habermas' 'emancipatory project', which promises a viable alternative to the status-quo oriented social science, they have placed the moral and ethical concerns at the centre of the IR theory.[20]

Unlike the Frankfurt School, the primary focus of other critical theories is on the practices and taken for granted assumptions about the international reality, namely the sovereign claims of the state and assertion about the systemic anarchy. For the postmodernists who stress that 'the reality is in a perpetual state of flux',[21] these 'core ontological givens' on which the mainstream IR theories rest account for the exclusionary practices by separating nations, classes, genders and races.[22] Postmodernists thus protest against the social and intellectual closure created by specific boundaries, which define 'what is inside and what lies outside' both in the case of the nation-state as well as the IR discipline itself.[23] Although the poststructuralist critique of traditional IR theories follows the 'deconstruction strategy'[24] based on the relationship between language and reality, it broadly concurs with postmodernism that all identities, including the sovereign state and the excluded others are 'effects of the operation of power and materialised through discourse.'[25] On similar grounds, feminism has challenged the gendered foundations of the positivist mainstream IR.[26] Since the majority of IR scholars engaged in theorising are men, the feminists question the positivist assumption of an unidentified and detached knowing subject (knower) and insist on allowing 'us (women) to become answerable for what we see."[27]

In all, the postpositivist critique of the mainstream IR theory postulates that 'meaning and understanding are not intrinsic to the world but, on the contrary, are continuously constructed, defended, and challenged.'[28] The 'third debate' eventually opened up the field to reflexivist approaches, which saw an unusual surge as reflected in the research and publications related to the IR theories in the wake of the end of the Cold War and failure of the dominant rationalist/positivist theories in predicting the collapse of the former Communist Super-power. Overly optimistic about the discipline's critical turn, Mark

Hoffman observed, 'unlike the 1950s and 1960s when Realism reigned supreme---it is now easier to say what International Relations is not than what it is.'[29]

In the following decades, however, the IR debate turned into an epistemological war with the rationalists led by Robert Keohane refusing to accord legitimacy to the postpositivists/reflectivists on the grounds that they do not share the commitment to the empiricist standards in their research agendas and fail to develop 'testable theories' without which 'it will be impossible to evaluate their research programme.'[30] Until they delineate such a research programme, Keohane admonished, 'they will remain on the margins of the field, largely invisible to the preponderance of empirical researchers, most of whom explicitly or implicitly accept one or another version of rationalistic premises.'[31] Like Keohane, other prominent mainstream IR theorists either raised concerns about the multiplications of theoretical perspectives and risk of 'paralytic relativism'[32] or castigated the critical approaches, particularly postmodernism for offering 'nothing in the form of alternatives'[33] save building castles in the air and criticising the 'mainstream paradigms.'[34]

The reflectivists, on their part, have contended that it is unfair to judge them using parameters set by the mainstream rationalists, given the epistemological position within which they operate is distinctly different. As noted, the rationalists are interested in parsimonious explanatory theory based on empiricism, falsification reasoning and 'correspondence theory of truth'.[35] The postpositivists/reflectivists, in contrast, 'question the value of facts and the meaning of objectivity for social inquiry'[36] and believe in the linguistic construction of reality. For some postpositivists, subjects and objects of reality are 'sociolinguistically constructed' and 'nothing exists outside of discourse.'[37] More important, positivists believe in the 'mind-world dualism', implying that there exists an objective social world 'out there' independent of or detached from the observer/researcher',[38] which is rejected by the postpositivists/reflectivists. For the latter, the subject (observer) and object (social world) construct each other, giving rise to what Steve Smith calls 'constitutive theory.'[39]

In view of the above fundamental differences over construction of reality and what constitutes knowledge, it is safe to argue that the dismissal of the reflectivist work as irrelevant to the discipline has more to do with the mainstream IR's concerns about sustaining the positivist epistemological consensus in the face of the de-constructivist challenge than any academically justifiable or intellectually tenable grounds. Even though some IR scholars have gone beyond the theoretical impasse by exploring the middle ground compromise position,[40] their efforts have so far yielded precious little. This is partly because of rationalists 'unwillingness to engage in any scholarly debate with the reflectivists and in greater part, their insistence on methodological monism, meaning acceptance of their (positivist) version of the scientific method. As a result, the discipline remains fragmented and pluralistic without a 'theoretical centre, or even a core problematique',[41] which has led some critics to wonder if this marks the end of International Relations theory or the IR itself.[42]

The purpose of presenting an overview of the 'third debate' involving the mainstream positivists and the postpositivist critics is twofold: firstly, to highlight the seemingly irreconcilable differences between the two theoretical camps in the divided discipline and secondly, to underline the fallout of the disciplinary crisis in terms of providing intellectual thinking space for the Indian IR scholars to reflect over the possibilities of developing alternative perspective drawn upon the country's unique philosophical traditions, historical experiences, spiritual heritage and cultural practices.

Western-centric/Eurocentric IR

Much like the previous IR debates, the positivist-postpositivist conversation is western-centric in its entirety. Whether it is the context in which the inter-paradigm debate turned into an epistemological duel or in the formation of the two opposing 'academic gangs'[43] or the issue of methodological pluralism over which they claim to differ, the non-western voices and experiences do not feature at all. Barring some discreet references in the critical theory inside/outside relationship framework, the non-western practices, traditions, historical struggles and above all, non-western thinkers find no mention either in the positivist position or in the postpositivist critique. The reason for this western-centric omission lies in a 'deeply rooted, almost subconscious tendency to deny very legitimacy and worth' of non-western values and ideas.[44]

While the rationalists/positivists invoke Thucydides, Hobbes, Machiavelli, Bodin, Grotius and Kant in support of their realist or liberal international theory, the reflexivists/postpositivists have turned to the critical European thinkers, notably Marx, Gramsci, Horkheimer, Habermas, Foucault, Derrida, Laclau and Mouffe to justify their opposition to the mainstream IR. Just as the rationalists locate IR's heritage in classical European thought, so do various strands of critical theory trace their origins to the crisis in the post-Enlightenment Western thought. Reflective of the common philosophical background, both sides concur that the Enlightenment was no less than the liberation/emancipation of humankind. In the words of Brown, 'Dare to know, and the truth will set you (us) free; this is the essential claim of the Enlightenment, and the desire for rational autonomy has inspired radical, progressive, left thought for two centuries – whether in the guise of liberalism, Marxism or social democracy; it has been an essential feature of the changes which have created modernity.'[45]

Modernity is thus the product of a process of the West's self-definition born out of 'dialogue with its own past'[46] and has little to do with the non-west. In other words, Western modernity is particular in itself but paraded as 'the universal point of reference in relation to which others recognise themselves as particularities.'[47] It is the universality claim of its particular historical experience that has made the West, particularly Europe, the target of postcolonial critique. Although a relatively new approach to the study of IR, postcolonialism aims to expose the Eurocentric construction of the world by explaining the 'relationship between Western representation and knowledge on the one hand and Western material and political power on the other.'[48]

Apart from contesting the Eurocentric IR based on a 'mythical, imaginary Europe'[49] and dichotomous representation of west and east, postcolonialism also attempts to investigate the contemporary relations of dominance and subordination in the light of the 'lingering colonial hierarchies of race, class and gender despite the winding down of the formal colonial period.'[50] With its focus on great power politics and security, the traditional IR theory 'naturalises these hierarchies and thus reproduces the status quo', whereas postcolonial studies offer a different standpoint to 'explore these concerns in international relations.'[51] The postcolonial approach to IR, however, suffers from inherent contradictions. The objects of study (i.e. imperialism and hierarchy) may differ from the mainstream IR, but its de-constructivist approach reflects the extent to which it is influenced by the Eurocentric perspectives and practices.[52] And this, arguably, explains why it has restricted itself only to critiquing Eurocentrism embedded in the discipline and chosen not to 'foster a non-western IR.'[53]

Unlike postcolonialism, which fairly fits into the postpositivist critical IR category, the English School, popularly known for its 'international society of states' approach, maintains equidistance from both rationalists/positivists as well as reflexivists/postpositivists. It posits a theoretical framework that goes beyond the binary oppositions and combines elements of realism, such as the primacy of the state, role of great powers and inter-state conflicts with the idea of international society based on shared norms, rules and institutions.[54]

The pluralistic model of the English School, according to its proponents, offers a coherent and advantageous method in 'understanding and explaining the world from a perspective which does stray from realism, but does not reject the primacy or necessity of the state in global affairs.'[55] Despite its growing popularity among IR scholars in recent years, the English School has come under increasing criticism for its Eurocentric bias. While some critics find its core claims about the centrality of the society of states to the contemporary world 'badly flawed',[56] others have called into question the 'founding myths of the English School' concerning the origins and expansion of international society. In this respect, the global diffusion of the English model of society has been described as 'coercive diffusion' on the grounds that the European state system spread across the world largely 'by defeating, subjugating, forming and deforming the societies and polities with which it came into contact.'[57]

Dependency-Structured Discipline

The above discussion of Eurocentrism reveals that the IR discipline is anything but international. If the standard account of the disciplinary history, tracing its origins to the 1648 Peace of Westphalia, the progenitor of modern nation-state sovereignty and highlighting a continuous tradition stretching from classical Athens to the present, reflects its parochial and ethnocentric features,[58] then its focus on great power politics ignoring the destructive consequences of proxy wars and intra-state conflicts in the periphery has rendered the discipline narrow and insular. The omission of the non-western voices is the product of Western world's dismissal of difference and non-recognition of agency of the 'other'. What is more, reasons for non-west's systematic absences reside in the Eurocentric assumption that non-European peoples are incapable of 'self-generation or auto-development' and they will develop only by following the 'naturalized Western path', which is reified as 'universal'.[59]

As a result, the IR has turned into a dependency-structured academic field wherein knowledge flows from the centre represented by a 'British-American intellectual condominium'[60] to the non-western peripheries. In the peripheries, there are many consumers and emulators of theories, concepts and methods produced by a few at the centre. In this entrenched hierarchical division of labour, the centre relies on the area studies specialists in the peripheries for scholarly materials to be filtered and cast in the western theoretical mould suiting to its policy requirements and universality of its knowledge claims. Regardless of whether the concepts and theories are relevant to the peripheries or not, they continue to import theoretical wisdom from the centre. It is, in brief, the asymmetric pattern of production and consumption that has reinforced the privileged status of the West and the intellectual marginality of the rest.

The channels through which the western concepts and theories travel to the periphery include textbooks, sponsored scholarships, and grants to non-western individuals and institutions. Equally important is the role played by the non-western scholars who receive training in Western educational institutions. In the words of Donald Puchala, they are 'social science socialised products of American graduate schools' that cannot be anything other than what they have been taught.'[61] Enamoured of the western ontology, many of them turn into first rate copycats as much in terms of 'unthinking emulators' as their ingrained aversion to the traditional knowledge system and cultural heritage of the country to which they originally belong. No wonder, it is these 'social science socialised' non-western IR scholars who unabashedly embrace the hegemonic practices and raise doubts over academic salience of ancient Indian texts like the *Vedas*, the *Upanishads*, the *Ramayana*, the *Mahabharata* and the *Bhagavad Gita*. Conversely, the persistence of the hierarchical mode of knowledge production and dissemination together with the proclivity of non-western scholars in the peripheries towards emulation or adaptation of the imported paradigms to local contexts account for 'poor connect' between the IR textbooks prescribed for students in Global South and ground realities.[62]

Unfortunately, scholarly efforts of the past few years to overcome the dependency structure of the discipline and the Western ways of knowing IR have not yielded desired results. As a recent study suggests, 'western dominance remains widespread, relying on implicit and mostly unquestioned knowledge (doxa) that presumes the superiority of Western degree programmes, journals, research methods, conceptual frameworks and even individual scholars.'[63] Those who called out the 'centredness' of IR and endeavoured to 'decenter IR from its Northern/Western anchors'[64] have offered no tangible alternatives except promoting conceptual frameworks rooted in the Global South.[65] So do the Global IR enthusiasts whose ambitious project of broadening the Western-centric IR to include the non-western representations with 'a commitment to pluralistic universalism'[66] is 'stuck in the critique-stage' due to the lack of agreement on how to proceed.[67]

It is in the wider context of disciplinary fragmentation and uncertainty surrounding its future that the Indic School of IR as a research programme is proposed in an attempt to provide an alternative framework premised on the notion of universality in contrast to the Western rationality and the Chinese theory of 'relationality.'[68] The latter was proposed by Yaqing Qin, founder of the Chinese School of IR, to understand world politics different from Western perspective, which is based on the assumption that actions of states are guided by rational calculations of self-interest. However, the explanatory weight of the Chinese theory of relationality needs to be assessed in conjunction with three other traditional Chinese concepts of Under-Heaven (*tianxia*), Great Harmony (*datong*), and the Kingly Way (*wangda*). If the Chinese style of multilateralism, especially in the Indo-Pacific region, is anything to go by,[69] it seems the concept of *tianxia* is used less as a relational norm than an instrument to legitimize a hierarchical tributary system with China at the Centre.[70]

Indic School of IR

The term 'Indic', after which the proposed IR School is named, refers to a geo-cultural space located in the east of the Indus River (originally the Sindhu). 'Greeks as early as Herodotus described it as '*indikç* (*chôrç*), an Indian place or land', while the Chinese Buddhist pilgrim Xuanzang (603–664) named it *Indu* and the Arabs called it *Al-Hind*.[71] In so far as the underlying ideas of the School are concerned, it is inspired by the philosophical insights, historical experiences, rich spiritual heritage and the unique intellectual traditions of the land, which 'the ancient Sanskrit geographies described it as a "Clime of the Bharatas" (*Bharatavarsha*).'[72] It relies on diverse sources, including the vast Sanskrit literature from the Vedas to the Mahabharata, Buddhist, Jain literature, the Puranas, post-Sangam literature, notably Tiruvalluvar's *Tirukkural*, as well as other 'regional languages and dialects of the subcontinent, most of which have older literary traditions than the languages of Europe such as English.'[73]

Drawing on a combination of the Rishi tradition of the land as well as philosophy of modern teachers like Sri Aurobindo and Swami Vivekananda, the Indic School of IR aims to develop a research tradition in many respects different from its Western counterpart. One of its prime objectives is to discontinue the practice of drawing historical parallel (for example, the idea of Kautilya being an Indian Machiavelli) and identifying similarities so as to justify the applicability of the Western paradigms or theories. Put differently, while the proposed IR School is not averse to engagement with the West, it considers adoption of western concepts and categories to fit the local setting as what Bhabha calls 'mimicry'.[74] Based on a set of core assumptions about the nature of world politics and the global visions informed by the 'Indic episteme',[75] it seeks to present a coherent and integrated framework comprising three inter-related components: historical, philosophical and axiological.

While the historical component represents the 'material base' of the Indic School in terms of identifying and collecting the related literature and sources for the purpose of 'thick description' and foundational narrative, its philosophical/epistemological underpinnings define the analytical framework designed to understand and explain the global political puzzle. Lastly, its cosmopolitan vision of *Vasudhaiva Kutumbakam* (the world is one family), and its knowledge claims guided by the principle of *Ekam Sat, Viprah Bahuda Vadanti* (Truth is one, but sages speak of it by many names) reflect the normative predispositions of the research programme.

Historical Context

Prof. Benoy Kumar Sarkar was the first Indian political theorist who drawing on multiple ancient texts, including Kautilya's *Arthashastra* and Kamandaka's *Nitisara*, brought to the fore 'the longstanding tradition of Hindu speculation on the subject of international relations.'[76] While his article titled 'Hindu Theory of International Relations' published in August 1919 in the reputed *American Political Science Review* drew scholarly attention to the Hindu idea of 'balance of power', the book titled *The Beginning of Hindu Culture as World Power* he had published three years prior to the article was the first-ever attempt to trace the Indian origins of the IR discipline. It begins by contesting the colonial narratives that portray Hindus of the fourth, fifth and sixth centuries living in 'splendid isolation' and then goes on to explain how 'internationalisation of Hindus' is reflected in 'the world of Kalidasa's poetry, which 'includes the whole of India and also the Indian borderland and Persia.'[77]

"If we exclude the Assyrian, Egyptian and Persian Monarchies of ancient times", Sarkar has argued, "the Maurya Empire of the Hindus (B.C. 321–B.C. 185) was, chronologically speaking, the first Empire in world's history, and that, internationally speaking, it occupied the first rank in the contemporary state-system." Similarly, the celebrated Empire of the Guptas (A.D. 330-606), according to Sarkar, was the 'First Power of the world' at a time when there was anarchy in China and Europe was immersed in her 'Dark Ages'.[78] 'Monarchs of Samudragupta-type', he further states, 'who may be compared easily with a Charlemagne, a Frederick or a Peter the Great, have flourished in India almost every second generation. Hindu folk-lore has known them as *Vikramadityas* and has invested their names with the halo of Arthurian romance.'[79]

In highlighting ancient India's cultural and commercial relations with the outside world, Sarkar maintains, 'it was the Indianism of Kalidasa's age' with which the Chinese Apostle Fa-Hien came in contact that led to the spread of Hindu culture in China and later in Japan.[80] Based on many such historical facts identified by him, Sarkar avers, 'Hindustan had never been shunted off from the main-track of universal culture. To come to India in the age of Guptas was to imbibe the internationalism of the atmosphere.'[81] Supporting Sarkar's contention, Western scholars have acknowledged that cultural practices and products from the Indic geo-cultural space spread far and wide in the first millennium, creating the 'quasi-global formation' in Southeast Asia.[82] As Sheldon Pollock writes, 'The story of how this formation arose—how Sanskrit traveled the vast distance it did and came to be used for literary and political texts, and what such texts meant to the worlds of power in which they were produced—has never been told in the historical detail it merits.'[83] Pollock has described this formation as 'Sanskrit Cosmopolis', which, he argues, 'recapitulated the geography of India' but was not created by any Indian military conquest in Asia.[84]

Philosophical Foundation

A brief overview of what Sarkar labels the 'world-sense' of ancient Indian rulers and thinkers helps define the context of the academic field but what would shape the future trajectory of the Indic School research programme is the spirit and outlook of Indian philosophy. 'Indian philosophy, including Indian logic, is a home-grown product, created by the natural genius of the people and capable of historical treatment', says Mahadev Rajaram Bodas in the edited volume titled *Tarka Samgraha of Annambhatta*, which was published in 1930.[85] Refuting the Western claims that there was 'importation of Greek philosophical ideas into India at some ancient time', Rajaram Bodas argues, 'It is tolerably indigenous and self-consistent, and that it does not need the supposition of a foreign influence to explain any portion of it.'[86] Indian systems of philosophy, he added, 'were gradually evolved out of a few broad principles by a succession of writers and under particular circumstances.'[87] This is similar to the position taken by Max Muller, who held that the 'Greek and Indian philosophies were autochthonic'[88] and neither of them borrowed their thoughts from the other. In the same vein, Betty Heimann, a German Indologist has observed, 'the significant fact that India has remained unchanged and uniform throughout all historic times, and that she has preserved her own consistent outlook in all her philosophical systems, however diverse these may seem.'[89]

As mentioned by Betty, Indian philosophy is made up of as many as nine systems including the *Nyaya System*, the *Vaisesika System*, the *Sankhya System*, the *Yoga System* the *Mimamsa System* and the *Vedanta/ Advaita System*.[90] While they differ over the questions related to epistemology and methodology, certain fundamental presuppositions are common to all these systems. Thus, 'the basic conception of *Karma*, of reincarnation and liberation, is recognized by all Indian thinkers without exception.'[91] From the Indic IR point of view, a diverse range of philosophical systems widens the scope of choices for scholars for developing theoretical assumptions and theory-oriented scholarship. In this connection, it is worth noting that four separate acts of knowing as identified by the great sage Gautama in the *Nyaya System* of philosophy, namely perception, inference, analogy and *Sabda* (statement of an authoritative person or text) aptly fit into the list of five different epistemological positions prepared by the Western scholars.[92]

Axiological/Normative Dimension

Axiology refers to the theory of value, and focuses on the question of what ought to be rather than what is. Just as it is ignored by the philosophy of science, which generally deals with epistemology and logic,[93] so has the mainstream IR theory neglected moral responsibility and ethical standards with the dominance of realism. For realists, as Steve Smith has pointed out, 'the international political sphere is one of necessity, regularity and danger, wholly unsuitable for the moral philosopher.'[94] While several IR scholars subscribe to the Weberian line of argument that 'scientific knowledge produces a rational, not an axiological obligation',[95] others consider it central to their 'cognitive endeavour and scholarly ethos as knowledge-producers and social agents.'[96] Writing on the eve of the US war on Iraq in March 2003, Steve

Smith, in an article, highlighted 'explicitly the relationship between academic study and ethics.' He forcefully argued that "there can be no such thing as a value-free, non-normative social science. I do not see any possibility (or desirability) of separating ethics from academic study."[97]

The ongoing debate within the Social Sciences in general and IR discipline in particular underlines the saliency of the axiological dimension of the Indic School, which is greatly influenced by the idea of ethical science embedded in the culture of the land. As defined by Sanatani scholars, ethical science refers to 'a definite and systematically arranged series of facts of conduct in their proper relations to each other and of the underlying principles of these relations. Another word for Ethics is morality, right conduct, and in order to know what is right, we have to understand something about the man and his surroundings.'[98] In brief, the Sanatani idea of ethical science is founded on the belief that the 'One Self is in all beings; every Jivatma (creature) is a portion, or reflection, of the One Self.'[99] What flow from this are the two complementary ideas of universality and acceptance of diversity. The latter is central to the land of seekers, and not believers where diversity is celebrated, unlike the Western practice of dismissal of differences and silencing or erasing of alternative perspectives.

The idea of universality represents its philosophical core encapsulated in *Aham Brahmasmi*, which explains the unity of macrocosm and microcosm. Reflective of this, the eminent historian Arnold Toynbee predicted in 1952, "India, the conquered will conquer the conquerors—The catholic-minded Indian religious spirit is the way of salvation for all religions in an age in which we have to learn to live as a single-family if we are not to destroy ourselves."[100] In any case, the knowledge tradition associated with the Indic space is not the monopoly of the people living in this part of the world; its meaning and message are universal and have the same resonance for all transcending sectarian as well as territorial boundaries.

The Indic School, therefore, aims to pool academic resources and involve like-minded IR scholars from across the world, similar to the way the English School of International Relations has evolved over the past decades. To conclude, the Indic School of IR is, doubtless, a work in progress, but it has the potential of what Hobson calls 'pioneering agency'[101] capable of auto-developing into a sustainable and widely acceptable alternative in the IR academic field, providing secure epistemological grounds amid the disciplinary crisis and fragmentation.

NOTES

1. Western scholars claim that the IR emerged as a distinct discipline in 1919 following the establishment of the first department and chair of international relations at the University of Wales in Aberystwyth by a local industrialist David Davies. The discipline to be studied then was, however, less of 'international' than the European interstate system. Tracing the origins of the discipline to the post-World War I Europe with the prime objective of preventing war is a part of the Eurocentric meta-narratives to 'celebrate the west as the highest normative referent in world politics'. John Hobson (2012), *The Eurocentric Concepts of World Politics: Western Political Theory*, London: Routledge, p. 15.
2. Stanley Hoffmann (1987), "An American Social Science: International Relations" in Stanley Hoffmann, ed., *Janus and Minerva: Essays in the Theory and Practice of International Politics*, Boulder, CO: Westview Press, pp. 3–24. The article was first published in *Daedalus* (Summer 1977), vol. 106, no. 3, pp. 41-60.
3. Reflexivity is different from being reflective. While researchers reflect on their data and make judgments about them, reflexivity takes this process a step further by examining the researcher's own beliefs, political opinions and other biases that could have an impact on the study's outcome. The term reflexivity in IR scholarship is "either generically and minimally construed as a form of self-awareness of one's own scholarly 'perspective,' or conceptualized in a more maximalist way as a methodological self-critique operating through an epistemic or theoretical bending back of one's thought". Inanna Hamati-Ataya (2013), "Reflectivity, Reflexivity, Reflexivism: IR's 'Reflexive Turn' – and beyond", *European Journal of International* Relations, vol. 19, no. 4, p. 675.
4. Steve Smith (October 2000), "The Discipline of International Relations: Still An American Social Science?", *British Journal of Politics and International Relations*, vol. 2, no. 3, p. 383.
5. There is considerable confusion among IR scholars as regards the usage of the term 'positivism'. While some characterize it as epistemology, others see it as a methodological position tied to an empiricist epistemology, which grounds knowledge claims about the reality on observation and experience. Empiricist epistemology, however, restricts knowledge by ignoring 'unobservable' such as the international structure, and describing experience independently of its interpretation. An alternative to empiricist epistemology is *rationalism*, which posits that knowledge of the world can be gained by using reason to interpret what we observe and experience. Steve Smith (1996), "Positivism and Beyond" in Steve Smith, Ken Booth K and M Zalewski, eds., *International Theory: Positivism and Beyond*. Cambridge: Cambridge University Press, pp. 11-44; Colin Wight (2013), "Philosophy of Social Science and International Relations" in Walter Carsnae,

Thomas Risse and Beth A Simmons, eds., *Handbook of International Relations*, London: Sage Publication Ltd, pp. 29-56.

6. Michael Banks (1985), "The Inter-Paradigm Debate" in Margot Light and A.J.R. Groom, eds., *International Relations; A Handbook of Current Theory*, London: Pinter Publishers, pp. 7-25.
7. Ole Waever (1996), "The Rise and Fall of the Inter-Paradigm Debate" in Smith et al., *Positivism and Beyond.*, p. 161. According to Waever, a combination of 'discipline history' (the attacks on realism being in complicit in political and moral disaster) and 'discipline external' (Vietnam War and student revolt in the U.S.) created a situation in which the discipline avoided its complete disintegration 'through the holding operation of the inter-paradigm debate', p. 158.
8. They are incommensurable because the two competing schools of thought are the two different views of the same world based on incompatible assumptions. In any case, the concept of paradigm borrowed from Thomas Kuhn's Philosophy of Science to designate three IR approaches is misleading since Kuhn's theory was never meant for application in the social sciences but only meant for natural sciences. Steve Smith (1995), "The Self-Image of a Discipline: A Genealogy of International Relations Theory" in Ken Booth and Steve Smith, eds., *International Relations Theory Today*, Cambridge: Polity Press, pp. 20-22.
9. Waever (1996), "The Rise and Fall of the Inter-Paradigm Debate" pp. 163-64. The main areas of difference between neo-realism and neo-liberalism include the effects of the anarchic international system, absolute versus relative gains, role of institutions in mitigating anarchy and prospects for international cooperation. These issue-based disagreements, however, do not matter so much given their ontological similarities as both the approaches essentially see the same world of international politics involving states as primary actors and egoistic value maximisers. David Baldwin (1993) *Neorealism and Neoliberalism: The Contemporary Debate*. New York: Columbia University Press, pp. 4-8; Smith, "The Discipline of International Relations", pp. 381-382.
10. Robert Keohane (1989), *International Institutions and State Power: Essays in International Relations Theory*, Boulder, CO: Westview, p. 161.
11. Yosef Lapid (1989), "The Third Debate: On the Prospects of International Theory in a Post-positivist Era", *International Studies Quarterly*, vol. 33, no. 3, pp. 235-254; Milja Kurki and Collin Wight, "International Relations and Social Science" in Tim Dunne, Milja Kurki and Steve Smith, eds., *International Relations Theories: Discipline and Diversity*, Oxford University Press, pp. 21-33.
12. The capital C and T is used to distinguish the Frankfurt School from the generic notion of critical theories that includes approaches critical of the legacy of Enlightenment or the project of modernity. The Enlightenment Project and meta-narratives it generated about the liberation of humanity by virtue of reason and scientific knowledge came under sustained attacks in the 19th and 20 the century Europe for bringing de-humanisation. As Habermas's theory of 'communicative action' suggests, the intent of the Frankfurt School Critical Theory is to reconsider the progressive aspects of the Enlightenment rather than abandoning its ideals. Other critical theories, notably post-modernism, however, do not share the view

that such reconsideration is required. Chris Brown (1994), "Critical Theory and Postmodernism in International Relations" in A.J.R. Groom and Margot Light eds., *Contemporary International Relations: A Guide to Theory*, London: Pinter Publisher, pp. 58-60.

13. Richard Devetak (1995), "The Project of Modernity and International Relations Theory", *Millennium: Journal of International Studies*, vol. 24, no. 1, pp. 28-51.
14. David Campbell (2013), "Poststructuralism" in Dunne, Kurki and Smith, eds., *International Relations Theories*, pp. 223-246; James Williams (2005), *Understanding Poststructuralism*, Chesham: Acumen Publishing Limited, pp. 1-24.
15. The notable social constructivists include Nicholas Onuf, Friedrich Kratochwil and Alexander Wendt who see the world as a construction and investigate the manner in which the construction has been achieved and possibilities of reconstruction within it. Although Wendt argues that ideas matter in IR as reflected in his famous statement, 'anarchy is what states make of it', reflectivists treat his work as closer to the rationalist mainstream because it shares methodological and epistemological assumptions with the neo-liberal institutionalism. See Smith, "The Discipline of International Relations', pp. 390-39; Alexander Wendt (1999), *Social Theory of International Politics*, Cambridge: Cambridge University Press.
16. Smith (1995), "The Self-Image of a Discipline", p. 26.
17. Richard Shapcott (2008), "Critical Theory" in Christian Reus-Smit and Duncan Snidal, eds., *The Oxford Handbook of International Relations*, Oxford University Press, p. 329.
18. Robert Cox (1981), "Social Forces, States, and World Order: Beyond International Theory, *Millennium*, vol. 10, no. 2, p. 128.
19. Ibid.
20. Inspired by the Frankfurt School founder, Max Horkheimer's use of critical reason in pursuit of emancipation or good society where individuals can realise their potential for autonomy, Habermas explored relationship between knowledge and human interests. Accordingly, he has identified three 'knowledge-constitutive interests': empirical-analytical sciences for prediction and control; historical hermeneutic sciences for understanding inter-subjective nature of social life; critically oriented sciences (Critical Theory) for emancipation and achievement of rational autonomy. Mark Hoffman (1987), "Critical Theory and Inter-Paradigm Debate", *Millennium: Journal of International Studies*, vol. 16, no. 2, pp. 231 – 249; Steven C. Roach (2008), *Critical Theory and International Relations: A Reader*, London: Routledge; Andrew Linklater (1992), "The Question of the Next Stage in International Relations Theory: A Critical-Theoretical Point of View", *Millennium: Journal of International Studies*, vol. 21, no. 1, pp. 77-98.
21. Jim George (1994), *Discourses of Global Politics: A Critical (Re)Introduction to International Relations*, Boulder, Colorado: Lynne Rienner Publishers, p. 29.
22. Anthony Burke (2010), "Postmodernism" in Reus-Smit and Snidal, eds., *The Oxford Handbook of International Relations*, pp. 359 -377.
23. Richard Ashley and R.B. J. Walker (1990), "Reading Dissidence/Writing the Discipline: Crisis and the Question of Sovereignty in International Politics", *International Studies Quarterly*, vol. 34, no. 3, pp. 367-416; R.B. J. Walker (1993),

Inside/Outside: International Relations as Political Theory, Cambridge: Cambridge University Press.

24. Deconstruction or decentering strategy is associated with the French philosopher Jacques Derrida who argues that identities are produced by reasoning in the inside/outside binary and it is the inferior/derivative 'outside' that is central to the constitution of the privileged/original 'inside'. Drawn on Derrida's logo-centric procedure of identity formation in binary oppositions, other poststructuralist scholars, notably Ernesto Laclau and Chantal Mouffe have later developed Poststructuralist Discourse Theory (PDT). This is based on the premise that all objects and actions are meaningful with the meaning being conferred by a system of differences. For an interesting discussion of PDT, see Thorsten Wojczewski (2018), *India's Foreign Policy Discourse and Its Conceptions of World Order*, London: Routledge, Chapt. 2; for Derrida's deconstructive reading, see David R. Howarth (2013), *Poststructuralism and After: Structure, Subjectivity and Power*, London: Palgrave Macmillan, pp. 38-54.
25. Campbell (2013), "Poststructuralism", p. 243. Discourse refers to a series of representations and practices through which meanings are produced and identities constituted. This concept is based on the belief that language is central to constitution of social life. Michel Foucault's works related to genealogy of knowledge show how power is implicated in knowledge systems and discourses as embodying social power. Michele Barrett (1992), *Politics of Truth: From Marx to Foucault*, Cambridge: Polity Press, pp. 124-155; Joseph Rouse (2005), 'Power/Knowledge' in Gary Gutting, *The Cambridge Companion to Foucault*, Cambridge: Cambridge University Press, pp. 92-113.
26. Marysia Zalewski (1993), "Feminist Theory and International Relations," in Mike Bowker and Robin Brown (eds.), *From Cold War to Collapse: Theory and World Politics in the 1980s*. Cambridge: Cambridge University Press, pp. 115-143; J. Ann Tickner (2014), "Gender in World Politics" in John Baylis, Steve Smith and Patricia Owens, eds., *The Globalization of World Politics: An Introduction to International Relations*, Oxford: Oxford University Press, pp. 264-278.
27. Annick T.R. Wibben (23 June 2017), "Look Who's Talking" in The Third Debate 25 Years Later: An International Studies Quarterly Online Symposium, pp. 12-13, https://dataverse.harvard.edu/dataset.xhtml?persistentId=doi:10.7910/DVN/P1IBFS.
28. Lapid, "The Third Debate", p. 242.
29. Hoffman, "Critical Theory and Inter-Paradigm Debate", p. 231. For a review of the contributions of critical theory to the discipline, see Nicholas Rengger and Ben Thirkell -White (2007), "Still Critical After All These Years? The Past, Present and Future of Critical Theory in International Relations", *Review of International Studies*, vol. 33, pp. 3-24.
30. Keohane (1989), *International Institutions and State Power*, p. 174.
31. Ibid., 173.
32. Fed Halliday (1995), "International Relations and Its Discontents", *International Affairs*, vol. 71, no. 4, p. 739; Fred Halliday (1996), "The Future of International Relations: Fears and Hopes" in Smith, Booth Zalewski, eds., *International Theory:*

Positivism and Beyond, pp. 318-327.

33. Kalevi Holsti (2016), *Kalevi Holsti: A Pioneer in International Theory, Foreign Policy Analysis, History of International Order and Security Studies*, Springer International Publishing: A G Switzerland, p. 23.
34. Stephen Walt (Spring 1998), "International Relations: One World, Many Theories", *Foreign Policy*, vol. 110, p. 34; See Randall L. Schweller (January 1999), "Fantasy Theory", *Review of International Studies*, vol. 25, no. 1, pp. 147-150.
35. Correspondence theory of truth refers to determining whether the facts of the world in an observer's statements true or false depending on their correspondence/ conformation to external reality.
36. Campbell, "Poststructuralism", p. 228.
37. Heikki Patomaki and Colin Wight (2000), "After Postpositivism? The Promises of Critical Realism", *International Studies Quarterly*, vol. 44, pp. 216-217.
38. Jackson has identified two opposing positions on the relationship between the researcher (the knower) and his/her study object (the known): *mind-world dualism* and *mind-world monism*. In the latter, the knower's subjective viewpoints and experiences are contiguous with the world he/she studies. In this case, it does not matter much whether there is or is not an objective reality 'out there', as its validation as such is inaccessible to us. Patrick Thaddeus Jackson (2011), *The Conduct of Inquiry in International Relations: Philosophy of Science and its Implications for the Study of World Politics*, Abingdon/New York: Routledge, pp. 35-36.
39. Martin Hollis and Steve Smith (1990), *Explaining and Understanding International Relations*, Oxford: Clarendon Press, pp. 1-7.
40. Kurki has, for instance, suggested that there is the need for broadening and deepening of the Humean conception of causation to overcome the disciplinarian division in IR, whereas Sil and Kazenstein have argued for *analytic eclecticism* as an alternative way of thinking about the relationship among cluster of analysis normally formulated in separate paradigms. See MiljaKurki (2006), "Causes of Divided Discipline: Rethinking the Concept of Cause in International Relations", *Review of International Studies*, vol. 32, pp. 189-216; Rudra Sil and Peter Kazenstein (2010), *Beyond Paradigms: Analytic Eclecticism in the Study of World Politics*, Basingstoke: Palgrave Macmillan.
41. Colin Wight (2019), "Bringing the Outside In: The Limits of Theoretical Fragmentation and Pluralism in IR Theory", *Politics*, vol. 39, no. 1, p. 78.
42. Tim Dunne, Lene Hansen and Colin Wight (2013), "The End of International Theory?", *European Journal of International Politics*, vo. 19, no. 3, pp. 405-425; Martin Giffiths and Terry O' Callaghan (2001), "The End of International Relations?" in Robert M.A. Crawford and Darryl S.L. Jarvis, eds., *International Relations - Still An American Social Science? Toward Diversity in International Thought*, Albany: State University of New York, pp. 187-201.
43. T J Scheff (1995) "Academic Gangs", *Crime, Law and Social Change*, vol. 23, no. 2, pp. 157-162.
44. Branwen G. Jones (2006), ed., *Decolonising International Relations*, Rowman & Littlefield, p. 12.
45. Brown, 'Critical Theory and Postmodernism', p. 57.

46. Roxanne L. Euben (Spring 2002), "Contingent Borders, Syncretic Perspectives: Globalization, Political Theory, and Islamizing Knowledge", *International Studies Review*, vol. 4, no. 1, p. 46.
47. Mike Featherstone (1990), ed., *Global Culture: Nationalism, Globalization, and Modernity*, London: Sage Publications, p. 12.
48. B. Moore-Gilbert (1997), *Postcolonial Theory: Contexts, Practices, Policies*, London: Verso, p. 34.
49. "Europe, like 'the West', writes Chakrabarty, "is demonstrably an imaginary entity, but the demonstration as such does not lessen its appeal or power." Dipesh Chakrabarty (2000), *Provincializing Europe: Postcolonial Thought and Historical Difference*, Princeton, NJ: Princeton University Press, p. 43.
50. Christine Sylvester (2014), "Post-Colonialism" in Baylis, Smith and Owens, *The Globalization of World Politics*, p. 145.
51. Geeta Chowdhry and Sbeila Nair (2002), eds., *Power, Postcolonialism and International Relations*, London: Routledge, p. 1.
52. Postcolonial scholars have, in fact, acknowledged their intellectual debt to the poststructuralism and postmodernism, and claimed that their study would assist the critical IR literature related to the politics surrounding global hierarchy. See Chowdhry and Nair, *Power, Postcolonialism*, pp. 25-27.
53. Sanjay Seth (2013), ed., *Post-Colonial Theory and International Relations: A Critical Introduction*, London: Routledge, p. 2.
54. Interestingly, the English school thinking rests on a triad of concepts comprising Hobbesian Realism, Grotian Rationalism and Kantian Revolutionism. It is argued that these three distinct spheres are at play in international politics. Barry Buzan (2001), "The English School: An Underexploited Resource in IR," *Review of International Studies*, vol. 27, no. 3, p. 473-474. For a historical account of the English School, see Tim Dunne (1998), *Inventing International Society: A History of the English School*, Houndmills: Palgrave.
55. Robert W. Murray (2013), ed., *System, Society and the World: Exploring the English School of International Relations*, Bristol: e-International Relations, p. 10.
56. Edward Keene (2004), *Beyond the Anarchical Society: Grotius, Colonialism and Order in World Politics*, Cambridge: Cambridge University Press, p. xii.
57. Fred Halliday (2009), "The Middle East and Conceptions of International Society" in Barry Buzan and Ana Gonzalez-Pelaez, eds., *International Society and the Middle East: English School Theory at the Regional Level*, New York: Palgrave Macmillan, p.18.
58. For the IR's foundational narrative, see Brian C. Schmidt (2013), "On the History and Historiography of IR" in Carsnae, Risse and Simmons, eds., *Handbook of International Relations*, pp. 4-11.
59. Hobson, *The Eurocentric Concepts of World Politics*, p. 6.
60. K.J. Holsti (1985), *The Dividing Discipline: Hegemony and Diversity in International Theory*, Boston, MA: Allen & Unwin, p. 103.
61. Donald Puchala (1998), "Third World thinking and contemporary International Relations", in S.G. Neuman, ed., *International Relations Theory and the Third World*, London: Macmillan, p. 139 cited in Pinar Bilgin (2008), "Thinking past 'Western'

IR?", *Third World Quarterly*, vol. 29, no.1, p. 12.

62. Navnita C Behera (2016), "Knowledge Production", *International Studies Review*, vol. 18, no. 1, pp. 153–155.
63. Beverley Loke and Catherine Owen (December 2021), "Mapping practices and Spatiality in IR knowledge Production: From Detachment to Emancipation", *European Journal of International Relations*, p. 5.
64. Meghana Nayak and Eric Selbin (2010), *Decentering International Relations*, London: Zed Books, p. 4.
65. See Arlene B. Tickner and Karen Smith (2020), eds., *International Relations from the Global South Worlds of Difference*, London: Routledge, 2020, pp. 1-15; L. H.M. Ling (2013), "Worlds Beyond Westphalia: Daoist Dialectics and the 'China Threat'", *Review of International Studies*, vol. 39, no. 3, pp. 549–568.
66. Amitav Acharya (2016), "Advancing Global IR: Challenges, Contentions, and Contribution", *International Studies Review*, vol. 18, pp. 4-5; Amitav Acharya and Barry Buzan B (2010), "Why is there no Non-Western International Relations Theory? An Introduction" in A Acharya and B Buzan, eds., *Non-Western International Relations Theory: Perspectives On and Beyond Asia*, New York: Routledge, pp. 1–25.
67. Maiken Gelardi (December 2020), "Moving Global IR Forward: A Road Ahead", *International Studies Review*, Vol. 22, no. 4, p. 830. Other such tricky issues raised by critics as regards the Global IR agenda include the developing and testing local theories, importance of problematising 'Global' and the idea of pluralist universalism. See Felix Anderi and Antonia Witt (2020), "Problematising the Global in Global IR", *Millennium Journal of International Studies*, vol. 49, no. 1, pp. 32-57.
68. See Acharya, "Advancing Global IR", p. 6; Hun Joon Kim (2016), "Will IR Theory with Chinese Characteristics be a Powerful Alternative?", *The Chinese Journal of International Politics*, vol. 9, no. 1, pp. 59 -79.
69. Aswini K Mohapatra (2 February 2021), "Asian Voice: An Unsustainable RCEP", *The Straits Times*, Singapore.
70. For See Zhao Tingyang (2005), *The Under-Heaven System: The Philosophy for the World Institution* cited in Willam A. Callahan (2013), *China Dreams: 20 Visions of the Future*, New York: Oxford University Press, pp. 52-53.
71. Sheldon Pollock and Benjamin Elman (2018), *What China and India Once Were*, New York: Columbia University Press, p. 6.
72. Ibid.
73. David Frawley (2011), *Hinduism and the Clash of Civilizations*, New Delhi: Voice of India, p. 128.
74. Homi K Bhabha (1994), *The Location of Culture*, London: Routledge.
75. A French philosophical term, 'episteme' has been variously defined by the Western scholars that need to be further explicated in the Indic geo-cultural context.
76. Martin J. Bayly (Summer 2017), "Imagining New Worlds: Forging Non-Western International Relations in Late Colonial India", *British Academy Review*", no. 30, p. 50.
77. Benoy Kumar Sarkar (1916), *The Beginning of Hindu Culture as World Power*,

Shanghai : The Commercial Press, p. 6.

78. Ibid., p. 1.
79. Ibid., p. 2.
80. Ibid., p. 5.
81. Ibid., p. 8.
82. Sheldon Pollock (2006), *The Language of the Gods in the World of Men: Sanskrit, Culture, and Power,* Berkeley: University of California Press, p. 11.
83. Ibid.
84. Sheldon Pollock (1996), "The Sanskrit Cosmopolis, 300–1300: Transculturation, Vernacularization, and the Question of Ideology" in Jan E.M. Houben, ed., *Ideology and Status of Sanskrit,* Leiden: E.J. Brill, p. 15.
85. Yashwant Vasudev Athalye and Mahadev Rajaram Bodas (1930), *Tarka Samgraha of Annambhatta,* Pune Bhandarkar Institute Press, Bhandarkar Oriental Research Institute Press, pp. IX-X.
86. Ibid., p. X.
87. Ibid., p. X.
88. Ibid., p. IX.
89. Betty Heimann (1937), *Indian and Western Philosophy: A Study in Contrast,* London: George Allen & Unwin Ltd., p. 47.
90. Satishchandra Chatterjee and Dhirendramohan Datta (2007), *An Introduction to Indian Philosophy,* New Delhi: Rupa Publications, pp. 26 -50. I am also thankful to my esteemed colleague and an eminent Sanskrit scholar, Prof. Rajneesh Mishra, Centre for Indic Studies, JNU, New Delhi for taking out time and explaining me different systems of Indian philosophy.
91. Heimann, *Indian and Western Philosophy,* p. 47.
92. Wight (2019), "Bringing the Outside In", p. 72.
93. See Alvin M. Weinberg (November-December 1970), "The Axiology of Science", *American Scientist,* vol. 58, no. 6, pp. 612-617.
94. Smith, "The Self-Image of a Discipline", p. 10.
95. Inanna Hamati-Ataya (June 2011), "The Problem of Values and International Relations Scholarship: From Applied Reflexivity to Reflexivism", *International Studies Review,* vol. 13, no. 2, p. 265.
96. Ibid., 260.
97. Steve Smith (2004), "Singing Our World into Existence: International Relations Theory and September 11", *International Studies Quarterly,* vol. 48, no. 3, p. 498.
98. *Sanatan Dharma: An Elementary Text-Book of Hindu Religion and Ethics,* (1916), Benares: The Board of Trustees, Central Hindu College, p. 129.
99. Ibid., p. 134.
100. Cited in Philip Goldberg (2010), *American Veda,* New York: Harmony Books, p. 25.
101. Hobson, *The Eurocentric Concepts of World Politics,* p. 6.

1

The Concept of Power in India's Strategic Culture

Praveen Kumar

This chapter begins by making two affirmations. One, the concepts of 'power' and 'strategic culture' have remained part of Indian political traditions. The issue has been an inability or unwillingness of the Western scholarship to identify and capture the historical events reflecting these ideas. Thus, when a writer like George K. Tanham stated (concerning India) that there is a lack of evidence of 'coherent' and 'systematic' national strategy,[1] he was selective in his approach in terms of his choice as well as interpretation of the historical phase where 'power' and 'strategic culture' could be seen to be in operation. Although this paper is not about the refutation of Tanham's understanding of 'power' or 'strategic culture' in the Indian context, it will factor in this aspect while explaining the Indian way to understand the power and strategic culture.

What is more important to highlight is that instead of finding the presence of a corresponding term in the national vocabulary, the endeavour should capture the form, essence, and functional aspect of the happening. In this aspect, concepts like power and strategic culture need to be situated in the Indian context. Besides, concepts are formulated in social science, not concerning parameters that would be static, but the latter is open to re-definition. The concept of power is a case in point.[2]

Second, the aforementioned claim can be established by offering evidence from Indian political writings and instances from Indian history. The instances should be accepted as evidence of testability in support of the claim that power and strategic culture should not be treated as a 'monopoly' of or 'patented' by Western literature. To emphasize this aspect is important because the second affirmation pertains to the understanding of the 'cycle of knowledge' that passes through the stages of theory building and testability. As any genuine knowledge is also sought to be legitimate, its acceptability may depend upon its scientific status. Hence, there will always be claims and counter-claims of the requirements of demonstrable 'pieces of evidence and 'proof" about a piece of specific knowledge.

With these affirmations, this paper proceeds to define 'power' and 'strategic culture' from the Indian perspective. Subsequently, an endeavour would be made to provide credible evidence that the inability of Western scholarship or scholars trained in Western traditions to identify the historical moments as evidence does not mean that the study of politics in India was unaware of the existence of these concepts. Also, any society or culture would not formulate and develop its knowledge simply to react to the counterclaims made by 'others'. Knowledge, including 'scientific' knowledge, needs to be pursued in the right earnest and should meet a given society's capability and relevance parameters. Secondly, the understanding of power is also to be contextualized with proper reference to Indian traditions and culture, as such concepts, most often than not, are only culturally embedded. To make these points, this study, in addition to the writings of Indian authors and thinkers, also draws from the ideas of Western writers. In a way, this is to provide a comparative understanding of the concepts.

Understanding Power and Strategic Culture in Select Literature from the West

A cursory glance at the Western literature would tell us that 'power' should mean dominance, and 'strategic culture', too, is about a nation's worldview or social behaviour that seeks and follows the goal of 'power maximization'. The whole understanding of strategic culture has developed in the context of the Cold War. The writers devoted volumes of literature to understanding the likely response of the two leading powers during the time of the Cold War, especially concerning their approach to the use of nuclear weapons.[3] Alastair Iain Johnston made it very clear when he wrote,

> "The former Soviet military was said to exhibit a preference for pre-emptive, offensive uses of force that was deeply rooted in Russia's history of external expansionism and internal autocracy. On the other hand, the USA tends to spread sporadic, messianic and crusading use of force that was deeply rooted in the morality of the early republic and a fundamental belief that warfare was an aberration in human relations. Such characterizations of the superpowers' strategic predispositions have been examined under the analytic category of "strategic culture".[4]

Johnston further writes,

> "The question of culture did not attract much attention in international security studies and international relations theory until the last ten to fifteen years, when interest in culture, strategic culture, and other ideational explanations for the behaviour of states has grown. Much of this new research is consistent with the conclusion of Joseph Nye and Sean Lynn-Jones that strategic studies have been characterized by American ethnocentrism and concomitant neglect of "national styles of strategy".[5]

A few things can be observed in the foregoing sentences. As has been stated already, the concept of strategic culture is specific to 'Cold War culture' and focused on likely nuclear hostilities between the USA and the Soviet Union. Second, understanding is relative and subjective, too, meaning that the mode of behaviour of one power is sought to be compared in terms of its likely aggressiveness or moderation with respect to the other. Also, understanding is perception driven. For the Western literature, strategic culture is more about understanding the mode of behaviour of states or organisations, in 'security and defence affairs'. The concept has a role more of an 'intervening variable' in foreign policy analyses.[6]

Similarly, the operational definitions of power, best characterised in the writings of social scientists like Robert Dahl, Bachrach, Baratz, and Steven Lukes, among others, would make it clear that 'power' works as an external 'force' against an actor to behave in a way that is to the liking of another actor. Dahl, in his theory of *Community Power* has attempted to understand that power is exercised in a community by (a) select individuals. Other individuals are made to follow the individual preferences of those who possess the power. Power, thus, would be understood as a relation between two actors A and B where A can make B do something that B would not otherwise do.[7] However, this concept of power also needs to be linked to individual capabilities to make others do something which they otherwise would not do. This is, in turn, linked to the resources that 'powerful individuals' may have at their disposal to make others to do what they wish them to do. Going by this logic, *prima facie,* those individuals who have more resources should also be more powerful, in comparative terms, again.

The dimension of power that Dahl has referred to would be understood as decision-making power. However, another element of power manifests itself as what is known as the power of 'agenda setting'. In this dimension, power operates at the level of actors who prevent certain decisions from being made, which they may feel are not in their interest. Bachrach and Baratz have explained this aspect in their analysis of 'two faces of power'. They argue that power relationships can manifest when three conditions are met—conflict of interests, which is different from the exercise of authority, compliance leading to a change in the other actor's behaviour, which is different from the application of force, and capability of one of the actors to invoke sanctions. They add that these are only necessary, but insufficient conditions for the power relationship to exist.[8] In addition to the power to make decisions, power also needs to be understood as "social and political values and institutional practices that limit the scope of the political process to public consideration of only those issues which are comparatively innocuous to A (the powerful actor)."[9]

There is yet another dimension of power that Steven Lukes has discussed in his book, "*Power: The Radical View*". While the first two dimensions could be understood as an overt and covert dimension of power, the third dimension is understood as the latent dimension of power.[10] Lukes does not discard the first two views of power. Incorporating the Gramscian idea of "hegemony", he, however, suggests that "power can also consist in the securing of consent to dominant power relations through the shaping of desires and beliefs."[11] The third dimension of power helps us understand that power relationships may still exist, even if overt or covert conflict may not be visible. Further, the processes and mechanisms involved in the power relationship 'need no longer be intentional and active'. According to Lukes, power in the third dimension may not be inimical to the preferences or the grievances of those who are subject to it.

In all these understandings of power, there is an element of 'repression' and 'repressor'. We may acknowledge here that the definitions of 'repressor' and 'repression' may change in different contexts. This, however, requires that we also need to, what Foucault stated: "expand the dimension of a definition of power".[12] Foucault attempted to move thinking about power beyond the view of power as repression of the powerless by the powerful. He intended to examine the way power relations operate routinely between people and institutions. According to him,

> "Power is not to be taken to be a phenomenon of one individual's consolidated and homogeneous domination over others, or that of one group or class over others. What, by contrast, should always be kept in mind is that power, if we do not take too distant a view of it, is not that which makes the difference between those who exclusively possess and retain it, and those who do not have it and submit to it. Power must be analysed as something which circulates, or rather as something which only functions in the form of a chain. It is never localised here or there, never in anybody's hands, never appropriated as a commodity or piece of wealth. Power is employed and exercised through a net-like organisation. And not only do individuals circulate between its threads; they are always in the position of simultaneously undergoing and exercising this power. They are not only its inert or consenting targets; they are always also the elements of its articulation. In other words, individuals are the vehicles of power, not its points of application."[13]

Thus, the representative literature from the Western world would consider power as some form of external force in the operation in which, persons, given their position in the societal relationship (intra-state or inter-state) are only a means to achieve the end of power or the powerful. Also, 'strategic culture', apart from being cold-war rooted, denotes an inherent tendency to overpower or dominate the other, most possibly against the wishes to the latter. As would be shown below, the understanding of power and strategic culture in Indian literature and history presents a broader idea of which this understanding is only a part. Also, this did not remain in the realm of idea, but there are instances from history that show that power in different forms and strategic culture in its broader meaning has remained part of Indian history and culture.

Power and Strategic Culture in Indian Tradition

The understanding of power and strategic culture, if seen from the Indian perspective, can have only two dimensions. Other aspects that have been discussed above are more a kind of sub-divisions or deeper analysis of the two dimensions, to be discussed below. The dimensions of power seen from the Indian perspective are physical and spiritual. The power in its spiritual dimension operates in the realm of 'reality' that requires transcending sensual perceptions. This enables humans to attain higher values and capabilities than what can be achieved in the temporal domain through physical means. The physical and spiritual dimensions of power are related and inter-dependent. However, in either respect, the Indian conception of power is not directed against 'fellow humans' to forcefully dominate 'the other' and depriving the latter of their ability to act. The power is more an enabler of an act than a 'restrainer'. The power in this sense would also mean that it is something, which is permanent and universal. The manifestation of power is in the form of an action, which is more concerned with the performance of duties than the enjoyment of power for power's sake. The power in its physical dimension operates in the lower realm, but eventually is absorbed and undertaken by the higher form, which is its spiritual dimension. Thus, power is more a means than an end in itself and its manifestation can be realised in what makes other nations/cultures to gravitate towards it than to be fearfully submissive before the physical strength alone.

To make these points clearer, representative literature from India would be analysed in the paragraphs below. The understanding of power can be located in literature like the *Vedas*, the *Ramayana* and the *Mahabharata*. This can be demonstrated scientifically. Lack of history writing on the part of the Hindus is not in itself a lack of evidence that strategic culture and power did not have a place in India's history, because "the accounts left behind and the chronicles accompanying the victorious Greek and Muslim armies speak of the bravery and strength of the Hindus".[14] The aspect of power can be effectively understood from the writings of Bankim Chandra Chattopadhyay, even though Bankim would be critical of the operation of force in Indian history, as the latter would not be used for the sake of 'liberty'. As Bankim would write:

> "For more than three thousand years, Aryans have fought against Aryans, or Aryans against non-Aryans, or non-Aryans against non-Aryans—Magadh has fought Kanauj, Kanauj has fought Delhi, Delhi has fought Lahore, Hindus have battled against Pathans, Pathans against Mughals, Mughals against the English—all of these people have fought against one another and continually stoked the fires of war in this country."[15]

Bankim would also place his faith in the historicity of literature like the *Ramayana* and the *Mahabharata*. In his understanding, Sanskrit literary texts may have myths and legends, however, they were useful as historical sources. This is evident in a project that Bankim undertook in *Krishnacharitra* where he endeavoured to establish the historicity of the character of Krishna. Bankim believed that the available texts on the life of Krishna contained 'numerous additions, abridgments, and recessions on the original'. If the later alterations could be separated, then the 'original historical account' on the life of Krishna could be known.[16] Bankim, however, firmly believed that such historical accounts could be established rationally and scientifically. Bankim's work also reflects upon the central theme of the 'law and politics' that according to Partha Chatterjee is the 'establishment of a criterion based on a judicious combination of force and mercy'. Bankim understood that in *Udyoga Parva* of the *Mahabharata*, Krishna deals with the same issue. Further, in the light of the narrative on the character of Krishna,

Bankim attempts to reconcile a philosophy of spirit with a rational doctrine of power, in his concept of *Dharma*.[17]

In the passages above, an attempt has been made to underline the fact that the concept of power, indeed, did find expression in Indian historical and political writings. Bankim's treatment of the *Mahabharata* and the character of Krishna make it amply clear. More importantly, power would find a scientific and rational base. This becomes clearer in the writings of ancient Indian political thinkers. Kautilya's *Arthashashtra*, again, is representative literature that throws good evidence on the fact that politics could be understood empirically and understanding of politics is firmly grounded in scientific understanding of the relationships of power.

If military power is a manifestation of national power, then ancient India did have a tradition of systematic categorisation of the Army. Six categories have been explained by various thinkers with the addition of the seventh one by Kautilya as *Autsahika* (living in different countries without any leader of invaders). The other six categories being those of *Maula* (hereditary or permanent), *Bhrtaka* (paid), *Shreni* (trained in the art of war), *Mitra* (soldiers of friendly kings), *Amitra* (soldiers of hostile or conquered kings and recruited like slaves) and *Atavi* (tribal soldiers).[18] It is significant to note that according to Kautilya, "it is power and power alone, which only when exercised by the king with impartiality and in proportion to guilt either over his son or his enemy, maintains both this world and the next."[19] Also, if strategic culture is about the maintenance of and manoeuvring of inter-state relations, the concept of the Mandala theory is significant evidence of the fact that Indians did have a culture of offensive and defensive strategy during their ancient history. Thus, as G.P. Singh writes,

> "The whole system of inter-state relations in ancient India was based on the equation which a king maintained with his friends and the attitude and policies which he adopted towards his foes."[20]

While in the passages above an attempt has been made to understand the physical dimension of power, power in its second dimension could best be understood in the ideas of Swami Ramakrishna Paramhans and his principal disciple, Swami Vivekanand. This power would be manifested in its most potent form in the form of knowledge that one would attain through the faculty of one's spirituality. Knowledge, generally understood, depends on what has been grasped through sensory experiences. However, to qualify to be valid knowledge, the knowledge also has to be scientific. Meaning, it should withstand the scrutiny of logic and rationality. It is required to be proved when its validity is questioned and there should be the regularity of pattern in terms of establishment of a cause-and-effect relationship. It is this form of knowledge, which was held as valid by Ramakrishna's principal disciple, Vivekanand, during his initial interactions with the former. However, under Ramakrishna's guidance, Vivekanand realised the 'existence' beyond sensory perceptions, and this is what would constitute true knowledge. This knowledge is real and is for the real, and is based on what can be realised. This knowledge is based on true experiences and is an outcome of the spiritual power that a person has developed within.

There are a few things, which need to be added here, to further explain the mode and method of attaining knowledge that Ramakrishna was maintaining. Ramakrishna's statements or assertions, if we can say so, were often contradicted by Vivekanand on the grounds of validity or acceptability on scientific grounds. Ramakrishna encouraged his disciples to question his 'assertions'. At times, even he would be ridiculed by Vivekanand while discussing issues like 'existence' or 'realisation' of God. Ramakrishna would advise him to apply 'reason and intellect' before accepting what was being told to him. Ramakrishna would often tell his disciples that "Test me as the money changer tests their coins. You must not believe me without testing me thoroughly."[21] Reason and intellect, which depend more on the senses, have a role to play in terms of moving towards what would constitute the knowledge. The knowledge is a quest for 'truth' or 'what is real' would, according to Ramakrishna, rather be based on 'superior understanding'. This superior understanding is "acquired through firsthand knowledge of the essence of the things."[22] This goes beyond reason. It is rather based on 'belief' or 'faith' which always has a solid foundation, which cannot falter. A knowledge acquired through reason can be proved to be wrong: however, not the knowledge, which is based on the consciousness of the real. Thus, Ramakrishna would hold that 'reason is weak, but the faith is stronger'. Vivekanand too accepted this form of knowledge as real, once he experienced this in the form of truth or real. Later, applying this understating on religion, Vivekanand held that religion, too, can be scientific.

If the senses cannot reach out to what lies ahead as reality, it is the limitation of the senses, and not to be denied that reality does not exist. The same would apply to religion or knowing God. As Ramakrishna would say, if one cannot see stars during the day time that would not mean that there are no stars.[23] This was very aptly put by Vivekanand in the following words:

> "...Sciences were but secondary. That which made us realise the Brahman was supreme, the highest knowledge. This idea we find in every religion, and that is why religion always claimed to be supreme knowledge. Knowledge of the sciences cover, as it were, only part of our lives, but the knowledge which religion brings to us is eternal, as infinite as truth it preaches."[24]

While the concept of power and strategic culture has been treated in some of its aspects in the preceding paragraphs, a caveat needs to be added at this stage. Given the scope of this paper, it would not be possible to list chronologically all the relevant literature from the Indian tradition dealing with these concepts, a project that is, nonetheless, required to be undertaken at some stage for the comprehensive treatment of these issues. But, here I would like to introduce an Indian personality that may look too many as out of place, given the nature of the concepts. That is M.K. Gandhi Ji. How power could be understood in both of its dimensions mentioned above and especially the spiritual dimension, which may rightly be claimed as the Indian concept of power, ought to be more significantly get its reasonable treatment in the writings of Gandhi. Gandhi's views provide both a critique of the Western sense of power and at the same time an explanation for the superiority of 'soul force' or 'truth-force' which may rightly be conceived to have a spiritual basis.

The first thing that one can notice in Gandhi is that power is about an asymmetrical relationship and grounded in the civilisation of a given nation. As Gandhi writes, "Formerly, when people wanted to fight with one another, they measured between them their bodily strength; now it is possible to take away thousands of lives by one man working behind a gun from a hill. This is civilization."[25] Gandhi further writes, "This civilization is irreligion, and it has taken such a hold on the people in Europe that those who are in it appear to be half-mad. They lack real physical strength or courage."[26] If Gandhi's analysis is to be applied, then the British did not take control of India and nor did they hold India because of their superior power, but they were in India "because we (Indians) keep them." If culture is about the psychological orientation of mind, then, according to Gandhi, "(Indian) agriculturists sleep fearlessly on their farms even today; but the English and you and I would hesitate to sleep where they sleep. Strength lies in the absence of fear, not in the quantity of flesh and muscle we may have on our bodies."[27]

Conclusion: Pieces of Evidence from Indian History

Ancient Indian traditions provide significant examples of power operating in its physical domain, even though the spiritual dimension of power was always considered to be more significant and got better treatment in Indian literature. For one, as Bankim suggests, if the scientific side of the literature such as the *Mahabharata* is looked into, one would get sufficient evidence of both, the power and the strategic culture. Second, if historical evidence is to be selected from the attempts that have been made to write and create history, then the reigns of the Mauryas, the Guptas, and the kingdoms in the South could be included to understand the Indian view on power and strategic culture. Hinduism, Buddhism, Jainism, and Sikhism fall in the domain of what rightly can be characterised as the spiritual dimension of India's power. As stated in some of the previous sentences, they do not act to deprive others of their freedom but are a natural attraction that makes others gravitate towards what truly can be identified as Indian culture. However, in the more recent past, India's freedom struggle provides forceful evidence that power in its twin dimension could be seen in its operational form wherein the most formidable force of the Earth could submit to the 'soul force' of the Indians. Thus, as far as concepts such as power and strategic culture are concerned, the issue has not been that Indians did not have a sense of them; rather, they remained indifferent to these aspects of politics. As has been noted in the opening remarks, the idea is not to react to certain knowledge forms which are claimed to be authentic, but a genuine pursuit of the knowledge that would come in the Indian way. As stated already, cultural contexts do matter.

NOTES

1. Tanham, George K. (1992), *Indian Strategic Thought: An Interpretive Essay*, Santa Monica, CA: Rand, p. v.
2. For instance, various authors have tried to capture different dimensions of power. See Dahl, Robert A. (1957), The Concept of Power, in *Behavioral Science* 2(3), July, pp. 201-215; Bachrach, Peter and Baratz, Morton S. (1962), Two Faces of Power, in *The American Political Science Review* 56(4), Dec., pp. 947-952; Lukes, Steven (2005), *Power: A Radical View*, Hampshire: Macmillan; Foucault, Michael (2000), *Power*, Ed. J.D. Faubion, Vol. 3 of *Essential Works of Foucault*, New York: The New Press; Angang, Hu and Honghua, Men (2002), The Rising of Modern China: Comprehensive National Power and Grand Strategy. English tr. of Chinese version, in *Strategy and Management*, No. 3; Morganthau, Hans J. (1948), *Politics among Nations: The Struggle for Power and Peace*, New York: Alfred A. Knopf; Nye Jr., Joseph S. (1999), Redefining the National Interest, in *Foreign Affairs*, Jul-Aug 1999, pp. 22-35. The list is only indicative. One can go on adding names like Kenneth Waltz and Susane Strange and Hedley Bull, among others.
3. The literature is in abundance. However, one can see the following works, among others: Lord, Carnes (1985), American Strategic Culture, in *Comparative Strategy*, 5(3); Pipes, Richard (1977), Why the Soviet Union Thinks It Could Fight and Win a Nuclear War, in *Commentary*, 64 (1); Gray, Colin (1986), *Nuclear Strategy and National Style*. Lanham, Md.: Hamilton Press; Gray, Colin (1981), National Styles in Strategy: The American Example, in *International Security*, 6 (2).
4. See Johnston, Alastair Iain (1995), Thinking about Strategic Culture, in *International Security*, 19 (4), p. 32.
5. Johnston, ibid. p. 33.
6. Meyer, Christoph O. (2004), *Theorising European Strategic Culture: Between Convergence and Persistence of National Diversity*, Brussels: Centre for European Policy Studies, No. 204, p. 2.
7. Dahl, Robert A. (1957), The Concept of Power, in *Behavioral Science*, 2 (3) July, pp. 202-203.
8. Bachrach Peter and Morton S. Baratz (1963), Decisions and Nondecisions: An Analytical Framework, in *The American Political Science Review*, 57(3), Sep. p. 633.
9. Bachrach and Baratz, ibid., p. 948.
10. Sadan, Elisheva, *Empowerment and Community Planning*, eBook available at www.mpow.org/elisheva_sadan_empowerment_intro.pdf, accessed on 01 Aug 2015, p. 37.
11. Lukes, Steven (2007), Power, in *Contexts*, Summer, p. 60.
12. Foucault, Michel (1982), "The Subject and Power", in *Critical Enquiry*, Vol. 8 (4), p. 778.

13. See Foucault, Michel (1980), *Power/Knowledge: Selected Interviews and Other Writings*, Ed. by Colin Gordon, Trans. by Colin Gordon, Leo Marshall, John Mepham, and Kate Soper. New York: Pantheon Books, p. 98.
14. Chaterjee, Partha (1986), Culture and Power in the Thought of Bamkim Chandra, in Pantham Thomas and Kenneth L. Deutsch ed. *Political Thought in Modern India*, New Delhi: Sage Publications, p. 60.
15. Chattopadhyay, Bankim Chandra (1965), *Bankim Racanavali*, Calcutta: Sahitya Samsad, p. 239. Cited in Chatterjee, Partha, 1986, ibid.
16. Chatterjee, Partha, ibid., p. 64.
17. Chaterjee, Partha. ibid., p. 77.
18. Singh, G.P. (2005), *Political Thought in Ancient India*, New Delhi: DK Printworld (P) Ltd., p. 109.
19. Kautilya *Arthashashtra*, Tr. by Shamsatri, R. Available at http://hinduonline.co/DigitalLibrary/SmallBooks/ArthashastraofChanakyaEng.pdf.
20. Singh, G.P., ibid., p. 119.
21. Nikhilanand, Swami (2015), *Vivekananda: A Biography*, Reprint edition, Kolkata: Advaita Ashram, p. 44.
22. Nikhilanand, Swami, ibid., p. 37.
23. Muller, Max F. (1898), *Ramakrishna: His Life and Sayings*, London: Theosophical Publishing Society, p. 98.
24. Vivekanand, Swami (2006), *The Complete Works of Swami Vivekananda*, Kolkata: Advaita Ashrama, p. 366.
25. Gandhi, M.K. (1938), *Hind Swaraj or Indian Home Rule*, Ahmedabad: Navjivan Publishing House, p. 32.
26. Gandhi, M.K., ibid., p. 33.
27. Gandhi, M.K., ibid., p. 40.

REFERENCES

Angang, Hu and Honghua, Men (2002), *The Rising of Modern China: Comprehensive National Power and Grand Strategy*. English tr. to Chinese Version in *Strategy and Management*, No. 3.

Bachrach, Peter and Baratz, Morton S. (1962), Two Faces of Power, in *The American Political Science Review*, 56(4).

Chaterjee, Partha (1986), Culture and Power in the Thought of Bankim Chandra, in Pantham Thomas and Kenneth L .Deutsch Ed., *Political Thought in Modern India*, New Delhi: Sage Publications.

Chattopadhyay, Bankim Chandra (1965), *Bankim Racanavali*, Calcutta: Sahitya Samsad.

Dahl, Robert A. (1957), The Concept of Power, in *Behavioral Science*, 2(3), July.

Foucault, Michael (2000), *Power*, Ed. J. D. Faubion, Vol. 3 of *Essential Works of Foucault*, New York: The New Press.

Gandhi, M.K. (1938), *Hind Swaraj or Indian Home Rule*, Ahmedabad: Navjivan Publishing House.

Gray, Colin (1981), National Styles in Strategy: The American Example, in *International Security*, 6 (2).

Gray, Colin (1986), *Nuclear Strategy and National Style*, Lanham, Md.: Hamilton Press.

Johnston, Alastair Iain (1995), Thinking about Strategic Culture, in *International Security*, 19(4).

Johnston, ibid., p. 33.

Kautilya *Arthashashtra*, Tr. by Shamsatri, R. Available at http://hinduonline.co/DigitalLibrary/SmallBooks/ArthashastraofChanakyaEng.pdf.

Lord, Carnes (1985), American Strategic Culture, in *Comparative Strategy*, 5(3).

Lukes, Steven (2005), *Power: A Radical View*, Hampshire: Macmillan.

Meyer, Christoph O. (2004), *Theorising European Strategic Culture: Between Convergence and Persistence of National Diversity*, Brussels: Centre for European Policy Studies, No. 204.

Morganthau, Hans J. (1948), *Politics among Nations: The Struggle for Power and Peace*, New York: Alfred A. Knopf.

Muller, Max F. (1898), *Ramakrishna: His Life and Sayings*, London: Theosophical Publishing Society.

Nikhilanand, Swami (2015), *Vivekananda: A Biography*, Reprint edition, Kolkata: Advaita Ashram.

Nye Jr., Joseph S. (1999), Redefining the National Interest, in *Foreign Affairs*, Jul-Aug 1999, pp. 22-35.

Pipes, Richard (1977), Why the Soviet Union Thinks It Could Fight and Win a Nuclear War, in *Commentary*, 64 (1).

Sadan, Elisheva, *Empowerment and Community Planning*, eBook available at www.mpow.org/elisheva_sadan_empowerment_intro.pdf, accessed on 01 Aug 2015.

Singh, G.P. (2005), *Political Thought in Ancient India*, New Delhi: DK Printworld (P) Ltd.

Tanham, George K. (1992), *Indian Strategic Thought: An Interpretive Essay*, Santa Monica, CA: Rand.

Vivekanand, Swami (2006), *The Complete Works of Swami Vivekananda*, Kolkata: Advaita Ashrama.

2

Grand Strategic Thought in the *Valmiki Ramayana*

Anoop Kumar Gupta

Contemporary discourse on India's strategic culture and grand strategy is very recent and vast. It is more or less confined to the study of strategic thinking and strategy in post-independence India. This debate has centred on whether India has a strategic culture or not. Some say that India does not have a strategic culture while others argue that India does have grand strategic thinking. Propositions and counter-propositions put forward by various scholars in this regard have significantly enriched the discourse.

However, in the beginning, contemporary discourse did not pay much attention to study, analyse, and explore the strategic culture of the Indic world. Later or sooner, in an attempt to discover the roots of Indian strategic culture, a lot of attention has also been paid to evaluate and interpret ancient Indian texts. Much has been written on the evolution of India's strategic thinking. Scholarly attempts have also been made towards a theorization of an Indic perspective. Kautilya's Arthashastra has emerged as a focal point in this regard. None the less, scholarly works that discuss strategic thought in ancient India more or less ignored the broad study of core strategic dimensions in the Ramayana separately. Though the Ramayana has been analysed from the social, political, moral, and philosophical points of view, there is a need to interpret it strategically. Strategic reading of the Ramayana could be another milestone as far as the evolution of an Indic perspective on strategic culture and international relations is concerned.

Understanding Strategic Culture

The strategic culture paradigm tries to explain the strategic behaviour of state actors based on its deep history and culture. As an alternative to classical realism and structural realism, cultural realism uses strategic culture as a tool to understand state behaviour. Alastair Iain Johnston's writings are important in this regard. He not only sketched out the strategic culture paradigm but also applied it to the strategic thinking and strategy of China.[1] According to Johnston, 'strategic culture is an ideational milieu which limits behavioural choices.'[2] He explained it as "ranked grand strategic preferences derived from central paradigmatic assumptions about the nature of conflict and the enemy, and collectively shared by decision-makers".[3] Further elaborating the concept he stated that strategic culture as a "system of symbols" comprises two parts. The first part consists of central paradigm of a strategic culture which includes basic assumptions about the orderliness of the strategic environment, that is, about the role of war in human affairs (whether it is inevitable or an aberration), about the nature of the adversary and the threat it poses (zero-sum or variable sum), and about the efficacy of the use of force.[4] The second part consists of assumptions at a more operational level about which strategic options are the most efficacious for dealing with the threat environment, as defined by answers to the first three questions.[5] For Johnston, strategic culture could be derived from the object of analysis, e.g., textual sources for potential answers to the central paradigm. Describing the method of analysis, he enquires how one should go about analysing the object of analysis. According to him, 'the best approach is to be fairly eclectic' and 'different methods might tap into different levels of meanings in the texts.'[6]

Discourse on Indian Strategic Thinking

Discourse on Indian strategic thought is recent but vast and diverse and even contains opposing and conflicting views. It begins with

George K. Tanham's writing in 1992 in which he put forward the proposition that India has produced little formal strategic thinking and planning.[7] K. Subrahmanyam and Jaswant Singh agreed with Tanaham's line of argument. K. Subrahmanyam emphasised that a strategic thinking deficit exists in India.[8] Discussing the lack of strategic thinking in India, Jaswant Singh emphasised that India simply abandoned the centrality of 'strategic culture' as the first ingredient of vigorous and bold national policies.[9] Reflecting his conservative and ultra-realist strategic thought, Bharat Karnad termed India as a 'reticent state'.[10] He also lamented that there is an 'absence of strategic imagination, verve, and ambition' in India.[11] He further stated that 'India over-emphasises its soft power' and 'little attention has been paid to hard power deficit'.[12]

However, many scholars in the politico-strategic community differed with this view and have countered the above proposition suggesting an alternative view stressing that India does have a strategic culture. In this regard, Rodney W. Jones stated that "India's strategic culture is not monolithic, rather is mosaic-like".[13] In his seminal work on Indian strategic culture, Kanti Bajpai claimed that "Indians do indeed think about grand strategy".[14] Bajpai proposed that Indian strategic thinking could be described in terms of three leading schools named Nehruvianism, Neo-liberalism and Hyperrealism and three minor schools based on Marxism, Hindutva, and Gandhianism. Writing on India's strategic culture, Shrikant Paranjpe concluded that the 'Indian' approach to strategic thinking may appear 'ambiguous' in nature to the extent that it does not seek to specify in concrete terms the road map of strategy and tactics...yet there is a utility in the deliberate ambiguity that is in fact the core of Indian strategic thinking.[15]

However, the mainstream discourse on Indian strategic culture has been more or less confined to the contemporary period. It was presumed that ancient or medieval India did not possess any canonical writings and was resultantly lagging behind in strategic tradition and that it was only in modern India and particularly after independence that grand strategic thought developed and flourished.[16] Kanti P. Bajpai and Harsh V. Pant have raised doubts about the existence of grand strategic thought and strategic culture not only in the ancient Indic world but also in the early or later medieval periods. They ask the question: "Is there an identifiable canonical text that has had a lasting influence?"[17] It was also argued that ancient Indian texts like the *Vedas*, the *Upanishads*, the *Ramayana*, the *Mahabharata*, the *Bhagavad Gita* and others do not fall into the category of 'canonical texts of antiquity' and 'it is almost impossible to show that these various texts have any valence amongst those who think about national strategy.'[18] The logical proposition that lack of familiarity and deep knowledge of ancient Indian texts among the Indian politico-strategic elite does not prove that these texts do not have grand strategic ideas and thought. Denying the existence of strategic culture in the Indic world on the above proposition would be a sort of academic injustice to these ancient Indian texts. This seems to be a kind of academic reductionism.

However, strategic thinking is not a new or just a modern phenomenon to India but has its roots since the dawn of civilisation. Strategic culture in India does exist since ancient times and one could find expression of strategic dimensions in one way or another in several ancient Indian texts like the *Vedas*, the *Ramayana*, the *Mahabharata*, and the *Arthashastra*. Various Indians, as well as Western scholars of Indology or international relations, have explained and analysed ancient Indian texts from a strategic perspective.

In his seminal work '*Hinduism and Ethics of Warfare in South Asia*', Kaushik Roy challenges the common Western narrative that pre-colonial India lacked military and strategic thinking.[19] He explores 'the evolution of theories of warfare from the dawn of civilisation in India.' He further suggests that 'better understanding of the legacy of ancient India's strategic theorising will enable a more accurate analysis of modern India's military and nuclear policies.'

In his article 'Chivalry and Warfare', B.N.S. Yadav associated the *Ramayana* and the *Mahabharata* with the chivalry tradition and the *Arthasastra* with diplomacy.[20] He stated that 'tradition of high chivalry' may be gathered from the two great epics—the *Ramayana* and the *Mahabharata*. For him, the early empires in northern India witnessed 'a sort of balanced and restrained chivalry.' He argued that in the *Arthasastra*, enthusiasm, and valour were subordinated to diplomacy.

In his seminal work, Torkel Brekke tried to explore the ethics of war and warfare in the Hindu tradition.[21] According to Brekke, there is lasting tension in the Hindu tradition between heroism and prudence. For him, the *Ramayana* and the *Mahabharata* witnessed the heroic ideal while the *Arthashastra* reflected the ideal of prudence. In an attempt to theorise the discourse, Brekke applies the Western terminology and stated that there is a tension between deontology and consequentialism in the Indian ideology of war.[22] According to him, Kautilya belongs to the consequentialist camp.

Raj Balkaran and A. Balter Dorn have explained the *Valmiki Ramayana* in terms of the 'Just War' doctrine.[23] According to them, modern 'Just War' criteria are as following: (1) A Just Cause, (2) The Right Intent, (3) A Net Benefit, (4) Legitimate Authority, (5) Last Resort, (6) Proportionality of Means, and (7) Right Conduct. Balkaran and Dorn emphasised that all seven modern Just War criteria are present in the *Valmiki Ramayana*. The first three criteria answer the question 'why use force?' The fourth criteria are related to the question 'who should authorise the force?' The fifth criteria involve the question 'when can force be used?' The sixth criteria answer the question 'what level of force?' And the seventh criteria are related to 'how and where to apply force? "Based on their comparative approach, both the authors advocate inclusion of Hindu thought into the global discourse on the ethics of war and peace."

In her thought-provoking article, Swarna Rajgopalan has explained the grand strategic thought in the *Ramayana* and the *Mahabharata*.[24] In an attempt to search for strategic insight into these two epics, she meticulously explores core values and instruments for creating security in both of them. Analysing the grand strategic thought in the Indian epics, she also puts forward a few logical propositions.[25] According to her, 'the legacy of the epics bears little resemblance to the realist world that scholars like Morgenthau described.' She concludes that the 'Indian penchant for claiming the high moral ground in international relations and the idealism of the Nehruvian era carry traces of the importance given to Dharma as the foundation and purpose of political action.' She also emphasised that the 'much-lamented absence of carefully articulated, meticulously executed grand strategic thought in Indian foreign policy may be consistent with our traditional political ethics as described by our epics. That is why, she remarks, 'classical grand strategic thinking might be said to have been an abomination from the perspective of the epics.' It seems that for Rajgopalan, epics are representative of high morality and idealism and lack modern realism and classical grand strategic thought. The Western paradigm of idealism and/or realism cannot be imposed on epics as they reflect a fine blending of both idealism and realism. Moreover, Gopalan did not explain the strategic thinking and strategy of Rama and Ravana separately, though both are entirely different.

Various attempts have been made at the institutional and individual levels to explore strategic dimensions in ancient Indian texts but there is a long way to go. Much has been written on Kautilya's *Arthashastra* and the Institute for Defence Studies and Analyses, New Delhi, has played a significant role in this regard. For a better understanding of the Indic perspective on strategic issues and international relations, there is a need for rigorous work to study various Indian texts and manuscripts separately and independently. Academic rigor is required to explore and establish the existence of strategic culture in these various Indian texts.

Strategic Culture in the *Valmiki Ramayana*

Kautilya's *Arthashastra* has been considered as a milestone regarding the evolution of an Indic perspective on strategic issues and international relations. Pre-Kautilyan strategic thought and post-Kautilyan strategic thought are also very important in this regard. The place of the *Ramayana* is very important in pre-Kautilyan strategic thought.

The *Ramayana* is one of the important epics and talks about various aspects of human life including social, political and strategic ones.[26] It is written in a storytelling format. Strategic thought in the *Ramayana* emerges with the development of its story. As the saga of Rama and Ravana unfolds, the strategic paradigms and strategic preferences of both protagonists surface clearly in the epic. On the other hand, Kautilya's *Arthashastra* discusses strategic dimensions directly without taking recourse of any tale-telling. It further develops systematically the strategic vision that was enshrined in pre-Kautilyan strategic thought. In this regard, L.N. Rangarajan stated that "Kautilya was not the originator of the Science."[27] Kautilya himself accepted in the very first verse of his work that he is only presenting the collection of previous *Arthashastras*. It is accepted that 'there were at least four distinct schools and thirteen individual teachers of *Arthashastra* before Kautilya.'[28] Kautilya himself recommended his students to learn *Itihas* (history) during their training period and for him, *Itihas* contains the study of the *Ramayana* and other texts.[29] Thus, the *Ramayana* is one of the important sources of pre-Kautilyan literature on statecraft and strategic vision. It has been ignored or least explored in the discourse on Indian strategic culture. It could be argued that systematic strategic thought in India begins with the Ramayana tradition and the *Valmiki Ramayana* is very significant in this regard.

The study of the *Ramayana* proves that it has strategic culture and strategy. This article is a combination of Indology and defence studies and particularly discusses the strategic aspects of the *Ramayana*. This article tries to explore the strategic dimensions in one of the great Indian epics. This is an attempt to reconstruct the *Valmiki Ramayana* for military science and strategic studies. The theoretical model of strategic culture and grand strategy has been used as a tool to revisit the *Valmiki Ramayana*. Pioneering work of Alastair I. Johnston on strategic culture and grand strategy has been of immense use in this regard. The article treats the *Valmiki Ramayana* as a textual document as it is available before us and tries to delineate the strategic paradigm in it. Though there are many versions of the *Ramayana*, this work is primarily based on the *Valmiki Ramayana* and has slightly taken references from other *Ramayana* traditions. This work focuses on exploring and understanding the core strategic values and strategic preferences in the *Ramayana*.

The study demonstrates and emphasizes that the strategic culture and strategy in the *Ramayana* is not monolithic. There are two paradigms of strategic culture in it, i.e., the strategic culture of Rama and the strategic culture of Ravana. A kaleidoscopic view of strategic thought and strategic preferences of Rama and Ravana demonstrate a different worldview regarding the core values, the concept of the adversary, nature of power, use of force and war-fighting strategy limitations.

Strategic Culture of Rama

The core value of Rama lies in the long Indic tradition of spiritual non-dualism. This non-dualistic philosophy of Rama is explained in the *Yog Vashistha* in great detail.[30] The text describes the spiritual journey of Rama and is written in the form of a dialogue between sage Vasistha and Prince Rama. The text begins with Rama as a seeker of spiritual liberation. It ends with the emergence of Rama as the one who is a *Jivanmukta* or spiritually liberated person. A *Jivanmukta* is described as a person who is enlightened, blissful, truthful, desire-less, benevolent, beyond worldly thirst, fearless and free from anger. A *Jivanmukta* follows the path of *Dharma*, i.e., to perform all necessary duties without a sense of involvement.

Dharma is righteousness and deeply rooted in this non-dualistic metaphysics. Rama's conviction in truthfulness and self-control was very profound that is why he emphasised that 'righteousness is paramount in the world and truthfulness is rooted in piety.'[31] For Rama, the path of *Dharma*, *Artha* (material gain) and *Kama* (worldly enjoyment) should undoubtedly follow in the wake of righteousness.[32] Rama stressed that one should abstain from pursuits in which *Dharma* does not find any scope and should undertake that pursuit alone from which follow *Dharma*. Rama underlined that following *Artha* (material wealth) without *Dharma* (righteousness) becomes hateful while following excessive addiction to *Kama* (sensuous enjoyment) which is incompatible to *Dharma* is not commendable.[33] *Dharma* is righteousness. It was a moral code of conduct. *Dharma* for him was to discharge one's duty according to righteousness. This *Dharma* of Rama is indicative of a peace-loving perspective and non-violent ethos. This ethos is indicative of a high moral standard.

The politico-strategic thinking of Rama is deeply connected with his core belief in non-dualistic philosophy. The king is the fountain of truth and righteousness and ever strives for the good of the state.[34] It was the duty of the king to follow and maintain *Dharma*. He is responsible to establish order, justice, security and public welfare in a given society and to eliminate the forces of injustice.[35] Realising the fear of anarchy, the *Valmiki Ramayana* attributes the rise and fall of a kingdom to the presence and disappearance of its ruler.[36]

For the protection and promotion of *Dharma* or righteousness, the strategic thinking of Rama gives due importance to statecraft, diplomacy and the security of the state along with utility and justification of force. Rama explained the principles of statecraft to his younger brother Bharata under the pretext of inquiring the welfare of his father and others.[37] Explaining the core value of statecraft to Bharat, Rama states that "having obtained his share and ruled in the right way over the entire globe, a wise king who holds sway over the earth and administers justice to the people in consonance with righteousness surely ascends to heaven."[38] Thus, Rama was stressing a fine blending between statecraft and righteousness. In Rama's strategic thinking nature of the adversary, the role of war, use, and limitation of force are determined and defined by the core values of *Dharma* (the right way).

What is the conception of the enemy and adversary in Rama's strategic calculations? For Rama, the basic norm for enmity and friendship was *Dharma* (moral code or righteousness) not the *Artha* (material gain) or *Kama* (worldly enjoyment). That is why the violator of *Dharma* is an enemy for Rama and the use of force against this enemy is just and fair. However, enmity is not a permanent feature of Rama's strategic culture. According to him, enmity ends with the end of the enemy. Rama knew that Ravana 'was full of unrighteousness and falsity'.[39] Still, Rama's conviction was that though Ravana 'made people cry by his tyranny' 'hostilities endure till death only'.[40] That is why he explained to Vibhishan (younger brother of Ravana) that Ravana is 'as well mine as yours' and asks him to organize the respectful funeral of Ravana.[41] Rama not only rescinds enmity towards Ravana after his death but also removes his weapons and armour and gives up his anger and assumes a gentle mien.[42] This is reflective of Rama's non-dual perspective towards all.

Here comes another question related to strategic culture discourse, i.e., the role of war and use of force in human affairs. For Rama, war is an aberration, not a desirable event. The use of force in Rama's strategic culture is related to the maintenance of *Dharma* and order for the public good. In Rama's strategic thought, the use of force in not related to personal whims and fancies. That is why he rejected the proposal of his younger brother Laksmana to use force to capture the throne of

Ayodhya when Rama was given exile of fourteen years by his father.[43] Rama suggested that Laksmana "give up this unworthy thought which is deriving its support from military heroism and take your stand on righteousness and does not resort to severity."[44] Here Rama clearly emphasised that mere chivalry and heroism could not be a cause for resorting to force.

Once righteousness, public order, and public interest are threatened, Rama did not hesitate to use force against the adversary and go to the extent of his annihilation. However, war and use of force are the last resort as far as the strategic preferences of Rama were concerned. Rama uses force against many *rakshasas* (devils) who were harassing innocent people because the king must protect his subjects.[45] On the advice of sage Vishwamitra, Rama kills ogress Tadka and two more ogres named Marica and Subahu who were interrupting the sacrificial performance of the sage. Sage Vishwamitra instructs Rama to kill the woman demon Tadka because 'there exists no righteousness in her.'[46] He explained that "for the protection of the people even that which is sinful or wrong must invariably be done by one whose duty is to protect...such is the eternal duty of those charged with the onus of administration."[47]

During his exile, the ascetic sages living in the Dandak forest requested Rama for protection against ogres.[48] Rama assured them that he would stop their persecution by the ogres.[49] Though Rama's wife Sita requests him not to kill the ogres and observe non-violence,[50] Rama expresses his firmness in keeping the vow of killing the ogres for the protection of the sages.[51] Accordingly, Laksmana lopped off Surpanakha's nose and ear and thereafter Rama kills Khara, Dusana and Trisira along with a large army of ogres. After the kidnapping of Sita by Ravana, Rama finally defeated and killed the King of Lanka. Thus, in Rama's strategic parlance, the use of force is defensive. He does not use force to expand his empire or to establish hegemony over others.

In his grand strategy, Rama was aware of four *Upayas* and a six-fold policy and used it according to the emerging situation. Rama used the instrument of *Danda* and *Vigrah* against various demons and finally against Ravana, but he did not underestimate the importance of *Sama* and *Sandhi* in his strategic calculation at the operational level.

To avoid conflict and confrontation, Rama also gave a chance to diplomatic efforts. In his initial conflict with the demons in the forest, Rama asked them to return and avoid war. Rama also tried to avoid a confrontation with Ravana. Hanuman as an ambassador of Rama gave an offer to Ravana that war could be avoided if he returned Sita to Rama. Rama again sent Angada to Lanka with the proposal that war could be avoided if Sita was returned to Rama.

As part of the six-fold policy, Rama gave due importance to *Sandhi*, i.e., alliances which EW described as external balancing in neo-realism. Rama was engaged in alliance building with Sugreev (the 'monkey prince' in exile). With the help of Sugreev and his army, Rama successfully developed a huge military build-up. Rama also gave shelter to Vibhishana and established a friendship with him. The role of Indra is also important in this regard. Ravana was Indra's enemy and Indra wanted to help Rama in his war against Ravana. Rama also accepted the help of Indra. This is reflective of the strategic conception that an enemy's enemy is a friend. Garuna also helped Rama. He emancipated Rama and Laksmana from Meghanad's Nagapash. External balancing was an instrument to protect people and to punish those who were harassing innocent people and violating the principle of righteousness.

However, before launching any military operation against the enemy, military preparedness and capacity building is necessary. Rama was aware of the fact that military weakness is fatal to the existence and security of the state. When sage Vishwamitra asked for princes Rama and Laksmana from their father, king Dashratha, to eliminate demon forces from the forest, Dashratha initially not only refused but also expressed his military weakness and incapability to deal with the demon forces of Ravana.[52] Dashratha admitted that he and his sons and army could not wage a war against the forces of Ravana.[53] This demonstrates the fact that the military power of the Ayodhya kingdom was comparatively weaker than that of King Ravana's Lanka. Dashratha himself accepted that he and his whole army could not face Ravana in conflict or war. Keeping this in mind, sage Vishwamitra paid attention to military preparedness and capacity building. He was well versed in different types of weapons and he "not only knows the use of all those missiles as one ought to but is also capable of evolving new ones".[54] Sage Vishwamitra gave techniques like *Bala* and *Atibala* to Rama and Laksmana.[55] After the killing of the woman demon Tadka, the sage also imparted the knowledge of using all the military weapons.[56] Rishi Agastya also transferred various powerful military weapons to Rama.[57] This is indicative of what is described as internal balancing in contemporary international relations theory.

Any grand strategy without Intelligence, surveillance, and reconnaissance is doomed to fail. These instruments also figured in the strategic planning of Rama for knowing and assessing the capacity of the enemy. Casting his eyes on all sides, Rama who was skilled in warfare, surveyed the army of ogre Khara.[58] Hanuman and Vibhisana played a crucial role in gathering Intelligence about the enemy. The search for Sita by Hanuman in Ravana's Lanka and his meeting with Vibhisana are very important in this regard. Hanuman was also aware of the four *Upayas* known as Sam, Daan, Bheda and Danda. He purposely decided to use force against Lanka's demons for knowing and assessing their hard power and military capability.[59] He not only wanted to ascertain who would predominate in an encounter between the enemy and ourselves, but also looked forward to determining the future course of action.[60] Hanuman also wished to meet Ravana so that he could read the design enshrined in his heart and ascertain his strength.[61] Hanuman's surrender before Meghanada was also part of his strategic calculation to have a direct conversation with Ravana.[62] On the advice of Vibhisana, Ravana decided not to kill Hanuman but ordered that his tail be set on fire and that he should be taken around the city.[63] Hanuman sees a strategic opportunity in it because he will get the chance to survey Lanka once more and understand its fortification.[64]

After joining Rama's camp, Vibhisana played an important role in providing crucial information about Ravana's military preparedness. The very first question that Rama asked Vibhisana was, "let me know in truth, the strength as well as weakness of the ogres."[65] Vibhisana's four ministers—Anala, Panasa, Sampati, and Pramati—also provided crucial intelligence regarding arrangements that had been made for the defence of Lanka.[66] Rama himself decided to climb to the top of Suvela Mountain along with Laksmana and the monkey troops to survey Lanka, its excellent gates and defensive walls.[67] The use of these instruments for strategy formulation at the operation level shows Rama's preference over prudence rather than sheer heroism.

Rama's war-fighting strategy was indicative of active defence, though it also witnessed an evolution. In his initial battles against various demons in the forest, Rama fought alone without the help of a regular army. All these battles with demons were limited in nature. In his war against Ravana, Rama organised a regular army of locals with the help of the monkey king, Sugreev. The movement of troops from the monkey kingdom of Kishkindha to the ocean shore, the building of a bridge across the ocean up to Lanka, various battle formations during the war with Lanka, and the war-fighting strategy are indicative of Rama's knowledge of military science and logistics. Regarding the movement of troops, Rama instructed monkey leader Nila to "lead the army speedily by a route full of fruits and roots as well as of honey and abounding in woods with cool shade and freshwater."[68] Rama's war-fighting strategy is mixed with conventional and non-conventional strategy against Ravana's forces. The monkeys were fighting with the help of stones and trees. On the other hand, Rama and Laksmana were fighting with bows and arrows and other weapons.

Rama gave importance to the medical wing in his army for the treatment of wounded personnel. Invoking Brahma's missile, Meghanad rendered Rama and Laksmana as well as a whole army of monkeys unconscious.[69] Jambavan then instructed Hanuman to proceed to the Himalayas and bring the four medicinal herbs, *Mrtasamjivni*, *Visalyakarani*, *Suvarnakarani*, and *Sandhani*.[70] Inhaling the unique fragrance of these powerful herbs, Rama and Laksmana as well as the monkeys were healed of their wounds, sprang to their feet and got rid of their pain.[71] It is important to note here that since the beginning of the fight between the monkeys and ogres, all the ogres were cast away into the sea as soon as they were killed that their numbers may not be known to the enemy.[72] This indicates the difference between Rama and Ravana's approaches towards their soldiers.

The strategic paradigm of Rama could not be simply explained in the traditional either-or format of idealism and realism. The strategic culture of Rama reflects a combination of both idealism and realism as far as the international relations theory is concerned. Strategic thinking and the strategic preferences of Rama are indicative of defensive realism. On the other hand, Rama's belief in non-dualistic metaphysics and his emphasis on righteousness witnessed high moral norms and idealism in his thinking. Rama's realism was rooted in his spiritual idealism.

Strategic Culture of Ravana

The core values of Ravana were materialism and material gain. Though Ravana was well versed in Vedic knowledge and was a devotee of Lord Siva, he used his knowledge and devotion to accumulate hard power and used this power to establish hegemony over others. Moral codes of conduct and human values have no place in Ravana's strategic thinking. Lamenting on the death of Ravana, his wife, Mandodari, herself acknowledged this fact. Mandodari deplored that Ravana proved to be a great source of annoyance to all the three worlds, threw all the worlds into disorder by oppressing them, tormented pious men, violated the moral order, employed conjuring tricks on the battlefield, bore away from various places the virgin daughters of gods, demons and human beings and perpetrated terrible deeds.[73] Ravana barely displayed any respect for others. When Kumbhinasi, daughter of Ravana's mother's sister, was taken away by king Madhu from Lanka, Vibhishana asked Ravana whether "this is surely the fruit of your sinful deeds as well as your perverse mind."[74]

Ravana hardly had any reverence for the dignity of women and was often 'overpowered by infatuation born of lust'.[75] He violated the chastity of the celestial nymph, Rambha.[76] Rambha's husband, Nalakubara, (son of Kubera) pronounced a terrible curse on Ravana that if "he will violate a woman who is unwilling to approach him, his head would split into seven pieces that very moment".[77] While returning home from his military campaign, Ravana bore away the virgin daughters of kings, *Rsis* (seers of Vedic mantras), gods and danavas.[78] All these women lamented and cursed Ravana that he would meet his death through the efforts of a woman alone.[79] While ranging over the Earth's surface, Ravana also insulted Vedavati who pronounced a curse on him stating that "for the sake of your destruction, I will be born again".[80]

Ravana was inclined towards the accumulation and maximisation of power. Maintaining and expanding material gain and hard power was a central theme in Ravana's strategic thought. To enhance his power, Ravana along with his younger brothers worshipped Lord Brahma who granted boons which would bring victory.[81] Ravana could not get absolute immortality as a boon from Lord Brahma but got immunity from death at the hands of Suparnas (eagles), Nagas (serpents), Yaksas, Daityas, Daanavas, Rakshasas, as also from gods.[82] Ravana was not scared of human beings and monkeys because he considered them too weak to challenge his power. Lord Brahma also gave another boon to Ravana that "you will assume any form at will."[83] Lord Sankara gifted Ravana the highly shining sword known as Candrahasa.[84] Ravana learned a hundred conjuring tricks from the demon Nivatakavacas.[85] Ravana's son Meghnad also performed seven sacrifices at Nikumbhila in Lanka for receiving boons from Lord Siva.[86] As a result of these sacrificial performances, Meghanad received a heavenly car, conjuring tricks to be applied in conflict, a pair of inexhaustible quivers full of arrows, a bow exceedingly difficult to resist and a powerful missile capable of exterminating the foe.[87] Meghnad also got power from Lord Brahma in exchange for releasing god Indra from his captivity.[88]

Ravana used this accumulation of power to expand his influence and empire. The first goal was to capture Lanka and in this regard, the lord of wealth, Kubera was forced to leave Lanka following which the Rakshasas occupied it and Ravana was installed as its ruler.[89] After assuming power in Lanka, Ravana "destroyed the gods, the Rsis, the Yaksas and the Gandharvas without restraint of any kind."[90] Ravana also overran the Nandana grove which was the pleasure garden of Indra.[91]

After receiving the message of Kuber to follow good conduct, Ravana not only killed the messenger but also declared that "I have made up my mind to conquer all the three worlds relying on the strength of my arms" and "I will send the four Dikpalas (guardians of the four directions) to the abode of Yama just on his account."[92] Ravana defeated all the four Dikpalas. Ravana overwhelmed Kubera, the lord of wealth, and seized his aerial car known as Puspaka.[93] Ravana also invaded the domain of Yama and destroyed his forces.[94] Ravana invaded the abode of Varuna, the god of water, and vanquished the sons of Varuna.[95] Ravana also invaded the realm of Indra.[96] Meghanada captured Indra using Maya (conjuring tricks) and declared his victory over him.[97]

Ravana ranged over the Earth's surface and oppressed many kings. Some kings who disobeyed Ravana's command perished and others surrendered to Ravana knowing his invincibility.[98] Ravana challenged King Marutta who finally decided to withdraw from battle and Ravana's triumph was declared.[99] Consulting one another and recognizing the enemy's strength, many fearless and exceedingly mighty kings like Dusyanta, Suratha, Gadhi, Gaya, and Pururava admitted to Ravana that they stood defeated.[100] In the process of conquering all the kings, Ravana also killed king Anaranya of Ayodhya and was cursed by him that the son of Dasaratha would end his life.[101] To overwhelm *Rasatala*, Ravana entered the ocean zone and subdued the Nagas, defeated the sons of Varun, vanquished Kalakeyas, killed his brother-in-law Vidyujjihva and challenged the powerful Nivatakavacas.[102] Ravana also challenged King Arjun, King Vali, and devil Nivatakavacas but could not defeat these three powerful kings. It can be argued that Ravana was trying to establish a unipolar power structure based on excessive use of hard power. The King of Lanka was moving towards a sort of global domination by dominating all the three worlds which could be termed as Pax-Ravana.

Describing Ravana's unlimited power, his wife, Mandodari, deplored that "you were the death, even to Death himself." Ravana was so drunk with power that he did not pay any heed to the 'salutary advice' of his well-wishers. Ravana ignored the 'counsel duly offered' by his brother Vibhisana and Kumbhakarna, maternal uncle Marica and his father-in-law, Maya.[103]

Ravana's conception of enmity and friendship is different from that of Rama's. Ravana was not ready to accept or consider anybody as superior or equal to him. Ravana has an envy ethos towards all those whom he found superior to himself. Explaining Ravana's hegemonic behaviour, the gods complained to Lord Brahma that he "is harassing the three worlds" and "hates the exalted or prosperous and seeks to overpower even Indra (the lord of paradise).[104] In this regard, *Valmiki* narrates that "approaching whomsoever he heard of as superior in might, irrespective of whether he was an ogre or a human being, Ravana, full of arrogance, challenged him to a duel".[105]

Ravana was more interested in dominating others rather than making them friends. He considered whosoever disagrees or opposes him as an enemy. He established a friendship with those people whom he could not defeat in battle. When Ravana tried to enter the abode of Lord Siva, Nandi asked him to 'turn back' because 'Lord Shankar is sporting on the hill' and the 'place has been rendered inaccessible to all created beings'.[106] Ignoring the advice of Nandi, Ravana laughed loudly at him and 'put his hand below the hill and lifted it in no time'; resultantly, 'the hill shook violently' and 'the attendants of the Lord trembled' and even 'Parvati also slipped and clung to Maheswara'.[107] Mahadev pressed the hill with His big toe and Ravana's arms were then crushed. Ravana's ministers advised him that "in all humility seek refuge in Him by singing His praises". Thus Ravana, respectfully bowing to Shankara, glorified God. Pleased with Ravana's praise, Mahadev released him and also gave him the gift of boons.[108]

Even king Arjun of Mahismati, monkey king Vali of Kishkindha and devil Nivatakavacas of Manimaypuri were no exceptions to the above proposition regarding Ravana's idea of friendship. Ravana did indeed have a friendship treaty with king Arjun, monkey king Vali and devil Nivatakavacas. Initially, Ravana wanted to fight and defeat all of them but failed and either got defeated like in the case of Arjun and Vali or was faced with deadlock as in the case of the Nivatakavacas (a class of demons) and finally offered a hand of friendship to all three of them. Ravana approached Nivatakavacas and challenged them to combat but there was neither victory nor defeat for any of the two sides.[109] On the advice of Lord Brahma, Ravana concluded an alliance with the Nivatakavacas.[110] In Ravana's strategic calculation, friendship building or alliance making was a function of utmost necessity or a result of his weaker position rather than a desirable thing.

Ravana's conception of the use of force was different from that of Rama. The offensive use of force as an instrument of war was an essential element of the strategic culture of Ravana. In the strategic preference of Ravana, war was an indispensable component of human affairs rather than an exception. In the strategic thinking of Ravana, the use of force was a means to establish hegemony and expand the empire. Ravana was thirsty for combat.[111] Ravana's usual statement or mandate to the kings of Earth was that either you ' battle with me or admit that you stand vanquished.'[112] Ravana was very fierce in combat and was so obsessed with victory over others that he killed even his brother-in-law named Vidyujjihva on the field of battle. Ravana himself recognised that he was intoxicated in the war for victory and was unable to distinguish between his people and others in combat while fighting.[113]

Ravana does not believe in peaceful coexistence. His sole aim was to expand his empire and establish hegemony over others by any means, be it hard power, conjuring tricks or deception. Ravana wishes to eliminate all his enemies. For Ravana, adversary is defined as an obstacle to the path to power and hegemony. Because of his lust for power and his hegemonic ambitions, Ravana did not like the multiple form of politico-strategic structure. Rather, he wanted to establish a unipolar structure based on excessive use of power. Coexistence and respect for others did not have any place in Ravana's strategic thinking. He dislodged his brother, Kuber, from power in Lanka and soon after initiated a drive for the expansion of his empire.

Application of the instruments of stratagem and deception against the enemy was a major component of the war-fighting strategy of Ravana. Straight warfare of the Yaksas was different from that of deceitful warfare of the Rakshasas and that is why the Rakshasas had the upper hand in their conflict with the Yaksas.[114] Meghanad applied conjuring tricks in conflict against god Indra and his son Jayant.[115] Meghanad also employed these conjuring tricks in the war against Rama.[116] Spy ogre Akampana suggested that Ravana adopt deception as a strategy against Rama and advised him to kidnap Sita by force as Akampana was of the view that "bereft of Sita, Rama will no longer survive in any case."[117] Demon Vajradamstra also emphasised the use of deception along with the use of force against Rama. He was convinced that if Rama and Laksmana fall into a trap, they needs must succumb to Ravana's wicked policy.[118] Mahodara suggested using stratagem as an instrument for achieving the desired goal without waging war with the powerful Rama. He was of the view that stratagem was the best course as the struggle with Rama will bring disaster. He suggested that "conquering his enemies without a contest, a mighty ruler of the Earth for his part fully enjoys for long renown and religious merit too as also prosperity and placidity, without meeting any danger."[119]

The military strategy of Ravana witnessed an evolution at the operational level. Ravana uses both strategic offence and strategic defence at different times. The military strategy of Ravana in his earlier military operations for expansion of his empire and hegemony over others was based on the strategic offence. On the other hand, the military strategy of Ravana against Rama was reflective of reactive options and strategic defence Here, Ravana's application of strategic defence and reactive strategy was more or less based on his strategic assessment of Rama's military capability. Ravana underestimated Rama's military capability and did not use all his military power against him. Ravana, Kumbhkarna, and Meghnada did not fight a war with Rama together.

There emerged a sort of strategic pluralism in Lanka as far as strategy against Rama is concerned. Four Upayas was known as an instrument of strategy. The point of discussion in Ravana's court in dealing with Rama's army was centred on choosing the strategic preferences among the four Upayas known as Sam, Daan, Bhed, and Danda. Ravana, along with many of his courtiers, was in favour of using the instrument of Bhed and Danda against Rama rather than Sam and Daan. On the other hand, Vibhishana and Malyavan were suggesting the use of Sam or persuasion as a strategy to deal with Rama's army. However, Ravana ignored the advice of Vibhishan and Malyavan and decided to use Bhed and Danda as strategic preferences against Rama. Spy Shardul suggested Ravana sow dissension in the enemy's rank and split Sugreev from Rama.[120] Ravana sends his spy messenger Shuk for that purpose but failed in doing so.[121]

Intelligence, surveillance, and reconnaissance were also very important in the strategic planning of Ravana for knowing the military preparedness of the enemy. He ordered his spies to "ascertain the plans of Rama as well of those who are nearest to him and who have got united with him through love".[122] Ravana knew that "an enemy whose movements and strength have come to be known through a spy is repulsed by wise monarchs with very little effort after being assailed."[123] In his earlier military operations against Devas (gods) and the four Lokpalas, Ravana did not give any importance to ICR elements. Akampana, Suka, Sarana and Sardula were involved in espionage and provided information about Rama's preparations to Ravana.

Strategic thought and strategic preferences of Ravana are reflective of aggressive realism in terms of contemporary discourse on international relations theory. Ravana seems to be one of the first exponents of aggressive realism as far as the international relation theory is concerned. However, the Western narrative of international relations theory did not give due importance to Ravana's strategic thinking in explaining and analysing realism.

Conclusion

The strategic culture in *Ramayana* is not monolithic because of strategic plurality in the *Ramayana*. The strategic thought and strategic preferences of Rama and Ravana were entirely different. Differences of opinion also appeared in the court of Ravana while he was discussing a strategic plan to deal with Rama's army. The cause of the difference between the strategic visions of Rama with that of Ravana lies in their different core values. The core values of Ram and Ravana were poles apart and opposed to each other. Rama's core value lies in the spiritual non-dualistic idea. Rama's strategic thinking was aimed at establishing righteousness, justice, and order and to protect people and subjects from evil forces. For Rama, the nature of the use of force, military preparedness and friendship building are defensive rather than offensive. Rama's strategic vision regarding internal and external balancing was not aimed at harassing or dominating others. Rama was opposed to hegemonic behaviour and did not wish to establish hegemony over others. Rama's military doctrine could be termed as an active defence. On the other hand, the core values of Ravana were materialism and the emphasis was on material gain. That is why the strategic thinking of Ravana was focused on accumulation of hard power and to establish hegemony over others. War is not an aberration but a desirable thing for Ravana. Aggressive use of force was an essential instrument for Ravana to expand his empire. Ravana's strategic propositions are reflective of offensive realism. The *Ramayana* tradition emphasized that the victory of Rama over Ravana indicated that the core values and strategic preferences of Rama were preferable to that of Ravana's.

The study of the *Ramayana* along with other ancient Indian texts could provide an alternative Indian paradigm of strategic culture and narrative in International Relations Theory (IRT). This would be useful in developing a non-Western approach and an Indic perspective towards strategic thought and IRT. The study of strategic culture in the *Ramayana* could be a milestone towards building an Indian version of International Relations Theory. Though the strategic culture is the product of numerous factors, *Ramayana*'s impact in terms of the strategic paradigm of Rama could be felt upon India's strategic thought and behaviour regarding the combination of peace-loving ethos and use of force as the last resort.

NOTES

1. Alistair Iain Johnston, *Cultural Realism: Strategic Culture and Grand Strategy in Chinese History* (Princeton: Princeton University Press, 1995); Alastair Iain Johnston, "Thinking about Strategic Culture", *International Security*, Vol. 19, No. 4, Spring 1995, pp. 32-64; Alastair Iain Johnston, "Cultural Realism and Strategy in Maoist China", in Peter J. Katzenstein ed., *The Culture of National Security* (New York: Columbia University Press, 1996) pp. 216-268.
2. Johnston, "Thinking about Strategic Culture", p. 46.
3. Alaistair Iain Johnston, *Cultural Realism*, p. ix.
4. Johnston, "Thinking about Strategic Culture", p. 46.
5. Ibid.
6. Ibid., p. 50.
7. George K. Tanaham, *Indian Strategic Thought: An Interpretive Essay*, (Santa Monica: Rand, 1992), p. 50.
8. K. Subrahmanyam, *Shedding Shibboleths: India's Evolving Strategic Outlook* (New Delhi: Wordsmiths, 2005), pp. 3-17.
9. Jaswant Singh, *India at Risk: Mistakes, Misconceptions and Misadventures of Security Policy*, (New Delhi: Rupa. 2013), p. 8.
10. Bharat Karnad, "Why India Is Not A Great Power (Yet)", (New Delhi: Oxford University Press, 2015), p. 2.
11. Ibid., p. 5.
12. Ibid., p. 11.

13. Rodney W. Jones, "India's Strategic Culture", Defence Threat Reduction Agency, Advanced Systems, and Concepts Office, 2006, p. 3.
14. Kanti Bajpai, "Indian Grand Strategy: Six Schools of Thought" in Kanti Bajpai, Saira Basit and V. Krishnappa, ed., *India's Grand Strategy: History, Theory, Cases,* (New Delhi: Routledge, 2013), pp. 113- 150; Also see Kanti Bajpai, "Indian Strategic Culture" in Kanti P. Bajpai and Harsh V. Pant ,ed., *India's Foreign Policy: A Reader,* (New Delhi: Oxford University Press, 2013), pp. 82-126.
15. Shrikant Paranjpe, *India's Strategic Culture: The Making of National Security Policy,* (New Delhi: Routledge, 2013), p. 9.
16. Kanti Bajpai and Harsh V. Pant, "Introduction" in Kanti P. Bajpai and Harsh V. Pant ed., *India's Foreign Policy: A Reader,* (New Delhi: Oxford University Press, 2013), pp. 4-5.
17. Ibid., p. 4.
18. Ibid.
19. Kaushik Roy, *Hinduism and Ethics of Warfare in South Asia: From Antiquity to the Present*, (Cambridge University Press, 2013).
20. B. N. S. Yadav, 'Chivalry and Warfare' in Jos J. L. Gommans and Dirk H. A. Kolff (eds.), Warfare and Weaponry in South Asia, 1000-1800, New Delhi, Oxford University Press, 2001, p. 67.
21. Torkel Brekke, "Between Prudence and Heroism: Ethics of War in Hindu Tradition", in Torkel Brekke, (ed.), *The Ethics of War in Asian Civilizations* (Abingdon: Oxon, 2006), pp. 113-144.
22. Ibid., p. 127.
23. Raj Balkaran and A. Walter Dorn, "Violence in the Balmiki Ramayana: Just War Criteria in an Ancient Epic", *Journal of American Academy of Religion*, Vol. 80, No. 3, September 2012, pp. 669-690, at http://walterdorn.net/165-ramayana-and-just-war
24. Swarna Rajgopalan, 'Grand Strategic Thought' in Ramayana and Mahabharata', in Kanti Bajpai, Saira Basit, V. Krishnapppa, *India's Grand Strategy: History, Theory, Cases*, (New Delhi: Routledge, 2014), pp. 31-62.
25. Ibid., pp. 56-58.
26 Srimad Valmiki Ramayana, Vols. I and II, (Gorakhpur: Gita Press, 1919, 13th reprint).
27. L.N. Rangarajan, *Kautilya: The Arthashastra*, (New Delhi: Penguin Books India, 1992), p. 3.
28. Ibid., p. 4.
29. Pandey Ramtej Shastri, Kautilya Arthashastra (Kashi: Pandit Pustakalaya, 1964), p. 17.
30. Yog Vashistha (in Hindi), (Gorakhpur: Gita Press, Samvat 2061).
31. Srimad Valmiki Ramayana, Vol. I, Ayodhyakanda, Canto 21, Verses 40-41, pp. 275-276.
32. Srimad Valmiki Ramayana, Vol. I, Ayodhyakanda, Canto 21, Verse 57, p. 276.
33. Srimad Valmiki Ramayana, Vol. I, Ayodhyakanda, Canto 21, Verse 58, p. 276.
34. Srimad Valmiki Ramayana, Vol. I, Ayodhyakanda, Canto 67, Verse 33, p. 415.
35. Srimad Valmiki Ramayana, Vol. I, Ayodhyakanda, Canto 67, Verses 8-36.

36. Srimad Valmiki Ramayana, Vol. I, Ayodhyakanda, Canto 67, pp. 413-415.
37. Srimad Valmiki Ramayana, Vol. I, Ayodhyakanda, Canto 100, pp. 499-505.
38. Srimad Valmiki Ramayana, Vol. I, Balakanda, Canto 25, Verses 17-19, p. 73.
39. Srimad Valmiki Ramayana, Vol. II, Yuddhakand, Canto 111, Verses 98-99, p. 629.
40. Srimad Valmiki Ramayana, Vol. II, Yuddhakand, Canto 111, Verse 100, p. 629.
41. Srimad Valmiki Ramayana, Vol. II, Yuddhakand, Canto 111, Verse 101, p. 629.
42. Srimad Valmiki Ramayana, Vol. II, Yuddhakand, Canto 111, Verse 124, p. 631.
43. Srimad Valmiki Ramayana, Vol. I, Ayodhyakanda, Canto 21, pp. 272-277.
44. Srimad Valmiki Ramayana, Vol. I, Ayodhyakanda, Canto 21, Verse 44, p. 275.
45. Srimad Valmiki Ramayana, Vol. I, Aranyakanda, Canto 6, Verses 11-14, p. 568.
46. Srimad Valmiki Ramayana, Vol. I, Balakanda, Canto 25, Verse 19, p. 73.
47. Srimad Valmiki Ramayana, Vol. I, Balakanda, Canto 25, Verses 17-18, p. 73.
48. Srimad Valmiki Ramayana, Vol. I, Aranyakanda, Canto 6, Verses 15-20, pp. 568-569.
49. Srimad Valmiki Ramayana, Vol. I, Aranyakanda, Canto 6, Verses 22-25, p. 569.
50. Srimad Valmiki Ramayana, Vol. I, Aranyakanda, Canto 9, Verses 9-33, pp. 572-574.
51. Srimad Valmiki Ramayana, Vol. I, Aranyakanda, Canto 10, Verses 15-20, p. 576.
52. Srimad Valmiki Ramayana, Vol. I, Balakanda, Canto 20, Verse 20, p. 63.
53. Srimad Valmiki Ramayana, Vol. I, Balakanda, Canto 20, Verse 23, p. 63.
54. Srimad Valmiki Ramayana, Vol. I, Balakanda, Canto 21, Verses 11-18, pp. 64-65.
55. Srimad Valmiki Ramayana, Vol. I, Balakanda, Canto 22, Verse 13, p. 66.
56. Srimad Valmiki Ramayana, Vol. I, Balakanda, Canto 27, Verses 4-24, pp. 77-79.
57. Srimad Valmiki Ramayana, Vol. I, Aranyakanda, Canto 12, Verses 32-37, p. 584.
58. Srimad Valmiki Ramayana, Vol. I, Aranyakanda, Canto 14, Verse 33, p. 609.
59. Srimad Valmiki Ramayana, Vol. II, Sundarakanda, Canto 41, Verses 2-4, p. 144.
60. Srimad Valmiki Ramayana, Vol. II, Sundarakanda, Canto 41, Verse 7, p. 144.
61. Srimad Valmiki Ramayana, Vol. II, Sundarakanda, Canto 41, Verse 9, p. 144.
62. Srimad Valmiki Ramayana, Vol. II, Sundarakanda, Canto 48, Verse 42-44, p. 166.
63. Srimad Valmiki Ramayana, Vol. II, Sundarakanda, Canto 53, Verse 2-5, p. 178.
64. Srimad Valmiki Ramayana, Vol. II, Sundarakanda, Canto 53, Verse 14, p. 179.
65. Srimad Valmiki Ramayana, Vol. II, Yuddhakand, Canto 14, Verse 7, p. 283.
66. Srimad Valmiki Ramayana, Vol. II, Yuddhakand, Canto 37, Verse 7-22, pp. 339-340.
67. Srimad Valmiki Ramayana, Vol. II, Yuddhakand, Canto 38, Verse 2-17, pp. 342-343.
68. Srimad Valmiki Ramayana, Vol. II, Yuddhakand, Canto 4, Verse 10, p. 240.
69. Srimad Valmiki Ramayana, Vol. II, Yuddhakand, Canto 73, Verses 68-74, p. 494.
70. Srimad Valmiki Ramayana, Vol. II, Yuddhakand, Canto 74, Verses 29-34, p. 497.
71. Srimad Valmiki Ramayana, Vol. II, Yuddhakand, Canto 74, Verses 71-74, p. 501.
72. Srimad Valmiki Ramayana, Vol. II, Yuddhakand, Canto 74, Verses 75-76, p. 501.
73. Srimad Valmiki Ramayana, Vol. II, Yuddhakand, Canto 111, Verses 48-55, p. 626.
74. Srimad Valmiki Ramayana, Vol. II, Uttarakand, Canto 25, Verse 28, p. 763.
75. Srimad Valmiki Ramayana, Vol. II, Uttarakand, Canto 17, Verse 3, p. 737.
76. Srimad Valmiki Ramayana, Vol. II, Uttarakand, Canto 26, Verses 40-42, pp. 767-768.
77. Srimad Valmiki Ramayana, Vol. II, Uttarakand, Canto 26, Verses 54-56, pp. 768-769.

78. Srimad Valmiki Ramayana, Vol. II, Uttarakand, Canto 24, Verse 1, p. 758.
79. Srimad Valmiki Ramayana, Vol. II, Uttarakand, Canto 24, Verse 20, p. 759.
80. Srimad Valmiki Ramayana, Vol. II, Uttarakand, Canto 17, Verses 31-32, p. 739.
81. Srimad Valmiki Ramayana, Vol. II, Uttarakand, Canto 9, Verse 48, p. 716.
82. Srimad Valmiki Ramayana, Vol. II, Uttarakand, Canto 10, Verse 19, p. 717.
83. Srimad Valmiki Ramayana, Vol. II, Uttarakand, Canto 10, Verse 25, p. 717.
84. Srimad Valmiki Ramayana, Vol. II, Uttarakand, Canto 16, Verse 44, p. 736.
85. Srimad Valmiki Ramayana, Vol. II, Uttarakand, Canto 23, Verse 16, p. 755.
86. Srimad Valmiki Ramayana, Vol. II, Uttarakand, Canto 25, Verses 2-7, pp. 761-762.
87. Srimad Valmiki Ramayana, Vol. II, Uttarakand, Canto 25, Verses 10-12, p. 762.
88. Srimad Valmiki Ramayana, Vol. II, Uttarakand, Canto 30, Verses 8-15, pp. 780-781.
89. Srimad Valmiki Ramayana, Vol. II, Uttarakand, Canto 11, Verses 1-52, pp. 719-721.
90. Srimad Valmiki Ramayana, Vol. II, Uttarakand, Canto 13, Verse 8, p. 726.
91. Srimad Valmiki Ramayana, Vol. II, Uttarakand, Canto 13, Verse 9, p. 726.
92. Srimad Valmiki Ramayana, Vol. II, Uttarakand, Canto 13, Verse 39, p. 727.
93. Srimad Valmiki Ramayana, Vol. II, Uttarakand, Canto 15, Verse 1-44, pp. 730-733.
94. Srimad Valmiki Ramayana, Vol. II, Uttarakand, Cantos 21 and 22, pp. 747-754.
95. Srimad Valmiki Ramayana, Vol. II, Uttarakand, Canto 23, Verses 20-54, pp. 755-758.
96. Srimad Valmiki Ramayana, Vol. II, Uttarakand, Canto 27, Verse 1, p. 769.
97. Srimad Valmiki Ramayana, Vol. II, Uttarakand, Canto 29, Verses 28-29, p. 778.
98. Srimad Valmiki Ramayana, Vol. II, Uttarakand, Canto 16, Verses 47-49, p. 736.
99. Srimad Valmiki Ramayana, Vol. II, Uttarakand, Canto 18, Verses 18-19, p. 741.
100. Srimad Valmiki Ramayana, Vol. II, Uttarakand, Canto 19, Verses 4-5, p. 743.
101. Srimad Valmiki Ramayana, Vol. II, Uttarakand, Canto 19, Verses 6-32, pp. 743-744.
102. Srimad Valmiki Ramayana, Vol. II, Uttarakand, Canto 23, Verses 4-19, p. 754-755.
103. Srimad Valmiki Ramayana, Vol. II, Yuddhakand, Canto 111, Verses 76-78, pp. 627-628.
104. Srimad Valmiki Ramayana, Vol. I, Balakand, Canto 15, Verse 8, p. 47.
105. Srimad Valmiki Ramayana, Vol. II, Uttarakand, Canto 34, Verse 2, p. 794.
106. Srimad Valmiki Ramayana, Vol. II, Uttarakand, Canto 16, Verse 10, pp. 733-734.
107. Srimad Valmiki Ramayana, Vol. II, Uttarakand, Canto 16, Verses 25-28, p. 735.
108. Srimad Valmiki Ramayana, Vol. II, Uttarakand, Canto 16, Verses 35-45, pp. 735-736.
109. Srimad Valmiki Ramayana, Vol. II, Uttarakand, Canto 23, Verses 5-9, pp. 754-755.
110. Srimad Valmiki Ramayana, Vol. II, Uttarakand, Canto 23, Verse 14, p. 755.
111. Srimad Valmiki Ramayana, Vol. II, Uttarakand, Canto 19, Verse 1, p. 742.
112. Srimad Valmiki Ramayana, Vol. II, Uttarakand, Canto 19, Verses 2-3, p. 742.
113. Srimad Valmiki Ramayana, Vol. II, Uttarakand, Canto 24, Verses 33-34, p. 760.
114. Srimad Valmiki Ramayana, Vol. II, Uttarakand, Canto 15, Verse 9, p. 730.
115. Srimad Valmiki Ramayana, Vol. II, Uttarakand, Cantos 28-29, pp. 773-779.
116. Srimad Valmiki Ramayana, Vol. II, Yuddhakand, Canto 50, Verse 49, p. 384.
117. Srimad Valmiki Ramayana, Vol. I, Aranyakand, Canto 31, Verse 31, p. 626.
118. Srimad Valmiki Ramayana, Vol. II, Yuddhakand, Canto 8, Verses 9-18, p. 254.

119. Srimad Valmiki Ramayana, Vol. II, Uttarakand, Canto 64, Verses 20-36, pp. 440-441.
120. Srimad Valmiki Ramayana, Vol. II, Yuddhakand, Canto 20, Verse 7, p. 286.
121. Srimad Valmiki Ramayana, Vol. II, Yuddhakand, Canto 20, Verses 9-34, pp. 286-288.
122. Srimad Valmiki Ramayana, Vol. II, Yuddhakand, Canto 29, Verse 19, p. 318.
123. Srimad Valmiki Ramayana, Vol. II, Yuddhakand, Canto 29, Verse 21, p. 318.

3

Indic Values of *Shanti* and *Shakti* in Modi's Pakistan Policy

Vivek Kumar Mishra

Introduction

Prime Minister Modi has made a difference in Indian traditional Pakistan foreign policy with his activism, effective operational diplomacy and visualising of a strong state and border policy. Modi's Pakistan policy can be best described as a unique combination of the *Shanti* (Peace) and *Shakti* (Power) paradigm of Bhartiya cultural values. This article attempts to analyse Modi's Pakistan policy based on the principles of Shanti and Shakti of Hindutva: the great nationalist ideology.

Philosophical Foundations

The foreign policy of each state is generally mediated through a set of core ideas and beliefs that policymakers use to justify their preferences and actions for serving the national interest. Hinduism is the guiding principle of Indian Foreign policy. Prime Minister Modi did try to connect foreign policy with *Bhartiya* values by stressing civilisational and cultural ties with the world. During his Lok Sabha election campaign in April 2014, he stated that Hindutva would be the guiding principle in Foreign Affairs. He stated, "I believe in Hindutva, which is based on the age-old concept of *Vasudhaiva Kutumbakam*.[1] "I believe that mutual respect for one another and cooperation should form relationships with foreign nations. And I am confident my Hindutva face will be an asset when dealing with foreign affairs with other nations."[2]

The word *Shakti* and *Shanti* originated from the Sanskrit terms, which mean power. The substance of both words have a clear appeal to India's cultural heritage, specifically to the Hindu heritage. The philosophical foundation of the *Shakti* and *Shanti* paradigm can be traced in the writings of many exponents of *Hinduism*. Modi has underlined the importance of power, stressing that India's historical weakness and colonisation highlighted the need to retain our ancient rich heritage by decolonising the past. He is of the view that *Shanti* and *Shakti* will go together in the arena of International relations.[3] The element of *Shakti* and *Shanti* fulfils the underlying logic of the realist theory of International Relations.

Bhartiya culture and civilisation embodies a unique blend of the *Shakti* and *Shanti* principles. This historical legacy has indubitably moulded the course of our policy and action. The *Mahabharata* can be used as a resource to explain peace and power paradigm, because the *Mahabharata* has stories that throw light on several principles of diplomacy. For example, Lord Krishna's mission as an envoy of the Pandavas to the court of the Kauravas for peaceful negotiations; the six months of intense diplomacy and negotiations before the war; and the display and demonstration of classical principles or virtues of diplomacy like truthfulness, precision, calm, patience, good temper, modesty and loyalty is a clear reflection of the *Shakti* and *Shanti* principles.[4]

Kautilya, in his *Arthashastra*, clearly pointed out "a wise king trained in politics, will, even if he possesses a small territory, conquer the whole Earth with the help of the best-fitted elements of his sovereignty and will never be defeated."[5] As a political realist, Kautilya stated that every nation maximises its power and national interest. Therefore, moral obligations have little or no force in actions among the states. Whether one state goes to war or remains at peace depends entirely upon the self-interest of or advantage to one's kingdom. War and peace are considered solely for the national interest.[6] The attitude of a ruler towards other states depends upon the special circumstances of each case.

Kautilya's six-fold foreign policy highlights some basic principles for attaining one's national interest and goals at the level of international politics based on political reality. According to Kautilya, the statesman should adopt the six-fold foreign policy, which includes peace (*Sandhi*) and power (*Vigrah*). Modi's foreign policy mirrors Kautilya's emphasis on a realistic, pragmatic, and intelligent use of power. While focusing on enhancing power as advised by Kautilya, Modi's believes in *Vasudhaiva Kutumbakam*. He feels that a judicious blend of power and peace approach in foreign policy can potentially turn India into a great power, i.e., *Vishva Guru*.[7]

The roots of the *Shanti* and *Shakti* paradigm can also be traced in the writings of Vinayak Damodar Savarkar, one of the principal exponents of *Hindutva*.[8] In his book, *Essentials of Hindutva*, he asserted that "national identity has important implications for the foreign policy of any country and adds, three critical criteria confer national identity: common blood, common laws and rites; and common culture." The explaination of national identity has important implications for foreign policy and national defence. Savarkar sees "a strong national identity as ultimately necessary for a strong national military." He writes in *Essentials of Hindutva*: "Moreover everything common in us with our enemies weakens our power of opposing them. The foe that has nothing in common with us is the foe likely to be most bitterly resisted by us just as a friend that has almost everything in him that we admire and prize in ourselves is likely to be the friend we love most."[9] According to Savarkar, *Hindutva* is not a word, but it is the spiritual or religious life of the Bhartiya people and the entire civilisation's history. Hinduism is only a derivative, a fraction, a part of Hindutva.[10] He has given more stress on nationalism, which is the instrument of national unity. In this context, he can be understood as a 'defensive strategist' focused on nationalism as an instrument of martial cohesion and national unity.

Savarkar's views are replicated by Madhav Sadashiv Golwalkar (Guruji), the second *Sar Sanghchalak* of the Rashtriya Swayamsevak Sangh, who writes, "Indians needed to recognise a truth that for real national honour and peace, there is no other way except the building of invincible national strength" because "the world is not prepared to listen to the philosophy, however sublime, of the weak."[12] Therefore, Indians should pay attention to our Hindu philosophy which tells us that *"man should be humble only when he is capable of humbling others."*[13] Hindutva is the civilisation that has made great cultural contributions to the world and Hindus as destined for global leadership.[14] Modi has intelligently applied Kautilya's principles of foreign policy and thoughts of Savarkar and Golwalkar and adopted the *Shanti* and *Shakti* paradigm in foreign policy to cultivate India's ability to engage power politics to fend off external aggression and security threat perceptions.

The *Shanti* and *Shakti* principles were strengthened during Prime Minister Atal Bihari Vajpayee's Government. Atal Ji foreign policy strategy was based on the leadership of the former military officer and Minister of External Affairs Jaswant Singh and National Security Adviser Brajesh Misra.[15] These practitioners thought that India's military power must be strengthened and a robust nuclear deterrent developed, with pragmatism as the best guide to a nation's foreign and security policy.[16] Modi has extended the Atal Bihari Vajpayee-led National Democratic Alliance government's (1998-2004) foreign policy by blending the *Shanti* and *Shakti* principles. He praised Prime Minister Vajpayee's decision to conduct nuclear tests in 1998 and lauded his public declaration of a 'No First Use' policy of nuclear weapons, striking a balance between *Shakti* and *Shanti*.

The BJP election manifesto of 2014 contains a section on foreign policy that states, "In our neighbourhood, we will pursue friendly relations. However, where we require...we will not hesitate from taking a strong stand."[17] It also emphasizes 'zero tolerance' of terrorism and 'extremism' and pledges to "deal with cross-border terrorism with a firm hand[18] and to build a strong, self-reliant and self-confident India regaining its rightful place in the comity of nations making alliances where necessary - a potentially significant promise, given India's longstanding wariness of alliances and preferences for non-alignment and strategic autonomy."[19] But, at the same time, the manifesto also emphasised: "soft power" designed to restore India to its proper place as *Vishwaguru*.[20]

Pakistan and Modi's Policy of Rebuild Neighbourhood

Prime Minister Narendra Modi's first foreign policy initiative was to rebuild neighbourhood relations in the South Asian region.[21] In this regard, he invited all the heads of the government of the South Asian Association for Regional Cooperation (SAARC) countries to participate in his oath-taking ceremony on May 26, 2014. This indicated that the neighbourhood is the top priority of Modi's foreign policy. Modi inherited very difficult relations with Pakistan after his predecessor suspended bilateral peace talks. However, he met Pakistan's Prime Minister Nawaz Sharif at his swearing-in ceremony in New Delhi, which led to setting up a meeting at the Foreign Secretary-level. It was an attempt to resume stalled dialogue after the Mumbai terror attack in 2008. He also greeted Nawaz Sharif on Pakistan's National Day and said that all outstanding issues between the two states could be resolved through bilateral dialogue in an atmosphere free from terror and violence.[22]

The Modi government in August 2014 formally objected to the meeting between the Pakistani High Commissioner and the separatist Kashmiri Hurriyat leaders in New Delhi and suddenly cancelled Foreign Secretary-level talks scheduled for August 25, 2014 in Islamabad.[23] The reason was that Pakistan continued to engage with the separatist Kashmiri Hurriyat Conference leaders, despite being cautioned by India against such activities.[24] Foreign Secretary Sujatha Singh conveyed to the Pakistan High Commissioner that Pakistan's continued efforts to interfere in India's internal affairs were unacceptable. Pakistan has to resolve all outstanding issues through a peaceful bilateral dialogue within the "Shimla Agreement" framework. The cancellation of Foreign Secretary-level talks conveyed a strong message to Islamabad.[25] The breakdown of the talks dashed the hopes raised by Modi's initiative of a positive turn in relations with Pakistan.

Pakistan incessantly violated the LoC and sponsored corss-border terrorism. Responding to Pakistan's periodic ceasefire violation across the Line of Control, India's Defense Minister warned Pakistan that it will make the "cost of this adventurism unaffordable."[26] Indeed, the Modi Government's position towards Pakistan has hardened because of the "zero-tolerance policy" on terrorism with the principle that "terror and talks can't go together." It is to be noted that the previous regimes reluctantly tolerated such meetings.

The Prime Ministers of both countries met at the SAARC summit held on November 26-27, 2014, at Kathmandu. Prime Minister Modi reminded all the members of SAARC about the Mumbai terror attack of 2008 and urged them to "work together to fulfil the pledge we have taken to combat terrorism and transnational crimes."[27] This was done because November 26, the day of the Kathmandu summit, happened to be the anniversary of the Mumbai attack. In the interest of building regional consensus on development, PM Modi avoided raising any of the sensitive issues that could offend any of his regional counterparts. However, the bilateral approach of Pakistan disrupted Modi's South Asian initiative. Pakistan's anti-India approach was the single most important factor behind the disappointing outcome of the Kathmandu SAARC Summit.[28]

Modi-Sharif Meeting in Ufa (July 10, 2015)

Prime Minister Modi met his Pakistani counterpart Nawaz Sharif on the sidelines of the Shanghai Cooperation Organization (SCO) Summit on 10th July 2015 in the eastern Russian city of Ufa. Both leaders agreed that India and Pakistan have a collective responsibility to ensure peace and promote development and condemned terrorism in all its forms. They agreed to cooperate to eliminate this menace from South Asia.[29] The meeting was focused entirely on terrorism and security issues, laying down a structure of talks between the National Security Advisers (NSA) of the two countries to discuss all issues connected to terrorism to be followed by meetings of the two 'countries' border management forces and then of the Director Generals of Military Operations.[30] It was also agreed that both countries "will expedite the Mumbai case trial, including additional information like providing voice samples" that were long pending on the Pakistani side.[31] India has handed over more than 14 dossiers of evidence, including the evidence used to complete the trial against terrorist Ajmal Kasab and others in India after the Mumbai attack. However, "Pakistan had not agreed to accept much of the evidence, as its judicial team was denied direct access to Kasab in custody before he was sentenced and executed."[32] The outstanding issue for India was cross-border terrorism and action against Zaki-ur-Rahman Lakhvi and other Mumbai attack accused. PM Modi raised India's concerns on terror and the release of Lashkar-e-Taiba leader Zaki-ur-Rehman Lakhvi, who was the operations commander of the Lashkar-e-Taiba and trained Ajmal Kasab and the other terrorists who attacked Mumbai, and given bail by a Pakistani trial court in April 2015, and has subsequently been exempted from personal appearances in court. However, Pakistan has not accepted the evidence given by India. Lakhvi and other terrorists were thus released.

The Pakistani army has never allowed the civilian government to have any decisive say in Pakistan's India policy, nor can they abandon the so-called strategic assets (jihadi organisations and their leaders) created and nurtured by them to keep India bleeding.[33] The Ufa meeting was followed by the terrorist attack at Dinanagar (Gurdaspur) on 27 July 2015, effectively derailing the scheduled National Security Adviser (NSA) talks.[34] Therefore, they did not want the NSA-level discussions to take place under the Ufa framework where terrorism was the main agenda, if not the only one, and India appeared to have built up a formidable amount of evidence in the form of dossiers as also living proof to expose Pakistan's army's covert war of terrorism against India.[35] Therefore, the NSA level talk was cancelled because of the differences in agenda of what the NSAs would discuss. India was adamant that the talks should be based on the Ufa spirit to discuss issues about terrorism and terrorism alone, but Pakistan wanted a broader agenda and wanted to include Kashmir.

India-Pakistan NSAs Meet in Bangkok

After the breakdown of talks based on the Ufa agenda, there was a breakthrough in November 2015 when the Prime Ministers of both countries had a meeting in Paris on the sidelines of the global climate change conference.[36] This was followed by a meeting of the National

Security Advisors of the two countries on December 6, 2015, in Bangkok, with an agreement for commitment to further dialogue.[37] The meeting's press release highlight' the discussions that include peace and security, terrorism, Jammu and Kashmir, and other issues, including tranquillity along the LoC".[38] It was also "agreed to carry forward the constructive engagement."[39] The meeting of NSAs in Bangkok and the External Affairs Minister Mrs. Sushma Swaraj trip to Islamabad to attend a conference on the future of Afghanistan were part of the government' decision to reset the engagement with Pakistan that has suffered after the cancellation of the above mentioned Foreign Secretary-level talks and NSA level talks. In the meeting, it was agreed that the governments would meet at four levels: Heads of States, External Affairs Ministers, National Security Advisors, and Foreign Secretaries within ten days.[40]

On December 25, 2015, Prime Minister Modi made an unannounced visit to Prime Minister Nawaz Sharif's residence at Raiwind on his way back from an official trip to Afghanistan.[41] It was the bravest decision since assuming power. The reason for his decision to stop over in Lahore was based on goodwill. Modi's surprise visit to Lahore was thus meant to build on this approach. However, the diplomatic innovations for peace again failed because of the structural impediment, i.e., terrorism, hosted, nurtured and deployed by Pakistan against India.[42]

Pathankot Airbase Attack

On January 2, 2016, *Jaish-e-Mohammed* terrorists attacked the Pathankot airbase in a pre-dawn strike days after PM Narendra Modi made an unannounced visit to meet Pakistan Prime Minister Nawaz Sharif in an attempt to strengthen relations between the two countries.[43] The Pathankot attack had two main aims. The first was to destroy MiG-21, Mi-25, Mi-35 fighter planes, and the other was that the terrorists wanted to destroy Indian military hardware. This attack derailed the peace initiatives, which boosted Modi's surprise stopover in Lahore.[44] The terrorist attack on the Pathankot Air Force base was a return gift from Pakistan in reply to Modi's visit to Lahore, an initiative to further the engagement and set in motion a peace process. After the attack, there were very limited options for New Delhi as far as its relations with

Islamabad were concerned. New Delhi then started an isolation policy to put international pressure on Islamabad to step up its efforts to stop cross-border terrorism against India.

In the context of counter-terrorism measures against Pakistan, Modi has given expression to the Indic values of *Shanti* and *Shakti* in several ways. Prime Minister Modi's policy of *Shanti* or peace with Pakistan is reflected in friendly gestures and policy initiatives, notably inviting then Pakistani Prime Minister Nawaz Sharif to the oath-taking ceremony, but Pakistan has continuously supported terrorist activities against India. Then Modi started diplomatic engagements against Pakistan to mobilise the countries which had commercial relations with Pakistan. The idea of concluding bilateral treaties on countering terrorism with countries from the Middle East (United Arab Emirates) or of visiting countries in Central Asia, as well as Saudi Arabia, to receive diplomatic support and initiate a common battle front against terrorism, represented the support of a diplomatic direction of "containment", assumed by Pakistan.

PM Modi's Initiatives to Isolate Pakistan after the Pathankot Attack

(I) India-Saudi Arabia Joint Statement

Prime Minister Modi has shifted the Pakistan policy with the objectives to strengthen India globally to isolate Pakistan under his policy of *Shanti*.[45] In continuation of his Gulf policy, Modi has signed a joint statement with Saudi Arabia. The Joint Statement issued after PM 'Modi's visit to Saudi Arabia in 2015 includes five extensive paragraphs on terrorism, called on all the states to reject the use of terrorism against other countries, dismantle terrorism infrastructure "where they happen to exist, and cut off any support and financing to the terrorists operating and perpetrating terrorism from their territories against other states, and bring the perpetrators involved in the acts of terrorism to justice."[46] Modi and Saudi King Salman bin Abdul-Aziz Al Saud have expressed strong condemnation of terrorism in all its forms and manifestations. "Affirming that the menace of extremism and terrorism threatens all nations and societies, the two leaders rejected any attempt to link this universal phenomenon to any particular race, religion or culture."[47] The two sides agreed to work together to adopt India's proposed

Comprehensive Convention on International Terrorism in the United Nations.[48] This is a very important development between the two countries, and Saudi Arabia should control the finance going to Pakistan's institutions, especially the madrasas, in the coming days. India is also hopeful that Saudi Arabia can persuade and pressure Pakistan to prevent it from using extremist groups for its advantage, especially against India. Prime Minister Modi was conferred the Arabian country's highest civilian honour – *The King Abdulaziz Sash.*[49] It was a diplomatic win for India because despite giving billions of dollars in aid and employing millions of Pakistanis, the Saudis have never bestowed their highest civilian honour on a Pakistani leader.[50]

(II) Terrorism and PM 'Modi's Address in US Congress (June 8, 2016)

In his address to the joint sitting of the US Congress on June 8, 2016, PM Modi stated that "India will never forget the solidarity shown by the U.S. Congress when terrorists from across our border attacked Mumbai in November of 2008."[51] He also stated, "not just in Afghanistan, but elsewhere in South Asia, and globally, terrorism remains the biggest threat. Its objectives are common: hate, murder, and violence.[52] In a not-so-veiled reference to Pakistan, Modi said that terrorism was "incubated in India's neighbourhood."[53] He said that terrorism has to be fought with "one voice" and commended the American Parliament for sending out a clear message by refusing to "reward" those who preach and practise terrorism for political gains, an apparent reference to the blocking of sale of eight F-16 fighter jets to Pakistan.[54] Modi expressed that "the need of the hour is to isolate those who sponsor terrorists and did not distinguish between "good" and "bad" terrorists as terrorism was not just a threat in Afghanistan, but elsewhere also in South Asia."[55]

(III) PM Modi's Independence Day Speech (August 2016)

Prime Minister Modi adopted the *Shanti* approach in the context of Pakistan from the Red Fort in New Delhi when he said that, "I want to present before the world two pictures that show the difference between those people who were brought up under the influence of humanism and those who reward terrorism. I want to tell the world and those who believe in humanity by narrating the two incidents that weigh the incident at Peshawar, where the terrorists had gunned down innocent school children in December 2014. Innocent boys and girls were killed; the temple of learning was soaked in blood by killing innocent children. There were tears in the eyes of our Parliamentarians. Indian school's children were crying, and every child in India felt the shock of the death of the children of Peshawar. This is our culture, borne out of humanism. On the other hand, terrorism is being glorified. When innocent people were killed in terrorist attacks, there were celebrations. What kind of life is this which is inspired by terrorism? How are governments formed through the inspiration of terrorism? The world will understand this difference clearly."[56] Repeating the charge against Pakistan for its support to terror groups in Kashmir, he said, the Pakistan government was glorifying terrorists, saying the Sharif government's actions were in sharp contrast to India's empathy with Pakistanis over terror attacks there, as after the Peshawar school massacre. The speech had a very strong component targeting Pakistan.

(IV) India's Balochistan Campaign

In his continued pursuance of the *Shanti* approach and isolation strategy, Modi stated in his Independence Day speech of 2016, "I want to greet and express my thanks to some people. In the last few days, Balochistan, Gilgit, Pakistan Occupied Kashmir people have thanked me, have expressed gratitude and expressed good wishes for me. The people who are living far away, whom I have never seen, never met - such people have expressed appreciation for the Prime Minister of India for 125 crore countrymen."[57] After the 2009 Sharm-el-Sheikh joint statement, the Balochistan insurgency assumed a prominent place in India's foreign policy discourse for the first time.[58] By raising the Balochistan issue, Modi has changed the rules of the game from the Indian point of view and gave a warning signal to Pakistan."[59]

India accused Pakistan of widespread human rights violations in Balochistan and Pakistan-occupied Jammu Kashmir (PoJK).[60] In a scathing attack on Pakistan during the 33rd Session of the UN Human Rights Council in Geneva, India said the main reason for disturbances in Kashmir was and is the Pakistan sponsored cross-border terrorism that stems from its territorial ambitions and has found concrete expression in repeated armed aggression. India's Ambassador and Permanent Representative at the U.N. in Geneva, Ajit Kumar, said that

"Pakistan is a country, which has systematically abused and violated the human rights of its citizens, including in Balochistan, as well as of the people of Pakistan-Occupied Jammu & Kashmir (POJK)."[61] In foreign policy terms, PM Modi's singling out of the Balochistan issue at an official political platform is unprecedented but will be seen by the Pakistan leadership as a counter-pressure in response to cross-border terrorism. Moreover, the Balochistan strategy gives India leverage and provides an option to respond forcefully to Pakistan's use of (terrorist) force against India without fearing nuclear escalation.

The growing international isolation of Pakistan resulted in frustration within Pakistan. PM Modi has spread his diplomatic dynamism worldwide at the bilateral and multilateral levels, which have diminished the credibility of Pakistan. "The USA has cut down the credit line" to its "trusted ally", as "Bangladesh and Afghanistan are openly talking about Pakistan as a terror-sponsoring state."[62] The Pakistani government was crumbling due to various internal reasons and adopted its best option to divert attention through anti-India sentiments in the form of the Uri attack. The Uri attack is the response to the growing isolation of Pakistan.

Uri Terror Attack

The Uri terror attack on September 18, 2016, on the Indian Army headquarters near the LoC has made relations tense on both states.[63] It was one of the biggest attacks on the Indian Armed Forces to date. During a speech at Kozhikode, Kerala, on September 23, 2016, Modi vowed that India would start a global campaign to isolate Pakistan. In his first public speech after the Uri attack, he termed Pakistan as one country in Asia conspiring to spill 'blood' across the continent and export terror to the world. Modi stated, "We will isolate you, and I will work for that this is the only country that is exporting terrorism in all corners."[64] This attack has broken the dam of "strategic restraint" in India. And yet, for over a week, India played it by the book, including sharing evidence with the Pakistan High Commissioner. But in the face of Pakistani denials, and worse, Pakistan's preposterous allegation that Uri was a "false flag" operation, India was left with no choice but to exercise the military operation in the form of a 'surgical strike' to send a strong message to Pakistan.

After the Uri attack, Nawaz Sharif raised the issue of Jammu and Kashmir in the 71st session of the United Nations General Assembly and praised Hizbul Mujahideen terrorist Burhan Wani who was killed in an encounter with security forces on July 8, 2016.[65] 'India's External Affairs Minister Mrs. Sushma Swaraj hit back on the same platform and called Pakistan a "terrorist state" which hosts the "Ivy League of terrorism"[66] and carries out war crimes against Indians through its "long-standing policy of sponsoring terrorism".[67] She also stated that "The land of Taxila, one of the greatest learning centres of ancient times "now hosts to the Ivy League of terrorism."[68] Mrs. Swaraj also pulled no punches in calling for identifying countries (she was indicating towards Pakistan) "that speak the language of terrorism, that nurture it, peddle it, and export it" and went on to show Pakistan a mirror by pointing to the "egregious abuses" by the Pakistani state against its people, including the brutality against the Baloch people."[69] This was the first time that India raised the issue of Balochistan at the UN.[70]

Shakti Strategy

On the *Shakti* side, Modi has taken many steps as well to balance things. However, his *Shanti* (peace) initiatives have failed just after the terror strike in Pathankot. The attack was an attempt to disrupt the peace initiative. Modi's efforts have always been reciprocated with friendship, but Pakistan's response was the terror attack in various parts of India.

(I) Surgical Strikes

The surgical strikes by India on terrorist camps across the Line of Control (LoC) in Pakistan were a perfect example of the *Shakti* strategy. In strikes just after midnight on September 29, 2016, "India airdropped commandos at the LoC, from where they crossed over 3 km into the Pakistani side, destroyed seven terrorist launch pads and killed 38 terrorists. The mission ended in a short four hours."[71] After the Uri attack, a strong negative sentiment brewed in the armed forces and the common people in India. So, in a break from tradition, the Director-General of Military Operations (DGMO), Lt. Ranvir Singh, announced on September 30, 2016, that army Special Forces had carried out "surgical strikes" in Pakistan-Occupied Jammu & Kashmir and destroyed seven terror launch pads of terrorists.

The peace and power strategy came into actual implementation after engaging in more than two years of regular diplomacy. Modi continued to engage with Pakistan even after cross-border terrorism continued.[72] India's choice of retaliation in the form of surgical strike responded positively by the international community. In a statement USA, there was no condemnation or censure of India's strike. The NSA Ajit Doval was in touch with his American counterpart, Susan Rice, further proving the growing realisation that India has had enough. US National Security Advisor Susan Rice reportedly said that "the USA expects that Pakistan take effective action to combat and de-legitimise United Nations-designated terrorist individuals and entities, including Lashkar-e-Taiba, Jaish-e-Muhammad, and their affiliates."[73] Countries like China, Turkey, and Saudi Arabia have so far refused to issue statements de-legitimising India's strike. The surgical strike put India into a league with the USA and Israel as "hard," militarily-capable democracies determined to combat terrorism and to punish states that do not fulfil their obligations to curtail terrorism.

India's pre-emptive strike across the LoC for counter-terror attacks has been complemented by proactive diplomacy that has sought to win new friends for India and weaken potential international support for Pakistan. Modi has the political confidence and international credibility to play the global concerns to India's advantage.[74] In devising and projecting the cross-border raids as a limited offensive to counter-terrorism rather than a confrontation with Pakistan.

The Policy of *Shanti* and *Shakti* after Surgical Strike

India is pursuing its ***Shanti*** strategy and has tried to isolate Pakistan from the world community. It has appealed for international condemnation and isolation of Pakistan for aiding and abetting terrorists and their organisations.

(I) Boycott of the 19th SAARC Summit

The biggest blow that India gave to Pakistan on the diplomatic front was its boycott of the 19th SAARC summit of 2016, scheduled at Islamabad. It was a major setback for Pakistan. Pakistan was completely isolated within the South Asia region after the Uri attack. After India's decision to boycott the SAARC summit, Bhutan, Afghanistan,

Maldives, and Sri Lanka also pulled out, citing "concerns on terrorism" and the lack of a "conducive atmosphere" for the forum.[75] Iqbal Chowdhury, the advisor to Bangladesh Prime Minister Sheikh Hasina, said that "India has got the legal, internationally-accepted right to make a response to any attack on her sovereignty and her soil"[76] All members of SAARC issued statements for creating a peaceful environment in South Asia free from terrorism. "It is a notable diplomatic success for India. When SAARC was started, India had been isolated. We were on guard than as it could have become India versus others. But now we have come to a stage where all countries are standing with India."[77]

(II) India-UAE Cooperation against Terrorism

The visit of the Crown Prince of Abu Dhabi to India as the chief guest at Republic Day, 2017, marks the culmination of an extraordinary engagement that PM Narendra Modi has had with the Gulf countries. By inviting the Crown Prince of Abu Dhabi, Prime Minister Modi gave a clear message that India is beefing up its ties with the UAE, which once was classified as Pakistan's closest allies. However, the relations may have given a serious cooling signal between Islamabad and Riyadh after Pakistan's decision not to join the Saudi-led intervention against Houthi rebels in Yemen. On March 25, 2015, a Saudi-led coalition of ten Arab States, including UAE, began an aerial bombing campaign against Houthi rebels in Yemen, who had taken control of Sana'a's capital.[78] The move has been widely viewed as an effort by the Saudis and their allies to preserve Sunni control of their volatile southern neighbour against the Zaidi Shia Houthis, supported by Iran. Pakistan's Parliament unanimously passed a resolution on April 10, 2015, and decided that the country would remain "neutral" in the Yemen conflict, signifying a sharp break between the two long-time partners.[79] The other important reason for changing the relationship between both the countries is that the UAE and other Gulf countries have increasingly been sceptical of Pakistan's ability to curb terror groups operating from its territory, especially after an attack on the convoy members of the country's royal family in December 2016 in Balochistan. The January 11, 2017 attack by the Pakistan-backed Afghan Taliban belonging to the Haqqani Network at 'Governor's House in Kandahar resulted in five UAE diplomatic staff deaths and the wounding of its ambassador to Kabul.[80] Such incidents demonstrate how the UAE and Pakistan might be moving in opposite directions.

Pakistan's government paints India as a permanent enemy and tends to expect its friends to view India through Pakistan's eyes as the UAE Crown Prince stands alongside Prime Minister Modi on the dais and UAE troops march alongside India's soldiers in Delhi on India's Republic Day Parade of 2017. Therefore it was a strong message for Pakistan to give up its stated position of treating India as its permanent enemy. This is indeed a great achievement of the nationalist government led by Prime Minister Modi.

The UAE would be the most vocal partner in the Gulf region to share India's concern on terrorism, which New Delhi hopes will send a signal to Pakistan. The Joint Statement mentioned terrorism more than 11 times. The 'Joint Statement' on counter-terrorism highlights that the two leaders articulated their unequivocal resolve to cooperate on counter-terrorism by adopting a zero tolerance policy towards the menace of terrorism.[81] The two sides agreed to coordinate efforts "to counter radicalisation and misuse of religion by groups and countries for inciting hatred and perpetrating acts of terrorism."[82] They emphasised the need "to facilitate regular exchanges of religious scholars and intellectuals and organise conferences and seminars to promote the values of peace, tolerance, inclusiveness, and welfare inherent in all religions."[83] Both leaders agreed that resolute and credible steps must be taken to eliminate safe havens and sanctuaries that provide shelter to terrorists and their activities. It is very significant that, without naming Pakistan, both leaders condemned efforts, including by States, to use religion to justify, sustain and sponsor terrorism against other countries. A large part of the joint statement addressed denouncing terrorism and strengthening cooperation in counter-terrorism operations and intelligence sharing. It is a result of the personal chemistry of PM Modi and his frequent interactions with the Gulf.

Pakistan's Support to Terror

There is no change of stance of Pakistan's attitude towards terrorism had not changed after Imran Khan became the PM.[84] "Despite Pakistan being grey-listed by the Financial Action Task Force (FATF), a presidential ordinance promulgated by the previous government that amended the Anti-Terrorism Act, 1997 to include global terrorists listed by the UN like the Jamaat-ud-Dawa (JuD) and the Falah-i-Insaniyat Foundation (FIH), offshoots of the banned Lashkar-e-Taiba (LeT), was allowed to lapse by the Imran Khan government."[85] Syed Salahuddin, the Hizbul Mujahideen (HM) supreme commander and head of the United Jihad Council (UJC), operates with impunity in Pakistan without any restrictions. In a press conference at Muzaffarabad on 27 October 2018, he stated that only a state-wide armed struggle could bring India to the table: "I wish every Kashmiri takes up arms against India, including my children."[86]

Pakistan's cross border terrorism remains a core concern in bilateral relations. India has consistently stressed the need for Pakistan to take credible, irreversible and verifiable action to end cross-border terrorism against India and fulfil its assurances, given to India at the highest level in January 2004 and reiterated several times, that territory under its control would not be allowed to be used for terrorism. It has also been emphasised by Indian government that India will continue to take firm and decisive steps to protect its national security.

Militants attacks in October 2017, against an Indian paramilitary camp near Srinagar, and in February 2018, against an Indian army base in the Jammu region, which killed five soldiers and a civilian. These attacks came amidst a period of increased cross-border shelling along the Line of Control, with more than 3,000 reported violations in 2017 and nearly 1,000 in the first half of 2018. Violent demonstrations and anti-India protests calling for an independent Kashmir also continued; over 300 people, including civilians, Indian security forces, and militants, were killed in attacks and clashes in 2017.[87] After months of Indian military operations targeting both Kashmiri militants and demonstrators, India announced in May 2018 that it would observe a cease-fire in Kashmir during the month of Ramadan for the first time in nearly two decades; operations resumed in June 2018. In addition, in May 2018, India and Pakistan agreed to a cease-fire along the disputed Kashmir border to restore the terms of their 2003 agreement.

Pulwama Terror Attack

A terrorist group—Jaish-e-Mohammad (JeM) perpetrated a heinous act of terror on a convoy of Indian security forces in Pulwama, Jammu and Kashmir, on 14 February 2019. In this terror attack, 40 security personnel were martyred.[88] The United Nations and other countries already proscribe the Jaish-e-Muhammed. Indian Intelligence agencies reported that Jaish was attempting other suicide terror attacks in various parts of India.

To reduce the chances of an escalation, India tried its best to build international opinion against Pakistan. This step was part of a broader strategy of apprising the international community about Pakistan's culpability in Pulwama to get general support for India's right to self-defence. It was believed in the Indian war room that once the international community came on board, Pakistan's retaliatory intent would be degraded. As a result, within 48 hours of the attack, 58 countries, including all the UN's Permanent Five (P-5), condemned the attack and offered support to India in the fight against terrorism.

Balakot Air Strike

Under his *Shakti* strategy, Modi responded to the Pulwama suicide attack on February 14, 2019, in the form of the Balakot air-strike. There was enough intelligence about training camps in the Balakot area of the so-called Azad Jammu Kashmir. The Indian Air Force conducted a well-directed air operation across the LoC on Jaish-e-Mohammad (JeM) terror camps in Balakot, Chakothi, and Muzaffarabad in the early hours of February 26, 2019. In a press conference, India's Foreign Secretary, V.K. Gokhale, dwelt on the Balakot strike and said that in this operation, "a very large number of JeM terrorists, trainers, senior commanders and groups of *jihadis* who were being trained for fidayeen action were eliminated".[89] He reiterated the India resolve "to take all necessary measures to fight the menace of terrorism" and called this a "non-military pre-emptive action" which was "specially targeted at the Jaish camp". The attacks were conducted with the help of the 'IAF's 12 mirage 2000 aircraft, on the three specific targets, nearly 300 militants were killed.[90] In counter-terrorism action, Pakistan has targeted military installations on the Indian side on 27 February 2019 by using its air force. Due to India's high state of readiness and alertness, Pakistan's attempts were foiled successfully.

The Balakot air-strike has proved the credibility of Prime Minister 'Modi's intent and consistency in resorting to power or coercive use of force in crises, particularly against Pakistan's sponsored terrorism. This has also compelled India's strategic partners and adversaries to think of the measure of the effectiveness of the able leadership of Modi.

The Modi government abrogated Article 370, which allowed an iota of autonomy to the state of Jammu and Kashmir. The President of India issued on 5 August 2019 the "Constitution (Application to Jammu and Kashmir) Order, 2019" under Article 370, that superseded the Constitution (Application to Jammu and Kashmir) Order, 1954."[91] The Jammu and Kashmir Reorganization Act 2019 proposed to create two Union territories (UTs), one to be called Jammu and Kashmir, and the other as Ladakh.[92]

Since his government came to power, Modi has been proactively engaged in countering cross-border terrorism in Jammu and Kashmir. However, Pakistan's continued support to terror groups and the changing environment of the state after the Pulwama and Uri attack has compelled the Modi Government to abrogate Article 370 by adopting the *Shanti* and *Shakti* strategy.

The Director Generals of Military Operations of India and Pakistan have issued a joint statement on 25th February 2021 and reiterated their commitment to a "strict observance" of all agreements.[93] The decision to give peace with Pakistan a fresh chance has Prime Minister Narendra Modi's personal imprimatur to follow his policy of peace with Pakistan.

Conclusion

Prime Minister Modi's Pakistan policy based on *Shanti* and *Shakti* principle's has become successful and capable of rendering concrete results in the medium and long run. The policy focuses on surrounding Pakistan, isolating it among the neighbouring states, and targeting its strategic partners. Modi has opened a new diplomatic line just after taking the oath through his diplomatic engagements, as compared to his predecessors, taking the initiative to change a status-quo disadvantageous for India. Modi has adopted *Shanti* (peace) and *Shakti* (power) strategy for dealing with Pakistan by exposing and isolating Pakistan internationally and focusing on the global attention on their nefarious designs, i.e., supporting cross-border terrorism against India and adopting coercive measures in the form of surgical and airstrikes.

The Balochistan issue is a strategic move that departs from the conciliatory approach on a festering issue for the last 70 years. The test of any foreign policy, especially when dealing with a country that sponsors terrorism as state policy, lies in its outcome. Modi's "peace through strength" policy in the Line of Control has been a success because it sent a clear and tough message to the Pakistani army: desist or die. Modi will be less willing to make any concessions to Pakistan unless there is an end to cross-border terrorism. Unlike his predecessors, he has not been willing to fudge the question of terror in the engagement with Pakistan. On the contrary, he insisted that Pakistan address India's concerns on terror as a priority in any talk or negotiation. If his predecessors, even if only reluctantly, accepted that they had no choice but to live with Pakistan's support for terror, Modi is thinking differently that he can bring about a change by the *Shanti* and *Shakti* approach alone.

NOTES

1. Lindsay Hughes, "India's Foreign Policy under a BJP-led Coalition Government", *Strategic Analysis Paper* (Australia: Future Directions International), April 28, 2014, p. 2.
2. "My Hindutva Face will be an Asset in Foreign Affairs", *The Indian Express* (New Delhi), 23 April 2014. Also cited in Ankit Panda, "Modi: Hindutva will Be an Asset in Foreign Affairs", *The Diplomat*, 24 April 2014. https://thediplomat.com/2014/04/modi-hindutva-will-be-an-asset-in-foreign-affairs/
3. Rajesh Basrur, "Modi's foreign policy fundamentals: a trajectory unchanged," *International Affairs* (OUP), No. 93, Vol. 1 (2017), p. 11.
4. Deep K. Datta-Ray, *The Making of Indian Diplomacy: A Critique of Eurocentrism* (New Delhi: Oxford University Press, 2015) cited in Pradip Kumar Gautam, "Understanding Dharma and Artha in Statecraft through Kautilya's Arthshastra", *IDSA Monograph* (New Delhi), Series, No. 53, July 2016, p.99.
5. Bharati Mukherjee, *Kautilya's Concept of Diplomacy* (New Delhi, Abhinav Publishers, 1998), p. 253.
6. Kalidas Nag and V.R. Ramachandra Dikshitar, "The Diplomatic Theories of Ancient India and the Arthashastra," *Journal of Indian History* (Trivandrum), Vol. 6, No. 1, 1927, p. 16.
7. Rajiv Bhatia, *The Arthashastra in Modi's India,* December 7, 2016, Gateway House,

India Council of Global Relations. https://www.gatewayhouse.in/the-arthashastra-in-modis-india/

8. Sumit Ganguly, "Hindu Nationalism and the Foreign Policy of India's Bharatiya Janata Party", *Transatlantic Academy Paper Series* (Washington: Transatlantic Academy), June 2015, p. 6.
9. Vinayak Damodar Savarkar, *Essentials of Hindutva* (New Delhi: Hindi Sahitya Sadan, 2003. First Published in 1923), p. 25.
10. V. D. Savarkar, *Hindutva: Who is a Hindu*? (Bombay: S.S. Savarkar, 1969).
11. Rahul Sagar, "State of Mind: What Kind of Power will India become? *International Affairs* (Blackwell Publishing Ltd.), Vol. 85, No. 4, 2009, p. 808.
12. Madhav Sadashiv Golwalkar, *Bunch of Thoughts* (Bangalore: Vikrama Prakashan, 1966), p. 270.
13. Madhav Sadashiv Golwalkar, *Bunch of thoughts* (Bangalore: Vikrama Prakashan, 1966), p. 273.
14. Kanti Bajpai, "Indian Conceptions of Order and Justice: Nehruvian, Gandhian, Hindutva, and Neo- Liberal", in Rosemary Foot, John Lewis Gaddis and Andrew Hurrell (eds.), *Order and Justice in International Relations* (London: Oxford University Press, 2003), p. 236.
15. Stephen Philip Cohen, *India: Emerging Power* (Washington DC: Brookings Institution, 2002), pp. 44-47.
16. Ian Hall, "Narendra Modi and India's Normative Power", *International Affairs* (OUP), Vol. 93, Issue 1, 2017, p. 122.
17. "Highlights of BJP manifesto 2014", *The Indian Express* (New Delhi), April 7, 2014.
18. Ian Hall, "Is a 'Modi Doctrine' Emerging in Indian Foreign Policy? *Australian Journal of International Affairs* (Taylor & Francis), Volume 69, Issue 3, 2015, pp. 2-3.
19. *Bharatiya Janata Party, Ek Bharat, Shreshtha Bharat: Sabka Saath, Sabka Vikas* (New Delhi, 2014), pp. 38-40. www.bjp.org/images/pdf_2014/full_manifesto_ english_ 07.04.2014.pdf
20. Ian Hall, "Narendra Modi and India's Normative Power", *International Affairs* (Chatham House: Oxford University Press), Vol. 93, No. 1, 2017, p.124.
21. S. D. Muni, "Narendra Modi's Foreign Policy: Rebuild South Asian Neighbourhood", *CLAWS Journal* (New Delhi), Summer 2015, p. 24.
22. "Stop Terror for Talks: Narendra Modi tells Nawaz Sharif on Pakistan National Day," *The Economic Times* (New Delhi), March 24, 2015. https://www.economic times.indiatimes.com/articleshow/46669906.cms?from= mdr&utm_ source= contentofinterest&utm_medium=text&utm_campaign=cppst
23. Government calls off India-Pakistan foreign secretary-level talks as Pak envoy meets Kashmiri separatists, *The Economic Times*, August 19, 2014.
24. Suhasini Haider, "India Pakistan Talks are Off", *The Hindu* (New Delhi), August 18, 2014.
25. Subhajit Roy, "Upset India Calls off Foreign Secretary talks, says 'unacceptable' Islamabad Terms it a Setback to Peace efforts", *The Indian Express* (New Delhi), August 18, 2014.
26. "India Warns Pakistan as tension escalates at LoC: Our forces will make Cost of your Adventurism Unaffordable", *The Indian Express* (New Delhi), October 9, 2014.

27. "Press Information Bureau, Government of India, Prime Minister's Office" http://pib.nic.in/newsite/PrintRelease.aspx?relid=111876.
28. Elizabeth Roche, "SAARC Summit Nears Failure as Pakistan, India Differ", *Live Mint*, November 26, 2014; "Pakistan Refuses to Sign Three Multilateral Pacts at SAARC Summit: Officials", *The Express Tribune* and *International New York Times*, November 26, 2014.
29. India, Pakistan vow to eliminate terrorism from South Asia, https://www.livemint.com/Politics/pPGO6qLbxns4HiF57WGlHP/India-Pakistan-vow-to-eliminate-terrorism-from-South-Asia.html
30. S. D. Muni, "The Ufa Fiasco: India Could Surely Do Better", *Economic & Political Weekly*, Vol. 50, Issue No. 36, September 5, 2015, p. 15.
31. S. D. Muni, "The Ufa Fiasco: India Could Surely Do Better", *Economic & Political Weekly*, Vol. 50, Issue No. 36, September 5, 2015, p. 16.
32. "Modi to Visit Pakistan Next Year", *The Hindu* (New Delhi), July 10, 2015.
33. S. D. Muni, "The Ufa Fiasco: India Could Surely Do Better" *Economic & Political Weekly*, Vol. 50, Issue No. 36, September 5, 2015, p. 16.
34. Vinod Bhatia, "Pathankot and Beyond - The Devil's Alternative, *Aakrosh* (New Delhi), Vol. 19, No. 71, April 2016, p. 65.
35. Ibid.
36. Sinderpal Singh, Dealing with Pakistan: Implications for India's Pakistan policy after Pathankot, *ISAS Insight* (Institute of South Asian Studies: National University of Singapore), No. 305, 18 January 2016, p. 2.
37. Ibid.
38. "India, Pakistan break the ice off-camera in Bangkok", *The Indian Express* (New Delhi), December 7, 2015.
39. Ibid.
40. Suhasini Haider, "India, Pakistan NSAs meet in Bangkok" *The Hindu* (Chennai), December 6, 2015.
41. "PM Modi lands in Lahore on a surprise visit, meets Pak PM Nawaz Sharif" *The Indian Express* (New Delhi), December 25, 2015.
42. C. Raja Mohan, "How Prime Minister Modi Can Sustain India's Pakistan Dialogue" *Carnegie India: Policy Outlook*, February 2016, p. 7.
43. "Uri terror attack: A look at past attacks in Jammu-Kashmir this year", *The Indian Express* (New Delhi), September 18, 2016.
44. Sumit Kumar, "The Pathankot Airbase Attack and the Future of India-Pakistan Relations", *The Diplomat* January 12, 2016.
45. "Why Modi's Visit to Saudi Arabia has a Clear Strategic Focus on Pakistan" https://scroll.in/article/806027/why-modis-visit-to-saudi-arabia-has-a-clear-strategic-focus-on-pakistan
46. "India-Saudi Arabia Joint Statement during the visit of Prime Minister to Saudi Arabia", *Press Information Bureau* (New Delhi), April 03, 2016. pib.nic.in/newsite/print release.aspx?relie
47. "India-Saudi Arabia Joint Statement during the visit of Prime Minister to Saudi Arabia", *Ministry of External Affairs* (New Delhi), April 03, 2016. http://mea.gov.in/bilateraldocuments.htm?dtl/26595.
48. Ibid.

49. "PM Modi conferred Saudi's Highest Civilian Honour", *The Indian Express* (New Delhi), April 3, 2016.
50. "Modi's Visit to Saudi Arabia", *Pakistan Today* (Islamabad) April 9, 2016.
51. "Text of the Prime Minister's Address to the Joint Session of U.S. Congress", *Press Information Bureau* June 8, 2016. http://pib.nic.in/newsite/PrintRelease.aspx?relid=146076
52. Ibid.
53. "As it happened: Terrorism is incubated in India's Neighbourhood, says Modi", *The Hindu* (New Delhi), June 8, 2016.
54. "Terror being incubated in India's Neighbourhood: Narendra Modi", *The Economic Times* (New Delhi), June 8, 2016.
55. "Terror being incubated in India's Neighbourhood: Narendra Modi", *The Economic Times* (New Delhi), June 8, 2016.
56. "Narendra Modi's speech on Independence Day 2016: Here's the full text", August 15, 2016. http://indianexpress.com/article/india/india-news-india/pm-narendra-modis-speech-on-independence-day-2016-here-is-the-full-text/
57. "Narendra Modi's Speech on Independence Day 2016: Here's the Full Text", *The Indian Express* (New Delhi), August 15, 2016. http://indianexpress.com/article/india/india-news-india/pm-narendra-modis-speech-on-independence-day-2016-here-is-the-full-text
58. Manzoor Ahmed and Baloch Aktar, "Political Economy of Balochistan Pakistan: A Critical Review", *European Scientific Journal*, Vol. 11, No. 4, May 2015, p. 274.
59. "Narendra Modi's Independence Day speech: PM throws down Balochistan Gauntlet", *The Indian Express* (New Delhi), August 16, 2016.
60. "India raises Balochistan at U.N.; hits out at Pakistan", *The Hindu* (Chennai), September 14, 2016.
61. Ibid.
62. Ashutosh Bhardwaj, "View from the Right: Punitive action: The Uri attack is a Response to Growing Isolation and Resultant Frustration within Pakistan", *The Indian Express* (New Delhi), September 28, 2016.
63. "18 Jawans killed in pre-dawn strike at Uri", *The Hindu* (Chennai), September 18, 2016.
64. "Will not forget Uri, Pakistan will be isolated: PM Modi", *The Shillong Times*, September 25, 2016.
65. "By invoking Burhan Wani, Nawaz Sharif has scored a self-goal; here's how," *The Indian Express* (New Delhi), September 22, 2016.
66. "Pakistan now host to 'Ivy League of terrorism': India at UNGA" *The Hindustan Times* (New Delhi), September 22, 2016.
67. "Pakistan is host to Ivy League of terrorism, Uri attack part of the continuous trail: Govt." *The Indian Express* (New Delhi), October 4, 2016.
68. "Pak a terrorist state, attracts aspirants from all over the world: India at UNGA" *Deccan Chronicle* September 22, 2016.
69. "At UN, India hits out at Pak with Balochistan volley", *The Hindu* (Chennai), September 26, 2016.
70. External Affairs Minister's address at the 71st UNGA, New York (September 26,

2016). http://mea.gov.in/Speeches

71. "4 Hours, Choppers and 38 Kills: How India Avenged the Uri Attack", *The Economic Times* (New Delhi), September 29, 2016.
72. "The Modi-Doval Doctrine of "Offensive Defence" Marks its Arrival." http://www.opindia.com/2016/09/the-modi-doval-doctrine-of-offensive-defence-marks-its-arrival/
73. Lalit K Jha, "Want Pak to Combat, Delegitimise Terror Entities: the US," *PTI*, September 29, 2016. http://www.ptinews.com/news/7920689
74. C. Raja Mohan, "Charting a New Course: Modi's Pakistan Policy", *ISAS Insight* (Singapore: Institute of South Asian Studies, NUS), October 11, 2016, p. 6.
75. Vivek Chadda, Rumel Dahia, Neha Kohli and Shruti Pandalai, "Uri Surgical Strike and International Reactions", *IDSA Issue Brief* (New Delhi), October 4, 2016, p. 9.
76. "India has Right to Respond to Attack on Sovereignty: Bangladesh on Surgical Strike", *The Times of India* (New Delhi), September 30, 2016.
77. "SAARC Boycott Success of Delhi's Diplomacy", *The Indian Express* (New Delhi), October 1, 2016.
78. "India has Right to Respond to Attack on Sovereignty: Bangladesh on Surgical Strike", *The Times of India* (New Delhi), September 30, 2016.
79. "Parliament Calls for Neutrality in Yemen conflict", *The Dawn* (Karachi), April 10, 2015.
80. Hussain Haqqani, "Zero-sum game is up", *The Indian Express* (New Delhi), January 27, 2017.
81. "India-UAE Joint Statement during State visit of Crown Prince of Abu Dhabi to India" *MEA* (New Delhi), January 26, 2017. http://www.mea.gov.in/bilateral-documents.
82. "India, UAE to Coordinate efforts to Counter Misuse of Religion for Inciting Hatred", *The Hindu* (Chennai) January 26, 2017.
83. Ibid.
84. Imran Khan's minister shares stage with 26/11 mastermind Hafiz', *The Times of India*, 02 October 2018. https://epaper.timesgroup.com/Olive/ODN/TimesOf India/PrintArticle.aspx?doc=TOIDEL%2F 2018%2F10%2F02&entity=ar03117 &ts=20181002004309&uq=20180921040217&mode=text
85. Banned groups', edit in *Dawn*, 27 October 2018, https://www.dawn.com/news/1441696/banned-groups.
86. Murtaza Shibli, 'Seventy Years of Accession', *The News*, 03 November 2018, https://www.thenews.com.pk/print/388859-seventy-years-of-accession,
87. Conflict Between India and Pakistan, Council of Foreign Relations", https://www.cfr.org/global-conflict- tracker/conflict/conflict-between-india-and-pakistan
88. Ministry of Foreign Affairs India (New Delhi) Brief, 25th September 2019. https://mea.gov.in/Portal/ForeignRelation/Bilateral_Brief_pakistan.pdf
89. Statement by Foreign Secretary on 26 February 2019', https://mea.gov.in/Speeches- Statements.htm?dtl/31089/Statement+by+ Foreign+ Secretary+ on+ 26+ February+2019+on+the+Strike+on+ JeM+training+camp+at+Balakot (Assessed on 27 February 2019).
90. Ashok Behuria, "Pre-Emptive Strikes: A Fitting Response to Pulwama" Air World

Service, (IDSA: New Delhi), February 27, 2019. https://idsa.in/system/files/news/ashok-pre-emptive-strikes-27-feb-2019.pdf

91. The Constitution (Application to Jammu and Kashmir) Order, 2019 C.O. 272 , *Gazette of India*, Ministry of Law and Justice, August 9, 2019, p. 1. http://egazette.nic.in/WriteReadData/2019/210049.pdf
92. Gazette of India, Ministry of Law and Justice, August 9, 2019, p. 1. http://egazette.nic.in/WriteReadData/2019/210407.pdf
93. *Ministry of Defence*, Joint Statement, 25th 2021, https://pib.gov.in/PressRelease Page.aspx?PRID=1700682

4

The Singularity of the India-USA "Bilaterals": An Investigative Exercise in Modi Doctrine and Public Diplomacy

Manan Dwivedi

Introduction

Cultural portrayals lead to the reflection of the reality and the attendant myth pertaining to any nation state particularly and in a region to be generally inclined. The cultural landscape of a nation can serve as the spawning centre for the political and social unison of a region within the context of its constituent political units. The myriad nations in South Asia also revolve around these parameters of a Mediascape-generated discourse which, apart from congealing the rubric of a nation state or a region, also, tends to create a divisive trend. The various myths and the historical facts attached to the lore of conflicts in the context of the India-Pakistan-China triumvirate serve a dual purpose which this paper will attempt to delineate in the form of a visual and cultural narrative.

This chapter will dwell upon the context of media generated hype and also about the much-needed constructs of nationalism and patriotic themes which do not actually militate against the conjoined theme of public diplomacy with the USA. The Government of the day in New

Delhi with its recent overtures towards a 'near-to-friendly' policy will form another argument.. This paper would develop the idea of Public Diplomacy as is being visibly attempted by the Prime Minister Modi's foreign policy dispensation. The role which the nation's mass media can play in firming up the case of state-led Public Diplomacy, will, be further elaborated and investigated through a brief content analysis of media reports in India through a selective utilisation of prominent national dailies and national satellite channel networks all across the Mediascape of India and the USA. The Media and the Public Diplomacy apparatus can be equated with the all-pervading commonality of national interest which will figure in this paper's narrative.

The making of a myth or the myth-making function is an essential component of the idiom of a national interest-seeking foreign policy making and implementation of the same. As a precursor element, the Western nations embarked upon a strategy of serving potential national interest-oriented specificities, wherein the respective establishments attempted to make the 'rest' swoon over and cooperate with their specific nationalities and national aims and objectivities. In a quintessential proactive and positive framework ordaining policy-making, the spawning of a myth becomes a prerequisite for the cementing of a narrative at a national and localized keel.

Wither Public Diplomacy and What is it?

Public Diplomacy is the creation of certain images and visages in order to spawn a sub-set of an exteriority in order to simplistically and in a Plain Jane manner augment the national interest of a nation state. And, it is an American construct forged as part of American soft power diplomacy in the interregnum between the two World Wars. Public diplomacy can be defined as a "Communication with foreign publics for the purpose of achieving a foreign policy objective."[1] The Internet and social media tools have given U.S. public diplomacy practitioners a new venue for such communication. Without the valuable on-the-ground presence of a diplomatic mission, however, its online presence is currently the chief route of direct access to Iranian citizens.[2] The establishment of this online presence has been in line with the State Department's development of a virtual diplomacy strategy entitled 21st

Century Statecraft which includes efforts to establish an online apparatus for nearly all U.S. diplomatic missions.[3] Manichaeism seems to be the order of the day wherein the satanic and evil narration and an intentional projection of a specificity of an image leads to the fulfilment of a national interest ordained objective of a nation.

Still, what needs to be realised is that the origin and the praxis of the nom de plume of Public Diplomacy is not about a mere bland satanization and vilification of the other; rather, it is a larger-than-life exercise to establish a national sentiment upon the vestiges of the global firmament. It definitively involves the propagation of a myth but the question which needs to be asked is what is wrong in the creation and the sustenance of a national myth with the all-apparent notion of providing an international platform for the history, tradition, economic, trade, societal and political achievements of a nation state such as USA and maybe India in the contemporary context of South Asia. One cannot deny the fact that it is the American diplomatic establishment that created the first effective edifice and a superstructure in order to propagate the national objectives. India too has followed suit with the media and diplomatic blitzkrieg initiated by Prime Minister Modi since the inception of the Delhi denomination in the momentous month of May 2014. The Modi denomination is attempting to develop a transformation between this diplomatic myth and reality in the Indian and American contexts.

Public Diplomacy in the USA

The art of selling and marketing a product, a theme or a cause is not chiefly attributable to a marketer of the market or a corporate salesman. The lore and praxis of marketing one's country and its history, tradition and linguistic construct is also a fulltime vocational engagement. The myth about India or the USA as a nation has to be globally and perforce propagated all across the public sphere in the international firmament. The ides of global politics perpetuated the USA's involvement in world politics and led to its disembarkment from its traditional isolationist perch, wherein, the American Founding Fathers' myth of "staying away from the entangling European alliances' was relegated to the political backburner. In the same continuum, it was through the auspices of President Franklin Delano Roosevelt, in the year 1936, that the "Good

Neighbour Policy" was initiated in the South American context which was a continuation of the Monroe Doctrine which was quintessentially American in origin, nature and functionality.

It so transpired that President Roosevelt visited the Argentinean capital, Buenos Aires, in 1936 with an impressive motorcade leading the way to the Argentine Parliament. An assurance was given to the Argentine nation and the rest of the Western hemisphere that nations could continue with their daily humdrum routine along with the larger umbrella of American 'super-puissance' in the region. A message was given to the rest of the world that the South American and Latin American regions were the USA's preserve and had to be sustained with American presence and large-hearted philanthropy. The larger issue of regional hyper power was reinstated with another significant development.

The art of Public Diplomacy was soon to be honed by the foreign policy establishment of the United States of America. During World War II, also, the American War Office and the State Department were given directions to mount a global campaign through the public management mechanisms. Such a global campaign would arraign all the American media and the cinematic apparatus which would amplify the fact of 'America being the most powerful and the richest nation in the international polity.' Other issues such as United States of America being the repository of fundamental freedoms, egalitarianism and decolonization along with the dignity and freedom issues of humankind were also paraded and portrayed globally by the U.S. War Office in conjunction with the American mainstream media. A conclave was developed between cinema producers, comic artists, pamphleteers and national dailies and radio in order to transmit combative messages against Nazi Germany and later on against the Soviet Union, leading to the quintessential Cold War confrontation.[4]

Thus, Public Diplomacy emerged as an instrumentality to advance American national interest globally through deft message campaigns thus bringing to the fore, the MMI (Military Media and Industry)[5] complex in the USA. The American instrumentality of soft war was unleashed all across the global firmament with a subterranean motif of propagating the all-pervading omniscience and the "City atop Mount Sinai" analogy which caught imagination of the larger world and of the developing nations. The aura and halo of the supersession and invincibility of the American Republic was soon to become one of the quintessential narratives in the Third and Middle World.

For instance, the creation of the superhero genre in the form of Superman, Captain America and Avengers through DC Comics was soon to become the emblem of the grand American stereotype. In the context of the super-hero termed as Superman, the narrative involves the idea of the "Other" which reaches Earth from the planet Krypton in order to grow up as an earthling after the fact that planet Krypton explodes in one self-destructive crescendo and there emerges a space capsule carrying a two-year-old boy child, Kal El[6] who, on reaching the Earth's atmosphere soon metamorphoses into a mutant super power-wielding earthling. He assumes the name of Clark Kent as his father teaches him to hone his super powers and hide them from the world and utilise them when he turns into the Man of Steel and the caped crusader which is the name by which the American and global media learns to call him. The myth of Superman is the precursor element in the context of the American state's soft power diplomacy which was further strengthened with other facets in the propagation of the power, pelf and efficiency of the grandiloquent American Dream.

As the Clark Kent character grows up, he fights manifold menaces and villains and soon emerges as an American and global beacon of liberty, non-proliferation, disarmament, peace, stability, democracy and all that is appreciable in the American liberal tradition and largely the American Dream. In the recent Hollywood release, *Man of Steel*, Superman's mother cajoles him after he has vanquished marauding villains as his initial foray into saving men saying, "Now, son, that you have vanquished the evil Zod and saved Earth, how would you support yourself in the world. So better look for a job once the job of saving mankind is over!"[7] Some motherly suggestion! Thus, the appellation of United States of America being the international super-cop with all the quintessential American beneficence becomes the "Ragtime raga" of the American experience. It is this do-gooder instinct and the fact of the USA being the symbolic custodian of human rights and world peace which was astutely propagated through World War II and the dreary Cold War days as the world very often reached the edge of World War III, was very often than not a forgone possibility.

Public Diplomacy through Indian and South Asian Lens

It is in the same context of the international razzmatazz that Prime Minister Modi has reinvented the artifice of public diplomacy in the Indian and South Asian context. His first message reflected the importance that New Delhi attaches to its immediate neighbours in the form of the South Asian countries despite the nagging and minute differences which India shares with some of them. The presence of all the South Asian and SAARC heads of state at the Modi inaugural in May 2014 was all about India according primacy to the SAARC comity of nations. The visits to Japan, Fortaleza, Bhutan and Nepal too portrayed a developing world perspective. The presence of President Obama on the occasion of the Republic Day celebrations in New Delhi too depicted the growing convergence between the Indian Union and the United States of America as several significant agreements were inked along with the ironing out of the details of the Nuclear Civil Liability Bill in India. All these formed part and parcel of an Indian striving which was much more than a standard photo opportunity with a trail of agreements and treaties to follow. What was awe-inspiring was the India-centric justification of this novel genre of media diplomacy which was undertaken very deftly by the Indian foreign policy establishment in order to erase the previous memories of reactive and larger policy paralysis of the previous regime in New Delhi.

Public Diplomacy: Known Frontiers in the USA

Though the term 'Public Diplomacy' has been part of the foreign policy skill set of Washington since the two World Wars, still some scholars attribute it to an innovation of the Cold War years. In one such enumeration, Jomane Chahine, hailing from McGill University, contends that, "The term—public diplomacy—only entered the lexicon of political and international affairs in the Cold War environment of the mid-1960s. It could however be argued that the essence of the practice—government communication with foreign publics—is as old as history itself."[8] The author further contends that, "The primary purpose of this dissertation is to argue that public diplomacy, as the specific form taken by the practice of government communication with a foreign audience in the latter half of the twentieth century, is a distinctive product of the development and ultimate intersection of several discrete though somehow connected concepts in social and political thought."[9]

Public Diplomacy is an artifice which is part of the mechanics of foreign policy in the country. The government of the day attempts to circumvent the internal dissensions in order to bring forth the objective of national interest in order to promote the avowed national interest of the nation. Diplomacy did not have an element of, "immediacy" in classical and traditional times. With the rapid upsurge in technological advancements and with the advent of geo-economic interdependencies, the idea of how a nation and its foreign policy was perceived and analyzed by international organizations and actors metamorphosed over the years. In a pre-eminent work on Public Diplomacy, the author attempts to delineate the inception of the idea of American Public Diplomacy which later went on to become the cornerstone of the policies of various foreign policy establishments in the world. 'The American Dream mythology,'[10] too, gets more than a reference in the work. It was John Truslow Adams who initiated and theorised upon the notion of the "Grandiloquent American Dream".[11] Justin Hart beautifully ekes out a detailed analysis of the notion of how Public Diplomacy was incepted in the American context with the visit of President Franklin Delano Roosevelt in 1935 in order to implement the "Good Neighbour Policy" of the USA.[12] The author narrates that the various shenanigans of the Office of War and the Intelligence agencies, which were in their incipient stage, led to the firming up of Washington's effort in creating a 'specificity' about the general visage and demeanour of the American Republic. The narrative is rich in details and ably investigates the 'internal workings' through a study of memos and correspondence in the American foreign policy-making establishment. The power struggles and the clashes of the men at the helm of affairs are sketched very evocatively and pithily within the historical setting of Public Diplomacy.

Justin Hart, the author, clinically brings out the internal clashes of personalities and the cloak-and-dagger nature of the earlier setting, which soon became commonplace and arrived in public view with the advent of World War II. The American war effort along with the Cold War propaganda of John McCarthy,[13] too, evoke an academic and policy interest in the receptive index of the reader. The entire 'cleaning up' instrumentality of the American establishment aimed at the communists too is too elaborately narrated in this work on U.S. Foreign Policy. The work examines the communications strategies of the American Government along with analyzing the origins of American "Soft Power". The book includes interesting and vivid portrayals of personalities such as Henry Luce, Archibald Macleish[14] and other framers of the initial edifice of American image-making efforts, culminating in the larger framework of Public Diplomacy. The entire diplomatic striving attains significant prominence with the pinpointing of original sources and primary research material which sheds more than able light on the subject. The twilight zone of the American overarch in the World War II years and the confrontation years in the Cold War years, too, gets an efficient rendition in the tradition of being a true blue researcher.

The Public Diplomacy Quest: An Innovative Policy Prescription

In the same tradition of myth-making, one can scarcely forget the J.P. Dutta directed war movie, "Border" in which a lot of gargantuan developments take place. One of them which can be cited here happens to be the consternation of the male actor, Jackie Shroff, who is an Air Force commander. He realizes that if the Longewalan post in the desert has to be protected in the face-off with a strong Pakistani thrust, then the Gnats, Hunters and MiG 21s had to be flown in to bombard the enemy tanks and armed cordons who had laid siege to the Longewalan post. Night falls while the 23rd Battalion of the Punjab Regiment led by Major Kuldip Singh Chandpuri is still found fighting for its life. Jackie Shroff, as the air–man, shouts out in exasperation that, "Bloody, these birds (planes) cannot fly in the night".

Thus, as first light hits the sky, the bombers decimate the Paki advance in a surreptitious slight of a flight. On the other hand,

Lt. Dharamvir Bhan's personal battle to come to terms with his father's memory as a decorated war veteran and his visage as his mother (Rakhee) turns up as a fleeting vision in order to adorn Dharamvir with a *sehra,* (the bridegroom's head dress) while Dharamvir breathes his last inclined against a destroyed tank. Thus, apart from the chilling portrayal of Chushul during the epic India-China war, the battle of the Longewalan post too enters the annals of military history as an indelible and remarkable page in the entirety of the patriotic tome. It is this myth-making which can be deftly utilized with the pantheon of daredevilry and the razzmatazz of the war heroes who laid down their lives or else survived as lasting testaments to the grit and determination of the Indian soldier. The Indian soldierly tradition can be aptly and effectively functionalised as the warring and determined myth of the nation and utilized judiciously as the star-spangled, tricoloured buntings fading into one another as E.L. Doctrow would write in his historical novel, "Ragtime".[15] Doctrow writes in his work that, "Tracks! Tracks! It seemed to the visionaries who wrote for the popular magazines that the future lay at the end of the parallel rails. There were long distance locomotive railroads and inter-urban electric railroads, street cars and elevated railroads, all laying their steel stripes on the land crisscrossing the hearts of the indefatigable civilization".[16] All these details of a twenty-first century USA on the move resonates with the provisions of the New Deal and the initializing of the gargantuan projects such as the Tennessee Valley Project being played out as pristine infrastructure all across the length and breadth of United States of America. Thus, as the public diplomatic agencies portrayed the capitalist and the market prowess coupled with the cultural strength and awe of the land of milk and honey, South Asia and India, in particular, can too take a leaf out of the book of public diplomacy as practised by United States of America though in a peacemaking tradition much befitting the land of Mahatma Gandhi and Gautama Buddha.[17]

The Indian-American Parable of Public Diplomacy

Prime Minister Narendra Modi has enthralled numerous nations through his shuttle-and-cultural diplomacy which gets ample reflection in the larger frame of the relationship with USA. The speech given by him in the plush environs of the Madison Square Garden is an ample reflection of the myth-and-the-lore intent of the New Delhi denomination vis-a-vis the stately Capitol Hill. The Prime Minister spoke eloquently much recently quoting from the songs of Bob Dylan which reflected the coming of age of the Indian people and its attendant youth segment. PM Modi said, "Today as I call upon the youthful segment of the American population, I can feel the sting of electricity which abounds in the cityscape of New York. In India, we are no longer the land of sadhus and serpents, though our cultural oeuvre remains intact. We play with the invention of the mouse now in the sense of its computer usage. In India, we are going to send rockets in space and along with this innovative society, we, are going to build toilets for impoverished masses in the rural hinterland of India as a proud nation."[18]

Thus, the larger-than-life diplomatic quantification by a deft diplomatic legerdemain by PM Modi has largely metamorphosed the reactive foreign policy of the nation into a brightly vibrant notion of proactive diplomacy. The marketing and selling of the larger visage of the nation has been hailed globally and domestically as the telling difference between the diplomacy of the Congress regime and the seething charge of public diplomacy by an astute diplomat into which Prime Minister Narendra Modi has transformed himself and his external affairs entourage. Thus, it is the novae foreign policy draft of PM Narendra Modi which scores as the soft power aspect of India's foreign policy.

President Trump's getting onto the saddle of power in the USA will see a transformation in the way the bilateral relationship develops between the twin nationalities. Sadanand Dhume, an eminent observer of India-US relations, writes very pithily in the American national daily, the *Wall Street Journal*, "Can Donald Trump and Narendra Modi yoke their countries more closely together in a common fight against radical Islam? The early signs look promising, but there's no guarantee of success. India needs to think more globally about the problem, while the U.S. must pay more attention to India's regional concerns."[19] Still, going by an issue-specific analysis of the India-US relationship, the countervailing role of India as a nationality containing PRC and the two legislative Bills and Executive Orders signed by President Trump in his first policy decisions can augur well for an Indian national security concern of curbing the menace of cross-border jihadi terrorism from across the nation's northern and western frontiers. This American disdain for global terror modules and concerns of an unadulterated immigration policy hold bright future prospects for a grandiloquent convergence between India and the USA in the near future of the larger international system.

President Trump declared in a radio chat show that "India is one of the oldest democracies of the world and is a natural ally of United States of America. All efforts of my Government will be aimed at forging "better" ties with India but in the near future I can assure India that the nomenclature of the Indian nation as being a better friend will soon be changed to, "the best friend" which United States can expect to have." In similar vein, President Trump gave the campaign trail clarion call to Indian Americans by addressing the Hindutva denomination of the Indian settlers with the catchy and efficient call of, "Abki Baar Trump Sarkar" in tandem with the Modi denomination's call to the nation of the order of, "Ab Ki Bar Modi Sarkar." This makes the genre of public diplomacy a clarion call in the garb of "New/Sound Byte Diplomacy" which brings out a historical, cultural and economic convergence between India and the USA.

Since the early engagement, between the New World and India, negative precedents have been established which were not conducive for cooperation and amalgamation between India and the New World, North America. American President Franklin Delano Roosevelt attempted to convince the British Prime Minister during the victorious days of World War II to free India. In the contemporary context, India and the USA are nations presently poised at an interesting liberal cusp. Idealism has a say in the way "interdependence" is being supported and has been increasingly witnessed in the relationship between India and the USA. Therein, both the nations are compatriots in the odyssey to mar the destabilizing intent of the forces of terrorism as an example. In the idealist bandwagon, democracy, constitutionalism, rule of law and unbridled individual entrepreneurship are, the cornerstones of the American Dream and its attendant founding myth. The idea of India, too, as a nation premised upon the democratic founding fathers such as Gandhi and Patel, partook of the demos-pathway immediately in the aftermath of the freedom struggle. Some foreign policy observers do not attach much significance to the aspect of democratization of American foreign policy, vis-à-vis, and nations all across the global firmament. Still, the fact remains that two democracies seldom go to war with each other and are quite friendly with each other.

In the context of the Indian nation, the USA used to relegate India to the strategic and diplomatic backburner as the larger South Asia was described by the U.S. State Department as "a mere blip on the radar screen of the American policy thought". The statement of Assistant Secretary of State, Robin Raphael, in the early Nineties blaming New Delhi for atrocities in the state of Jammu and Kashmir, too, served as part of the "negative narrative" of the India-US relationship. Much before the India-US dissonance on the nuclear cooperation front, the hyphenation of India with Pakistan soured the pitch of the India-US, relationship before it could grow out of the shadow of the Cold War. Prime Minister Narendra Modi too has declared that "these shadows of hesitance between the twin nations should be done away through the Cs of candour and convergence."[20] The American President also has termed the India-US "bilaterals" as the "defining partnership of the century". One American President who was a Democrat and went against New Delhi's national interest in the sphere of nuclear issues, was Bill Clinton. Hillary Clinton, the other Democrat, is poised for a showdown with the unpredictable and presumptive candidate amongst the Republicans, that is, Donald Trump.

The recent visit of the American Secretary of State to India made the Indian External Affairs Minister question the diplomat when the Minister raised the theme of neighbourly contributions in the context of terror activities on Indian territory. The pinpointing of the Lashkar-i-Toiyaba and Jaish-i-Mohammad by the Indian Minister made the American Secretary of State take notice of the Indian concern.[21] As a positive development from USA, the country has also lobbied for making New Delhi's entry a convenient reality in the Nuclear Suppliers Group. India too has been open to a friendly handshake and is doing a quid pro quo. New Delhi has pledged one billion dollars for various sectors in Afghanistan which has been well received in American circles.[22] The American standpoint in working towards conflict resolution in Afghanistan will receive a fillip from these Indian steps. As India has emerged as one of the largest donors of civilian aid to Afghanistan, the State Department spokesperson has contended that India is helping Kabul defend itself better and restore security for its people.

Apart from raising the complaint of cross-border terrorism with the USA, one of the post-May 2014 foreign policy standpoints of the New Delhi government has been the intelligent coupling of the Defence and commercial aspects of the partnership. According to Professor B.M. Jain in his work titled *"The Age of Uncertainty"*,[23] in 2016, the role of "Complex Interdependence" in the firming up of the partnership between India and USA, has been taken up energetically. The work utilizes the thesis of "Alter casting", wherein, both the nations can began to be cast in each other's selves, in the larger perspective of the relationship. Signalling, brandishing of a sword, a forceful march-on, a retreat into the high-up hills, (if the terrain of the battle is akin to Balaclava)[24] or the fluttering of a white surrender flag, are part of the diplomatic acts. This posturing has to be carried out in any exchange between two nations.[25]

The MEA release reports that there were major exchanges in 2015 before the visit of President Obama in January 2016 as a state guest in New Delhi. The relationship's foundation was laid in cordial terms in the form of the "electricity" generated by PM Modi in his speech at the UN General Assembly in September 2015 along with his oratory at the Madison Square Garden. This innovative style of Public Diplomacy transpired much before the San Jose-Shark tank event with American software firms being asked to invest in India. The MEA release further reports some of the 2015 engagements, "There were a number of high-level delegations in both directions in 2015. In January, Secretary of State John Kerry led the U.S. delegation to the Vibrant Gujarat Summit in Ahmedabad. In February, U.S. Secretary of Treasury Jacob Lew visited India for the fifth meeting of the Economic and Financial Partnership Initiative with our Finance Minister. U.S. Secretary of Transportation Anthony Foxx and the Secretary of Defence Ashton Carter, too, visited India in the middle of 2015."[26]

South Asian Milieu

The latest entrant to SAARC, that is Afghanistan, which is culturally linked to India as the story of the eternal Kabuliwala engrosses us with memories of the dry fruit trader in Kolkata. It is about the supine Kabuliwala selling his dry fruits one hot afternoon in Kolkata and remembering his daughter as he befriends a girl of the age of his daughter in Kabul. The Indian connection with Kabul persists with the idea of India lending a helping hand of support, succour, aid and capacity-building assistance to a war-ravaged Afghanistan including the entire edifice of the GWOT[27] and the Indian stance and policy on it. The torched and tarred memories of the gory partition also keep India and Pakistan in an inconvenient truce despite having fought four wars. The Indian recrimination of the plight of personages like Mallala[28] in the interstices of a failing Pakistan and the threat which it poses to a stable and increasingly progressing India, remain as matters of regional and global concern as SAARC too objectifies to attain the collectivity as practised and enjoyed by the likes of MERCOSUR and the European Union. Individually, nations such as Bhutan, Nepal, Bangladesh and Maldives can partake of their respective social-cultural pies and move on to a larger collective both bilaterally and also as pegs in a larger regional order.

Prime Minister Modi's B2B clarion call can ignite the interests of the so-called micro states in South Asia where the sobriquet of a benign hegemony can be done away by the Indian foreign policy-making establishment. The relationship between India and Bhutan is historic. The new government is committed to make this even stronger. The strength of a democracy is very important for that region and its people. The stronger India will be, the better it will be for Bhutan and other SAARC nations. A strong and stable India is needed to make sure that we can help our neighbours with their problems."[29] Prime Minister Modi ignited the passions during his first visit in his uncanny public diplomacy pattern when he stated that terrorism divides but culture and tourism unites in the context of the hilly Kingdom of Bhutan.[30] The significance attached to Bhutan conveys a stolid message that the conundrum caused by the benign neglect in the Indian establishment is a development of the past and the new dispensation in New Delhi considers the South Asian nations as being second to none, Bhutan and Nepal being the correct instances in the context of regional cooperation.

In the context of Bangladesh, the issue of the enclaves has been considered anew by the Modi Government where stark resemblances can be drawn between the 1971 Land Boundary Protocol and the 2011 land boundary agreement with Prime Minister Manmohan Singh. Also, the Indian help to Maldives during the regime of Abdul Gayoom along with the help rendered to the island nation in the 2004 tsunami and the stance related to Nasheed's political fortunes shed ample light to the India-Maldivian 'bilaterals'. Sri Lanka too has rescinded agreements on the exchange of fishermen and the Indian federalized touch in its regional foreign policy too has come into prominence in the context of the Bengalis in Bangladesh and Tamils in relation with the Emerald Isle with India lending all the vocal support for the promulgation of legislation to end the executive and autocratic presidential system in Colombo. The regional-federalism paradox has been conveniently picked up by Prime Minister Modi as he intends to provide autonomy to the states as they interact with their immediate neighbours in South Asia.

Conclusion

The pre-eminence imparted to small South Asian nation states was to serve as an ideal staple mechanism for the Modi Government to flag off issues, ink agreements and solve differences with the neighbourhood while the larger Look East policy adorns the regional mantle as the "Act East" Policy. The entire striving of the New Delhi dispensation can be further buttressed by the content of the speech which PM Modi delivered at the Madison Square garden in Manhattan. The speech can be related thus: "He brought the roof down with crowd-pleasing jokes about how a country that was once regarded as a land of snake-charmers was now spinning the world around its finger with a (computer) mouse and how India had sent a spacecraft to Mars for seven rupees a kilometre when it cost 10 rupees a kilometre in Ahmedabad."[31] The Indian Prime Minister further narrated that "It was the idea of Sulabh Shochalayas ruling the roost in India. Also, the air of New York has a peculiar electricity about it which only proactive elders and agile youngsters can bring to a city." [32]

Thus, apart from all this diplomatic razzmatazz, the act of delivering the United Nations General Assembly speech in Hindi too served as an avidly observed and commonly commented upon *'First'* dovetailing with the Republic Day visit of President Obama to the Indian capital winding up in a much-televised spectacle of, "Chai Pe Charcha". The act of quoting from Bob Dylan also brought into context the changed facets of a traditionally ensconced Indian diplomacy in the Nehruvian mould since the days of the decades of Congress rule. Observers and political pundits might be quick to belittle these steps and diplomatic initiatives as being too much in the higher end and being devoid of substance and being all about spectacle, still the novae and fresh nature of the diplomatic approach leaves an indelible mark on the foreign policy motifs of the India Union. It is this quaint quest with the amalgamation of the local with the global which has ignited the fancy and expectations of the global polity and geo-economics. If the 'visceral' and 'the colour, verve, vibrancy and the gaiety' of the cultural conjoindness can be eclectically firmed up and reach a converging fruition, then, the quest for a feasible and functional Public Diplomacy strategy can be on the anvil in the relationship with United States of America, with, India leading the odyssey with a 'benign benefaction.'

In the larger context, in April 2015, Prime Minister Modi unveiled his Rawls Theorization by claiming to post Indian objectives as being supportive of the weakest nations in the larger chain of the developing and developed world. He reiterated as part of his drive in Paris and with the Rafale manufacturers in Toulouse, France, that mere growth stories premised upon bland statistics cannot amount to India's diplomatic standpoint but foreign positing with the attribute of a human face, sentiment and hope will form the substratum of India's diplomatic face. The same runs true for the trade quotient embedded in the cultural and trade practicalities of the USA with India unassumingly heralding a conjoined front for the twin rule of law-abiding, liberal and democratic nationalities of India and the USA. The initiation and precursor role of India as a soft power instrumentality and a natural leader can serve as a recurrent reality for Washington. This is one stolid policy prescription that can be proffered over here.

NOTES

1. Wallin, Matthew, "The New Public Diplomacy Imperative", American Security Project, 2012. Available at: http:// americansecurityproject.org/featured-items/ 2012/the-new-public-diplomacy-imperative/
2. U.S. Department of State Official, Telephone Interview, 2013, April 12.
3. Hanson, Fergus, "Revolution @State: The Spread of eDiplomacy", Lowy Institute, 2012. Available at: http://lowyinstitute. cachefly.net/files/hanson_revolution_ state_web.pdf
4. Henry Kissinger, "Diplomacy" (New York: Simon and Schuster, 1994), pp. 40-60.
5. Ben H. Bagdikian, "The New Media Monopoly" (New York: Beacon Press, 2004), pp. 10-20.
6. Richard Donor, "Superman: The Movie," Warner Brothers, 1978.
7. Zack Snyder, "Man of Steel," Warner Brothers, 2011.
8. Joumane Chahine, "Public Diplomacy: A Conceptual Framework" Department of Art, History and Communication Studies, McGill University, Montreal, 2010.
9. Ibid.
10. James Truslow Adams, *"The Epic of America,"* New York: Simon Publications, 2001, pp. 1-20.
11. Ibid.
12. Justin Hart, *"Empire of Ideas: The Origins of Public Diplomacy and the Transformation of US Foreign Policy"* (London: Oxford University Press, 2001), pp. 20-40.
13. MACARYTHISM refers to an American historical tradition in which the idea of culling out of practicing and active communists was to be metamorphosed into a realistic Government paradigm, wherein, artists, playwrights, actors and authors, University professors and academics and other public personages were targeted, questioned and castigated for their communist linkages as part of the larger program of global and domestic containment.

14 Ibid

15. E.L. Doctrow, *"Ragtime"* (New York, Random House, 2007), pp. 1-10.
16. Ibid.
17. Dipanjan Roy Chaudhary, "PM Modi Makes Strong Pitch For India's Permanent Seat in UN Security Council", *Economic Times*, April 15, 2015.
18. "PM Modi's speech at the Madison Square Garden," https://www.youtube.com/ watch?v=tKx3OlHrV9I (Online: Web), Accessed on 1 February 2017.
19. Sadanand Dhume, "The Promise of a Modi-Trump Alliance," *The Wall Street Journal*, December 5, 2016.
20. Shubajit Roy, "Shedding Hesitations of History: PM Modi Points to Future in his Address to US Congress," *Indian Express*, June 6, 2016.
21. "On Terror and Pak, Meeting of Minds With US: Sushma Swaraj" *Indian Express*, 6 December 2014.
22. "India US Relations", https://www.mea.gov.in/Portal/ForeignRelation/ USA_15_01_2016.pdf (Online: Web), Accessed on 2 February, 2016.
23. B.M. Jain, *"Indo-US Relations in an Age of Uncertainty: An Uneasy Courtship,"* (New York: Routledge, 2016), pp. 2-20.

24. Alexander Wendt, "Anarchy is What States Make of it: The Social Construction of Power," *International Organization*, Volume 46, No. 2, Spring 1992, pp. 391-425.
25. Ibid.
26. MEA Document on US Visits to New Delhi, 2016.
27. GWOT can be comprehended as the Global War on Terror which was initiated by President Bush's Foreign Policy establishment in the aftermath of the September 11 attacks. It was a creation of a string of pearls in order to encircle the entire gamut of nations and civilities affected by the menace of global terrorism.
28. Mallala Yousufzai, "I am Mallala: The Girl who stood up for Education and was shot by Taliban," (Little Brown and Company, 2013).
29. India Today Correspondent, "Modi addresses Bhutan's Parliament, Says a Stronger India Better For Bhutan too," *India Today*, June, 2014.
30. Ibid.
31. Chidanand Rajghatta, "PM Narendra Modi Enthralls a Rapturous Crowd at the Madison Square Garden," *The Times of India*, September 8, 2014.
32. Ibid.

5

Cultural Continuum of India's Foreign Policy

Abhishek Srivastava

Introduction

No nation exists in a vacuum. To be able to survive in an increasingly competitive world order, a country needs a coherent foreign policy that clearly relays its interests, objectives and the ways to achieve them vis-à-vis other states. The foreign policy again is not the result of one particular factor, but has a multitude of factors inherent in it, like the national interest, domestic and international milieu, military capabilities, geography, economy and the national culture.

Prime Minister Modi, ever since coming to power in 2014, has taken on the task of engaging India with the world with unparalleled vigour. South Asia or India's immediate neighbourhood, and Central, South-East, and East Asia or the Extended Neighbourhood have found the utmost importance in PM Modi's foreign policy. His novel way of diplomacy consists of the use of cultural underpinnings of Asia and highlights the ancient and civilizational ties that these nations shared in order to gradually increase its own stature in the region.

This chapter will begin by discussing the role of history in the foreign policy formulation of India and then trace the roots of contemporary foreign policy in India's culture and philosophic traditions. It will look at India's growing use of cultural diplomacy and its success/failure per se.

The role of the past in shaping the present and future identities and interests of the nations can be best understood by the Constructivist theory of International Relations. The theory helps in understanding how the history of a state plays role in socially constructing states' identities which in turn shape the foreign policy objectives of the state and its perceptions and relationships with other states. The national identity also plays a major role in influencing the behaviour of any state in a given situation and determines whether it will be co-operative or aggressive in its interactions. Accordingly, it can be deduced that culture is relevant to the constructivist theory of IR as it is a set of socially-shared beliefs which in turn form the basis of the national identity.

Cultural Basis of India's Foreign Policy

India's post-independence foreign policy was mainly characterized by its profession of non-alignment and promotion of a self-sufficient model of economy. While the immediate reasons of these can be easily identified as the need to preserve the hard-earned freedom and to cast off the imperial yoke by developing rapidly, these policies can be traced back to ancient Indian political thought. While it would be a mistake to view foreign policy in a cultural vacuum, it is difficult to ignore it entirely as most of India's policies from Panchsheel, Non-alignment, anti-imperialism and anti-racism have a strong cultural element and are largely a continuation of the political thought formulated in the *Mahabharata*, *Arthashastra*, *Manusmriti*, *Panchatantra*, *Bhagwad Gita* and teachings of religions like Buddhism, Hinduism and Jainism.

Indian political tradition carries a strong revulsion towards the adoption of any policies leading to the extremities and it is from this that a strong preference and advocacy of the middle path is seen. Some examples of this can be seen in the form of the advocacy of a middle path between abolition of private property and capitalism and Buddhism's teaching of following the 'Middle Path' or 'Madhyamika' between extreme penance and indulgence. A strong influence of this was seen on Nehru when he said "India has absorbed and harmonized different religions, even the conflicts between science and religion... maybe it is our destiny to help reconcile the conflicting ideologies of today."[1] The impact of this idea of the middle path is very evident in the policy of non-alignment that India adopted at the onset of the Cold War. India not only chose to follow the middle path between Western liberal democracy and Soviet egalitarianism but also decided not to join either of the two camps. This enabled India to maintain a spirit of bonhomie with other nations and to try to diffuse the tensions between the two superpowers during conflicts like the Korean War and the Suez Crisis.

The principle of *Vasudaive Kutumbakam* found in the *Maha Upanishad* emphasizes the importance of welfare of all. It was in following this denunciation of aggressive warfare and the proclivity for welfare of all that India cast off a neutral stand during the Cold War and played an active part in the negotiations.

Other than this, being non-aligned provided India the leeway to analyze the merits and demerits of every situation and formulate its standing based on its own reason, rather than blindly following the ideology of the leader of the bloc. This emphasis on reason can be traced back to the *Mahabharata* which emphasizes that *Dharma* should be based on reason. The Indian culture and spiritualism as enshrined in the scriptures such as the *Vedas* and *Vedanta* aptly encapsulate the diversity prevalent in India since ancient times. In the *Chhandogya Upanishad*, it is written, "*Ekam Sat, Vipra Bahudha Vadanti*"—the Truth is one, but the wise speak it in different ways.[2]

India has long been a land of diversity and has allowed different cultures and religions to flourish side by side. This can only be made possible if the people of the country have a strong tolerant ethic. Not only is India the birthplace of four major religions of the world—Hinduism, Buddhism, Jainism and Sikhism—it was this spirit of toleration that allowed the assimilation of the Christians, Jews and Islamic rulers in Indian society. This has also manifested itself in India's historical attitude towards refugees, which has always been welcoming as seen in the case of offer of asylum to the Dalai Lama and the refugees from the erstwhile East Bangladesh during the 1971 war. The spirit of toleration also led India to reject the division of the world into two blocs during the Cold War as such a division rested upon the intolerance of the ideology of the other bloc.

What is perhaps the most defining part of India's foreign policy is its emphasis on peaceful and negotiated settlements of disputes and its belief in the futility of war. The *Mahabharata*, *Arthashastra*, and *Panchatantra* all argue that war should only be used as a last resort when all other ways of amicable settlement of disputes such as conciliation, gifts, etc., have failed.

Later proponents of non-violence were of course the Buddhists and Jains and Asoka, who on becoming a Buddhist renounced war as an instrument of foreign policy and emphasized on friendly and diplomatic relations with his immediate neighbours. Mahatma Gandhi later became a champion of the cause of non-violence during the independence struggle and preference for it was seen in India's attempts to negotiate with the Portuguese in Goa, China and Pakistan. An important component of IFP, the Panchsheel or the five principles of peaceful coexistence is undeniably moulded by the traditions of non-violence and toleration in Indian political thought.

India has the distinction of never having attempted to invade another country throughout its history, and no prominent Indian thinker advocates the use of force or coercion to disseminate Indian culture and values outside its own boundaries. Kautilya gives the idea of a '*Dharma Vijayin*' or the righteous conqueror who is implored to rule in accordance with local customs and traditions after conquering their territory and not to uproot the people's original ways of life, as Western imperialism tended to do. This feeling of anti-imperialism became more pronounced by the 200-year-long colonial experience and the sufferings and injustice witnessed by India. India's emphasis on Afro-Asian unity during the Cold War and being a strong supporter of decolonization movements in countries like Indonesia and a staunch opponent of the apartheid regime in South Africa, all stem from its own colonial experiences.

Former Indian P.M. Mr. Atal Bihari Vajpayee once said that "you can change your friends but not your neighbours".[3] It is a seemingly simple statement, but carries huge implications as far as the foreign policy of India is concerned. India is located in a tumultuous neighbourhood and shares boundaries with two particularly antagonistic countries—China and Pakistan. The need to cooperate and try to maintain friendly relations with them in order to maintain peace and stability in India itself cannot be overemphasized. The need to constantly engage with neighbours through diplomatic and ambassadorial channels was first underlined by Kautilya in his Mandal theory in the *Arthashastra*. The *Arthashastra* also emphasizes that peace is to be preferred over war and efforts should first be made to reconcile with the enemy. The adoption of this scheme of thinking was witnessed in the period preceding the 1962 Indo-Sino war, in Nehru's firm belief in the diffusion of tensions with China through dialogue.

Religion has also always played a vital role in promoting exchange of ideas since ancient times. Chinese philosopher-diplomat Hu Shih once said that India conquered China culturally for over 20th centuries without ever sending a soldier across its border; the statement is often taken to highlight the rich history of cultural ties between the two civilizations.[4] Similarly, Emperor Ashoka, after adopting Buddhism, sent his son and daughter to Sri Lanka as emissaries to spread the message of the religion there.

India has had the fortune of being the birthplace of several thinkers and philosophers who have contributed vastly to the export of India's culture to the nations beyond. The first such personality that comes to mind is undoubtedly Mahatma Gandhi, who not only won India its independence from the British, but also organized successful struggles in South Africa and served as an inspiration for other great world leaders like Nelson Mandela and Martin Luther King Jr. Today, the whole world knows India as the birthplace of Gandhi who was a trailblazer of the use of truth and non-violence to achieve political ends. Swami Vivekananda, while recognizing the syncretised tradition of India, emphasized on the essential oneness of all religions. He left his mark on the world by his opening statement at the Chicago Parliament of Religions where he addressed the gathering as 'Brothers and Sisters of America', thus underlining his message of universal brotherhood. One of Aurobindo Ghosh's dreams for India was the 'spiritual gift of India to the world', which would lead to more and more countries turning towards India and her teachings.

Cultural Diplomacy of India

India thus undoubtedly harbours a huge potential as far as exploiting its vast cultural reserves are concerned. India shares deep historical ties with South Asia and South-East Asia and the processes of cultural exchanges and assimilation are not unknown to the region.

Culture, according to Joseph Nye, along with values and policies, is one of the characteristics of a nation's soft power. Soft power essentially refers to spreading a country's influence beyond its borders without resorting to the hard power of the military or any other form of coercion. Soft power entails attracting other nations and having a persuasive power over them. Jeffery Haynes talks about how religious and cultural groups can influence a nation's foreign policy by lobbying with the policy makers to incorporate religious beliefs and cultural values in the foreign policy.

India is still widely recalled as the 'Golden Bird', as a land of spices, gold, diamonds, merchants and traders. India is also widely recognized as the land of non-violence, diversity, tolerance, yoga, Ayurveda. While all these elements are present in the international cognition, as such, it is the realization of the importance of these and India's willingness to utilize them that remains to be seen.

As mentioned earlier, immediately after independence, Nehru chose to follow the policy of non-alignment keeping in the mind the ancient Hindu and Buddhist political and religious thoughts. Due to the importance that these traditions lay on peaceful co-existence, and the futility of war, India played an active role in diffusing the tensions between the two superpowers in the various arenas of conflict, while at the same time adopting the policy of Panchsheel or the five principles of co-existence which were, mutual respect for each other's territorial integrity and sovereignty, mutual aggression, mutual non-interference in each other's internal affairs, equality and cooperation for mutual benefit and peaceful co-existence. The Indian Council of World Affairs was set up in 1943 as a think tank to promote India's relations with other countries through research, discussion, etc., in cultural issues. However, India's drive to maintain peaceful and stable relations with everyone led to neglect of the capitalization of hard power and it suffered a humiliating defeat in the Indo-Sino war in 1962. The soft power was also under-utilized. Thus, India failed to emerge as either a major hard power or a major soft power.

This changed after the collapse of the USSR towards the end of the Cold War in 1991 and the economic crisis which drove India to liberalize its economy and establish relations with East Asia in an effort to look for new friends and markets. It was in this scenario that India's cultural and civilizational links with these nations came to be recognized and actively promoted.

According to Ian Hall, five new developments can be identified in what he terms "new Indian public diplomacy" since 2000. They are: efforts to reach out to overseas Indians; building connections with foreign business interests; foreign aid and development programmes; promoting events to showcase and "nation-brand" India; and, using new social media to reach out to younger generations.[5]

Previously neglected, the Indian Diaspora came to be widely recognized as a vital aspect of spreading India's soft power across the globe. It is present in a number of nations and at several vital positions and hence becomes very important in spreading Indian culture. Pravasi Bharatiya Diwas is celebrated to cultivate the Diaspora as cultural ambassadors.[6] PM Modi has made it a point to address the Indian community during his foreign visits. The most spectacular of these can be seen in the images of PM Modi addressing full houses at the Madison Square Garden in the USA and Wembley Stadium in the UK.

While earlier prime ministers were not averse to the use of culture to strengthen India's relations with other nations, none of them quite realized its prospective usage and this is where PM Modi deserves due credit. His foreign policy is largely guided by the twin objectives of diluting the mutual distrust by underscoring the similarities and to use culture to sugar-coat political decisions. He has drawn inspiration from the ancient ideals of India's role as *Vishwaguru* or the world leader and *Vasudaiva Kutumbakam*.

The major ways by which India has been expanding its cultural influence include the active promotion of Yoga, Ayurveda and highlighting and emphasizing religious links with its Asian neighbours.

Yoga is an ancient Hindu practice and is practised widely across the world. At the UN General Assembly meeting in September 2014,

Modi called yoga 'an invaluable gift from our ancient tradition to the world'[7] and then went on to get 21 June recognized as International Yoga Day. This recognition will certainly lead to an augmentation of India's cultural capital across the world and enable nations to see India as land of practices that can adopted for spiritual and health benefits. Yoga is also being used to spread the message of peace in conflict situations. The Art of Living Foundation has been travelling to conflict-ridden areas to promote peace and harmony by the practice of Yoga. Related to yoga is the emphasis that has been given to the ancient Indian treatise on medicine, Ayurveda. The Modi Government set up the Ministry of AYUSH for the promotion of Ayurveda and has been holding Ayurveda seminars with nations such as The Netherlands. It has also gradually become increasingly popular in the developed world with about 2,000 Ayurvedic retreat centres having been developed around the world.

India has also laid stress on religious links in ties with nations such Nepal, where the Ramayana Circuit was inaugurated in 2018 to promote religious tourism between the two nations. A bus service was started between Janakpuri in Nepal and Ayodhya in India as part of this circuit; Janakpuri being the birthplace of Sita and Ayodhya that of Lord Rama. This will certainly go a long way in strengthening the historical and traditional relations between Nepal and India and highlights how the religious traditions of the two are dependent on each other. Modi, on one of his visits to Nepal, also visited religious and holy places such as Jabalpur, Muktimath and Pashupatinath. In a nation that is visibly moving towards China, this gesture went a long way in increasing the popularity of Modi among the people who thronged in their hundreds and thousands to the civic reception organized for him in Janakpur.

PM Modi had remarked that 'without Buddha, this century cannot be the Asian century.'[8] In the post-reform period, good relations with the countries of East and South East Asia have been imperative for India and one way of strengthening ties is using the image of the Buddha. The use of Buddhism in cultural diplomacy of India has become so vital because it provided the basis for the adoption of a common culture, thoughts, ideas and practices among people in India, Japan, Korea and China and thus became an important factor in providing the culturally disparate Asia with some sort of cohesion. While there are a few practising Buddhists in India today, India can veritably claim the legacy of Buddhism as it originated here and various important sites associated with the Buddha like Bodh Gaya, Sarnath and Nalanda are located in India. India hosted the International Buddha Purnima Diwas in 2015 to commemorate the birth, enlightenment and *Mahaparinirvana* of Buddha.

The revival of Nalanda University is also of special significance for students from Buddhist majority countries as scholars from across Asia came to study here throughout history. Buddhism is also important in Indo-Lankan ties where the Buddhist ties date back to Ashoka's time; a cultural centre was inaugurated at Jaffna by PM Modi. He also laid down the foundation stone of a Swaminarayan temple in Abu Dhabi, which will be the first traditional Hindu temple in West Asia. In his address at the inauguration, he said that he hoped the temple would spread the message of '*Vasudaiva Kutumbakam* to people across the world'[9] and would definitely act as a harbinger of the message of harmony, peaceful co-existence and tolerance—the cornerstone of ancient Indian political thought—in the nation.

The Government of India also proposed Operation Mausam to develop the Spice Route with Kochi at the centre in a bid to counter China's maritime silk route and to develop maritime connectivity from Africa, Arabian Peninsula and South Asia to South East Asia. The ancient spice route was so called because it was the course that the spice and gem traders traversed. In addition to increased trade connectivity, is also provided an impetus to the spread of religions like Judaism, Christianity and Islam through the Indian Ocean Region.

Indian Culture to Tackle Global Issues

The world, as we know it today, is a very different place from what it was when our ancient scriptures were written. Not only is it afflicted by a multitude of problems such as climate change, sustainability of development, water conservation, and rising incidents of state and non-state violence, there is also a lack of consensus on how to deal with them. Many Indian scholars, in this scenario, have begun highlighting the endurance of the various facets of Indian culture and literature to solve the many problems faced today.

Fourteen of 20 megacities of the world are facing a water scarcity or drought conditions today and as many as four billion people already live in regions that experience severe water stress for at least one month of the year. Nearly half of those people live in India and China and with their ever-growing populations, these problems will only rise.[10] Hence, ways of water conservation attain utmost importance. Indian culture focuses on *bhakti*, which entails the worship of god, and includes, among others, worship of Nature. In the *Manusmriti* is found an abject proscription of impure objects like urine, spit, blood or poison being cast into water bodies. Rivers are objects of worship in the Vedas and this shows the importance that rivers have always enjoyed in India. Also found across North India, in cities like Delhi are step wells known as *Baolis*, which were used in olden times to provide water for drinking and agriculture. Then come *Johads* or small-scale dams found in Rajasthan, which were used to capture water and to replenish the water table. These were in place in ancient India, but fell into gradual ruin. Both *baolis* and *johads* are effective means of water conservation and according to experts can be easily replicated in areas having similar climatic and physiological conditions as India.

We are living in an age where the possibility of the exhaustion of essential resources is very real and looms large over humankind. Indian culture has always focused on sustainability and the yogic principle of *Aparigraha*, or attachment to material things, is an example of this. *Aparigraha* entails keeping only what is necessarily needed by one, and living in harmony with nature. The Bishnoi community of Rajasthan is a pioneering example of protection of nature; protecting wildlife forms as part of their faith.

India's climate pledge is also in line with its history and tradition of harmonious co-existence with nature. As has already been mentioned, Indians have always regarded the flora and fauna of the globe as part of their family. Hindu scriptures consider each organism in the world to be equally pertinent in the scheme of nature and mandate the preservation of sacred groves and forests. The *Matsya Purana* celebrates the planting of trees as a festival and condemns those who cut and destroy forests and trees.

The 2018 Global Peace Index shows that the world in 2018 is less peaceful than at any other times in the last decade.[11] The rise of ethnic violence, terrorism and conflicts among nation-states have marred the peace of the world and Indian literature again has some wisdom to share on this issue. Indian sages held the view that peace in society is not possible without the individual's well-being and for this, popular welfare and equitable distribution of resources is imperative. The happy and satisfied individual is the basis of a peaceful society which further leads to a stable and secure national and international arena. The methods of peaceful diplomacy are propagated in both the *Arthashastra*, and the *Mahabharata* and this finds echo in Article 51 of the Indian Constitution according to which, the state shall endeavour to maintain international peace and security and encourage settlement of disputes by arbitration.

While India has certainly made great strides in engaging in cultural diplomacy, there is much room for improvement. India faces challenges in this cultural engagement from both internal and external quarters, and if India's cultural reserves are spectacular, so are the problems and challenges.

Domestically speaking, India's cultural traditions of tolerance and inclusivity have come under a cloud of doubt due to the rising incidents of communal violence and lynching. What is ever more concerning is the image of the Indian leadership abroad. Western media houses refer to PM Modi as a 'Hindu nationalist' and the BJP as a 'Hindutva party', which renders all the appeals of religious and cultural assimilation made by the Government to nothing more than a farce in the eyes of the target audience as this challenges the multicultural narrative that forms the basis of the 'culture' that India seeks to promote abroad.

India, which has traditionally been a land to offer protection to the persecuted and to give them asylum, was very lukewarm in its response to the Rohingya refugees and managed to attract worldwide condemnation by threatening to deport them back to Myanmar.

At the systemic level, the major challenge that India faces is in the form of China. China and India both have very vibrant cultures and are vying for extending their influence to the whole of Asia and this puts them in the crosshairs of each other. China's culture is perhaps its most valuable source of soft power and consists largely of

Confucianism, Taoism and Martial Arts, and it has capitalized on these by offering scholarships to foreign students, giving humanitarian aid and establishing Confucius institutions in different parts of the world. China has also sought to revive the age-old Asian connectivity by the One Belt One Road initiative. China has also proactively used Buddhism to extend its reach to East and South East Asia. It has so far had the upper hand when it comes to using cultural diplomacy and this is because of various reasons. Firstly, India is seen as a regional hegemony in South Asia and her neighbours harbour a deep distrust of her intentions. Hence, in a way to counter the Indian hegemony, more and more nations such as Sri Lanka and Nepal have turned to China. Secondly, China does not have the complicated history that India shares with her neighbours which makes it easier for it to move forward with them rapidly without any major impediments. Thirdly, soft power needs to be complemented by hard power and this is where India severely lags behind China. India's rise is also hindered by its limited outreach. While in 2013, China had over 500 Confucius institutions and language centres across the world, India had just 35.

Conclusion

Notwithstanding the hindrances stated above, India has recognized the vast potential of its culture in cementing ties with Asian nations and those across the Indian Ocean as well. What makes India particularly attractive is its vibrant democratic culture, institutions of free speech, freedom of religion and a constitutional protection of the rights of individuals. These are areas where India has an upper hand over China.

Another important point to keep in mind is that unlike the hard power of the military, soft power works in the long run and results take some time to materialize. How efficient has India's use of its culture been can only be evaluated after a few years since the focus on culture is relatively new in Indian diplomacy. That being said, India should take effective steps to ensure that the multicultural ethos of the nation is not threatened. India would also do well to address the legitimate concerns of its smaller neighbours to prevent them from turning to China.

NOTES

1. Jha, N.K. (1989), Cultural and Philosophical Roots of India's Foreign Policy, *International Studies*, 26(1), pp. 45–67. https://doi.org/10.1177/002088178902600 1003
2. Mahapatra, Debidatta Aurobinda (2016), From a latent to a 'strong' soft power?, The evolution of India's cultural diplomacy, Palgrave Communications, 2, 16091. 10.1057/palcomms.2016.91.
3. *The Economics Times*, May 09, 2003.
4. Pethiyagoda, Kadira (2017), China-India relations: Millennia of peaceful coexistence meet modern day geopolitical interests. Brookings.
5. Mahapatra, Debidatta Aurobinda (2016), From a latent to a 'strong' soft power?, The evolution of India's cultural diplomacy, Palgrave Communications, 2, 16091. 10.1057/palcomms.2016.91.
6. Ibid.
7. PM Modi's address to the 69th session of the UN General Assembly.
8. Address by PM Modi at the International Buddha Purnima Diwas celebration 2015.
9. *The Hindu*, February 11, 2018.
10. Leahy, Stephen (2018), From not enough to too much, the world's water crisis explained, *National Geographic*.
11. Global Peace Index 2018.

REFERENCES

Mahapatra, Debidatta Aurobinda (2016), From a latent to a 'strong' soft power?, The evolution of India's cultural diplomacy.

Palgrave Communications, 2, 16091. 10.1057/palcomms.2016.91.

Jha, N.K. (1989), Cultural and Philosophical Roots of India's Foreign Policy, *International Studies*, 26(1), 45–67. https://doi.org/10.1177/0020881789026001003; 'The growing role of Buddhism in India's soft power strategy (2018), World Economic Forum. https://www.weforum.org/agenda/2018/07/the-growing-role-of-buddhism-in-india-s-soft-power-strategy/

Jha, Hari Bansh (2018), Modi's cultural diplomacy: Bearing fruits in Nepal, Vivekananda International Foundation. https://www.vifindia.org/2018/september/17/modi-s-cultural-diplomacy-bearing-fruits-in-nepal

'Ramayan Circuit gets a new bus service', *The Hindu*, May 12, 2018.

Modi Deploys his culture skills in Asia (2015), Brookings.

Stobodan, P. (2016), Asia's Buddhist Connectivity and India's role. Institute for Defence Studies and Analysis. https://idsa.in/issuebrief/asias-buddhist-connectivity-and-indias-role_pstobdan_190216

Hazarika, Obja & Mishra, Vivek (2016), Soft Power Contestation between India and China in South Asia.

Pratap, Bhanu, India's Cultural Diplomacy: Present Dynamics, Challenges and Future Prospects, *International Journal of Arts, Humanities and Management Studies*.

Ganguly, Meenakshi (2017), India's response to Rohingya crisis is timid, Human Rights Watch.

Jha, N.K. 'Peace and Security: Traditional Indian Perspective', *South Asia Politics*, Vol. 3, No. 12, April 2005, pp. 21-25.

'The three wonders of the world solving modern water problems', *The Guardian*.

Pandey, Arundhati (2017), What India can teach the world about sustainability, World Economic Forum.

Wernick, Adam (2015), India brings back its ancient wisdom to fight its modern environmental problems, Public Radio International.

Tripathi, Satyendra, Climate Change and India's Traditional Lifestyle and Practices: Potential for Mitigation. India Foundation.

Agoramoorthy, Govindasamy, and Minna J. Hsu, "Ancient Hindu Scriptures Show the Ways to Mitigate Global Warming through Responsible Action," *Anthropos*, Vol. 106, No. 1, pp. 211–216. *JSTOR*, JSTOR, www.jstor.org/stable/23031817.

6

International Relations in Ancient India: Kautilya's Arthashastra Revisited[1]

Shounak Set

There appear among mankind unique individuals from time to time who by dint of their merit shape the course of history and leave their imprint on the everlasting altar of time. Standing tall on the obscure porch of ancient India is the enigmatic figure of Kautilya, variously referred to as Vishnugupta or Chanakya (370–283 BC approx.). While differing and contradictory accounts pertain to his origins and historicity, scholars are largely unanimous that Chanakya, having been insulted by Emperor Dhana Nanda, usurped the throne and installed Chandragupta Maurya, leading to the foundation of the pan-Indian Mauryan empire. Then he proceeded to collate the insights gained from the philosophy and practice of statecraft; thus, was the genesis of the magisterial treatise of the *Arthashastra* which is composed of 15 sections each devoted to a specific aspect of government. Kautilya's thinking, which dates back to nearly 2,500 years ago, is therefore a testament to the pinnacle of human excellence in intellect and imagination. His *magnum opus*, the *Arthashastra*, praised by many for its breadth, examines a wide array of topics ranging from fiscal policy at one end of the spectrum to public administration at the other and even deals with gender relations. For reasons of scope and space, this study confines itself to Kautilya's ideas pertaining to International Relations (henceforth IR) and investigates their relevance for the modern era. Works from classical antiquity like the *Arthashastra* merit scrutiny not merely for their profound philosophical insights transcending the confines of space and time but also because they can provide a cognitive tool for analysing the present and anticipating the future. Thus, this commentary aims to clarify his extraordinary originality and transcendental universality and distil its potential significance in terms of contemporary applicability.

Ancient India was home to a sophisticated diplomatic tradition characterised by a ruthlessly realistic state system which insisted that foreign relations be determined by self-interest rather than by ethical considerations. Fourth-century BC India represented a complex mosaic of kingdoms, protectorates and dependencies. While most of these were politically autonomous, if not independent, they were united through a common culture anchored in Hinduism and constrained by codes and conventions emanating from political and commercial contacts with each other. Unsurprisingly, stronger parties attempted to dominate weaker ones, but even if successful, they rarely interfered with the convention and customs of their vassals. However, the outstanding fact was that there was no hegemony and the political landscape was chronically anarchic and volatile. This situation changed in 321 BC when Chandragupta Maurya founded an empire in lands which are in modern times Northwestern India, and would gradually extend through much of the Indian subcontinent. He relied upon an eclectic and innovative combination of Persian, Greek as well as indigenous practices of statecraft, largely theorised and systematised by Kautilya, his preceptor, political advisor and prime minister, successively. Thus was born the glorious Maurya Empire, midwifed by Kautilya, which guaranteed security and stability over an extraordinarily large area in which peace ensued and trade flourished. This area, because of the relative slow pace of travel on land and sea, was comparable to Greece during the Peloponnesian War, and arguably in a way equivalent to today's entire world. This resulted in India's first ever political unification and ushered in an age of peace and prosperity. The *Arthashastra* painstakingly elaborates the means and methods for establishing a state and preserving its power in the strategically competitive milieu and in the face of adversarial powers with the inherent danger of political subversion and social instability.

The Kautilyan idea of IR is embodied through the Mandala theory, which envisages a comity of states classified on indices of comparative hostility and amity.[2] The Mandala has often been misinterpreted literally as an arrangement of states in concentric circles, with the singularly most important actor *(Vijigishu)* constituting the epicentre of international affairs, its nearest rival being the principal antagonist (*Ari*) and geography determining allies and adversaries. The idea of Mandala is, however, indicative of the complicated interstate inter-linkages contingent upon varying degrees of amity and animosity where each state is a Mandela itself; the mandala then as a microcosm reflects the range of allies and adversaries of a state whereas the mandala as an international structure is the macrocosmic aggregation of these unit-level mandalas. Survival if not self-aggrandizement by states in a fiercely competitive strategic milieu is the functional assumption of this formulation where sovereignty of a state is personified through its respective regent. In the contemporary world, survival and gaining power is widely acknowledged as the elemental interest of a state and exercising sovereignty through territorial enforcement is the primary expression of that; the subject of territorial security informs most of Kautilya's political thought, and serves as an incisive guide for national security in the present era marked by ascending porosity of borders and increasing importance of non-state actors. In essence, the Kautilyan framework can be not just relevant, but even superior to existing approaches of international relations.

Conventional international relations, as an academic discipline, is premised largely on the intrinsic equality of states, and this accentuates the intellectual impoverishment of the discipline by widening the divergence between theory and praxis as the inequality among states and other actors in the current era has assumed unprecedented levels. Kautilya's conceptualisation of international relations is delightfully devoid of such debilitating deficiencies as he considers state behaviour to be contingent on relative power. The *sadhgunyas* are a classification of six different policies outlined by Kautilya as a framework of foreign policy pivotal on the differential power level of the states, which operate through four principal mechanisms, the *chaturupayas*. The latter constitute modes of diplomatic exercise whereas the former represent policy principles guiding the overall range of action. Agreement for peace (*Sandhi*), bandwagoning (*Samsraya*), duplicity (*Dvaidhibhava*), war (*Vigraha*), limited offensives or marches (*Yana*), indifference or neutrality (*Asana)*, combined together constitute a six-fold policy or *sadhgunya*, the cornerstone of the Kautilyan scheme of diplomacy. The first three are prescribed for weaker states against stronger states, the next two befit stronger parties and the last is reserved for states of equal power. The practical application of these is through various contextual combinations and permutations of the four *upayas*, i.e., conciliation (*sama*), gift (*dana*), coercion (*danda*) and dissension (*bheda*), and subject to political expediency and optimal utility. The *Arthashastra* elegantly classifies several subdivisions of the six-fold policy and elaborates on different circumstances along with appropriate pay-offs for the actors involved.[3] This classification schema by itself is not insignificant if the intellectual elegance of the model is considered; and when the antiquity of the setting is acknowledged, it establishes itself as a stupendous achievement.

Kautilya's accurate grasp of the distinction between means and end cannot and should not be underestimated. Situated in the ancient era of more than two millennia ago, this is remarkable as even modern Realist scholars have suffered from this serious shortcoming. They identify the goal of foreign policy as 'national interest', but conflate it with power and suggest that states seek power as an end in itself.[4] Kautilya unambiguously defines 'power' as the means of foreign policy as varying from 'happiness', which is the end and is measured by welfare, and prosperity of the state, which in the modern era can be construed through indicators of living standards and social cohesion. Thus, power for Kautilya is beyond being simply the currency of politics; it is the precise means to the end, which is happiness. It can be crudely taken as the index for measuring the success of foreign policy and is complemented through order and welfare of the state. Because of this, happiness cannot be completely comprehended without accounting for parameters like internal stability, standard of life, social cohesion and so on, and all of these cumulatively influence the power of a state in the international environment. This ecumenical approach deserves a special note when commentaries on the shortcomings of disciplinary straitjacketed examinations of international relations have become the pervading feature of the academic discourse of the discipline.

The contemporary world is marked by its fluidity as the axis of global power shifts from the West to the East and emerging players challenge established actors. Hence, although these concepts retain an element of perennial significance, the current era of power transition and power diffusion contributes to their critical salience. IR has for a long time revolved around the dichotomous binaries of 'hard power' versus 'soft power'. Power, whether 'hard' or 'soft', is however rendered meaningless if it cannot be leveraged to advance the national interest; thus, 'smart' power entailing adroit application of hard and soft powers in tandem for optimum effect becomes essential to the scenario. Significantly, since its advent in the 1990s, the very conceptualisation and application of 'smart' power has remained a largely Western phenomenon; the Kautilyan injunctions, however, contain the seeds of a radical revision of smart power on indigenous terms apt for non-Western states. Epistemologically smart power enhances the role of agency and privileges it as an independent variable. Kautilya views power as the Trinitarian function of (a) deliberation or decision-making, (b) treasury and military and (c) resoluteness. Such a conceptualisation of power involves active application and utilisation of the various elements of the state following accurate and discernible analysis of conditions and political climate; strikingly similar yet analytically distinct from Joseph Nye's formulation of 'smart' power which calls for contextual application and synthesis of elements of hard and soft power with a favourable outcome being the focal point of reference.

Kautilya acknowledged the prohibitive expenses of war and cautioned for intrigue and secret offensives in a manner not dissimilar to the Chinese master strategist, Sun Tzu, who held that the best victories were the ones where aims were achieved without bloodshed.[5] The *Arthashastra* counsels *'kutayuddha'* and *'mantrayudha'*, corresponding to covert operations and diplomatic offensives as instruments of state policy, and these acquire significance for the modern era where war continues by other means following its prohibition by the UN Charter of 1945. The emergence of phenomena like 'law fare' and 'asymmetric conflict' in recent times is a poignant rejoinder to these timeless principles, as the incipient complications and novel tendencies overwhelm the ideas and institutions which, anchored in assumptions of the previous century, strive to regulate the values and resources in the transforming global environment. Curiously, despite the relative neglect of the text in the modern era, several diplomatic and military practices resemble Kautilyan maxims, illustrating the remarkable sophistication of this ancient classic. The Cold Start doctrine of the Indian Armed Forces, for instance, visualises short but intense and integrated punitive strikes at the tactical level against Pakistan without escalation to a full-fledged war and thereby reflects an uncanny resuscitation of the millennia-old practice of '*yana*' pursued by stronger powers against weaker powers as an act of compliance or coercive diplomacy short of war. Aid diplomacy in modern times, similarly, is reflective of the Kautilyan concept of' *dana*'. Kautilya cautions the conqueror against substituting his virtues for the vices of the defeated enemy for administering conquered territories. Arguably, the latter postulate portrays a notion similar to the maxim of 'winning hearts and minds' of affected populations in the face of insurgencies, as was evident from the U.S. occupation of Iraq and the U.S. offensives henceforth.

Kautilya theorised an international system along with its subsystems, structural dynamics, typologies and mutual interaction of the key actors, distinguished by incredible intellectual elegance and a precise policy framework. The *Arthashastra*, marked by its moral relativism and ingrained farsightedness, has led him to be compared with Machiavelli on one hand and Aristotle and Plato on the other for the systematic treatment unencumbered by theological platitudes. Unsurprisingly, then, Kautilya is alternately praised and condemned for stark pragmatism and amoral viciousness. In the same breath, Kautilya's masterpiece has captivated scholars and practitioners alike over the ages. If Modelski declares, "Kautilya's *Arthashastra* remains with us as an impressive monument to man's ability to reason, clearly, if abstractly, about the most complex problems of social and international affairs"[6] then a leading Indian diplomat remarks, "...the importance of the concepts and the ways of thinking that the *Arthashastra* reveals is useful because in many ways, the world which we face today, is similar to the world that Kautilya operated in when he built the Mauryan Empire to greatness..."[7] Thus, despite its antiquity, the *Arthashastra* remains an everlasting political classic, on account of its brilliant exposition of statecraft. Kautilya's *Arthashastra* hence remains a treasure for its ageless political wisdom and profound knowledge of human nature that remains unblemished with the passage of time; it then becomes a talisman for charting the course through the tempest that is 21st-century international relations.

NOTES

1. R. Shamasastry, *Kautilya's Arthashastra*, Mysore Publishing House, Mysore, 1951.
2. Kautilya, *The Arthashastra*, Penguin, New Delhi, 2000.
3. Jayantanuja Bandyopadhyaya et al., *Kautilya's Mandala as an International System*, School of International Relations and Strategic Studies, Jadavpur University, Calcutta, 1991.
4. Roger Boesche, 'Kautilya's Arthashastra on War and Diplomacy in Ancient India', *The Journal of Military History*, 67(1), 2003, pp. 9–37.
5. George Modelski, 'Kautilya: Foreign Policy and International System in the Ancient Hindu World', *The American Political Science Review*, 58(3), September 1964, pp. 549–560, at http://www.jstor.org/stable/1953131
6. Shivshankar Menon, 'Study of Arthashastra Important to Understand Our Strategic Culture', Press Release, Institute for Defence Studies and Analyses (IDSA), New Delhi, October 8, 2013, at http://idsa.in/pressrelease/StudyofArthashastra ImportantShivShankarMenon.html

7

Liberal-Idealist Contemplation in the Non-Western World: A Study of Ubuntu in Africa

Sandipani Dash

Introduction

Ideational inadequacy and connected operational inefficacy of the West dominated the contemporary world order and has evoked renewed interest in ancient cultural ethos originating in the non-Western regions. The pre-colonial idea of Ubuntu carries a revealing legacy in the pursuit of humanism in Africa, which has been subjected to the centuries-long process of domination and brutality unleashed by external forces, more specifically the Western powers. The continent has, however, witnessed a fundamental transformation in recent decades. Resurging Africa has indeed started re-engaging with the external world, opening up the scope for stressing its cultural connectivity with other non-Western civilisational entities, for their active engagement in the idea-shaping exercises of global affairs on humane terms.

Keeping the above in perspective, this chapter has examined Liberal-Idealism as an analytical construct emanating from the Western world. It has subsequently contextualised the Liberal Idealist tradition in the regions beyond the West. In addition, the paper has conceptualised Ubuntu, for searching the ideational expanse of the existing structure of global affairs.

Liberal-Idealism in the Western World

Liberal Idealism is a dominant idea in the global affairs discourse, owing to its origin to the celebrated concept of perpetual peace expounded by Immanuel Kant.[1] Running through Woodrow Wilson's reiteration justifying America's entry into World War I in 1917 and then the enunciation of fourteen principles as part of his vision of an inter-war world order, it culminated in the Democratic Peace Theory and Liberal Peace Thesis in the post-Cold War context.[2] It essentially posits the inevitability of democratic governance for ensuring global peace. For bringing peace through the introduction of structural democracy in select parts of the non-Western world, orchestration of regime change becomes the principal strategy of the extra-regional powers, especially the US-led actors of the West. Hence, an inescapable question arises: are gradually evolved democratic institutions, or the arbitrarily crafted ones, essential for global peace? To put a more fundamental question, how liberal and ideal are methods of applying Liberal Idealism in the practice of global affairs?

Interventionist endeavour towards establishing democratic institutions in Libya is an instructive case. The unilateral military intervention of the West in this North African country, ignoring the mediatory role of the African Union, has caused enormous domestic and regional destabilisation. The then U.S. President, Barack Obama, under whose leadership the North Atlantic Treaty Organisation forces carried out the military operation, admitted that failing to prepare for the aftermath of the ousting of Libyan leader Col. Muammar Gaddafi was the worst mistake of his presidency.[3] However, American institutional liberalists like Robert Keohane, in the beginning, interpreted regime change through military means in Libya as one of the major indicators of the 'revival of moralism' in post-Cold War world politics.[4] The *moralpolitik* supposition of this exercise is demystified, with timely revelation on the American scheme of capturing oil resources[5] and the French Government's covert operation for killing Gaddafi in Libya.[6] The exogenous imposition of the apparent political morality has recreated many such conflict theatres and insecurity zones in the non-Western world.

The idea and practice of establishing democracy and peace through topward compelling methods have so far received enough critical reflection and enormous discredit. Roberts views liberal state-building and peace-building as a "post-Cold War neo-imperial agenda of intervention" in which states in post-conflict environments are being built in the image of the West. For Roberts, such an approach which is invasive and imperial has failed and will continue to fail as long as there is a failure to recognise and understand that "transitional impositions of democratic practice cannot be substituted for or replace, in the short-term, political behaviour derived from needs, experiences, histories, and evolutions quite different from those from which Western democracy is derived."[7]

Similarly, Darby, using a post-colonial critique of liberal peace-building notes that it is a colonial enterprise that marginalises the experiences, approaches, and understandings of non-Western societies and does not connect with their everyday lives.[8] Darby notes that as long as peace-building initiatives are determined from "above and outside", they are "cast in the mould of colonialism."[9] Richmond observes that "The whole apparatus of peace is sometimes colonial and racist in that it implies the transference of enlightened knowledge to those who lack the capacity or morality to attain such knowledge themselves."[10]

Patrick Tom argues that the practice of international peace-building is grounded in the idea of the superiority of the liberal peace over other forms of peace, especially, local ones. He illustrates the case of Africa, where communities are rarely consulted about what kind of politics or state they want and, as such, are being presented with no choice, but liberal peace. For him, this assumes *a priori* that this is what they want and thus ends up looking like a colonial project. He adds that the liberal peace project has failed to achieve its aims including a democratic setting in which people's welfare and human rights are promoted. As such, it does not look like a very humanitarian practice, but as something that has been designed to recreate colonialism.[11] Patrick suggests that if liberal peace-building is to be "saved", it ought to be saved from its "cheerleaders" who offer prescriptive strategies without a critical reflection on their viability and acceptability in post-conflict environments and have witnessed local resistance to them. While the liberal peace model has worked well in the West, it is crucial to question whether transplanting it wholesale to non-Western societies with different cultural and historical backgrounds from it will work. War-torn societies need to be "saved" from problem-solving approaches that are biased towards these societies and ignore local agency, capacities for peace-making, order, and recovery. The locals' voices need to be heard,[12] since as insiders they "possess the historical, cultural, and linguistic resources that outsiders lack, and that are essential not only to understanding the root causes of conflict but also to search for sustainable solutions."[13]

The Democratic/Liberal Peace Thesis marginalises experiences, approaches, and understandings of non-Western societies. This exclusivist variant of Liberal Idealism systemically permeates the ideational structure of global affairs, which bears for centuries together, the ascendancy of the West, especially prolonged dominance of the Anglo-Saxon powers like Britain and the USA. R.J. Rummel gave a compelling story of the horrors that occur in modern societies. He depicts how 'democide' has been very much a part of human history. Among other examples, his depiction includes the massacre of Europeans during the Thirty Years' War, the relatively unknown genocide of the French Revolution, and the slaughtering of American Indians by colonists in the New World.[14] Liberal-Idealist discourse emanating from the West, in effect, raises a human facade for the pursuit of domination and brutality that is constantly unleashed under the existing hierarchical global order, which is based on the presumption of supra-state anarchy.[15]

The anthro-economic foundation of this Anglo-Saxon eclecticism essentially lies in individualistic economic freedom and Euro-centric cultural determinism. A globalist project is rooted in the Weberian thesis of 'Protestant Ethics and Spirit of Capitalism', which has overwhelmingly shaped the Western capitalist worldview. Max Weber, in his seminal treatise *The Religion of India: The Sociology of Hinduism and Buddhism* published in 1958 argued, "Capitalism would remain weak in India because the ancient religions of India have no element of the Protestant ethic, a necessary element for the growth and development of capitalistic thoughts."[16] Weber further put forward, "The irrational approach of Indian religious traditions, consisting of such dogmas as the *samsara* (illusionary world) and *karma* (doctrine of divine compensation), created a system that was highly traditional and progress-inhibiting."[17] Pre-dating Weber by more than a century, another such powerful thinker like Hegel, who has immensely contributed, in addition to Immanuel Kant, to idealist philosophy in the West, in his 1830-1831 *Philosophy of History* lectures at the University of Jena stated:

> The Negro...represents the natural man in his completely wild and untamed state. We must lay aside all thought of reverence and morality—all that we call feeling—if we would rightly comprehend him; there is nothing harmonious with humanity to be found in this type of character. The copious and circumstantial accounts of Missionaries completely confirm this.....[18]

The notional premise of such an awful sense of Euro-cultural superiority is monotheistic theological traditions that have gained traction in many parts of the world, including the West. Though carrying global pretensions, the Western version of liberal idealism consequently remains completely dismissive of the ideational and behavioural specificity of the non-Western World.

Contextualising Liberal-Idealist Tradition beyond the West

The Liberal-Idealist narrative of established International Relations (IR) has barely taken note of the historical experiences and ideational traits of the regions far from the West. It is a continuation of the larger problem that has systemically gripped the theory-building exercises of the discipline since non-Western specificity has received scant recognition in the literature on IR. However, any reflection on the skewed empirical-normative basis of the so-called universal theories of International Relations does not ignore the truth that the non-Western world, like the West itself, is not a homogenous construct. This spatial category has a diversity of units and inhabitants.[19]

Illustrating the analytical gaps in IR theories in general and Liberal-Idealism in particular, Amitav Acharya fairly pleaded, "Liberalism also needs to acknowledge the significant variations in cooperative behaviour that do exist in different local contexts, and that no single model of integration or interactions can account for all or most of them."[20] His basic contention is that the literature on pre-Westphalian international systems has ignored interactions anchored on trade, ideas (including political ideas) and culture, where empire, hegemony, or explicit and continuous power balancing is absent. For him, international systems of that time could develop out of ideational interactions as much as material ones such as war and conquest. [21]

There is scope for incorporating pre-existing practices and values in Asia and its adjoining regions into the Liberal-Idealist analysis of global affairs. For instance, South-East Asia and the Indian Ocean, with a long history of commerce and flow of ideas, but without unity by conquest, are seldom studied as international systems.[22] Contemplation on the roots of democratic dialogue in India, as reiterated by Amartya Sen in his masterpiece *The Argumentative Indian: Writings on Indian History, Culture, and Identity* published in 2005, is again very instructive. Sen first identifies that democracy, as practised in India, is not just about elections, but also about civic discourse, including a 'willingness to listen to different points of view'. This maintains the 'long and written-up argumentative tradition' of India.[23]

Furthermore, the expression *Vasudhaiva Kutumbakam* (the world is a family) reflects the humanism of ancient India. It comes from a famous Sanskrit verse of the Hindu text *Maha Upanishad*,[24] saying *Ayam nijah paroveti ganana Laghuchetasam, Udaara Purushaanam tu vasudhaiva Kutumbakam*. Dr. Karan Singh attributed a near meaning to it through his properly translated words, "Division between 'mine' and 'yours' is a small and narrow way of looking at reality, indulged in by people with immature minds. For those of the greater consciousness, the entire world is a family."[25] He further interprets the consequent comprehension of the human race as an extended family, due to realisation of divine inhabitation in all human beings.[26] Such a spiritual humanist outlook has made India's ancient philosophers perceive unity in all mankind. The highest good is to be found, not in the domination of one race or nationality by another, but in a cooperative commonwealth in which the 'welfare of the entire world' or the 'good of all beings' (*Sarvavutahita*) is assured.[27] In essence, the Indian tradition has always nurtured the idea of an interlinked neighbourhood with a sense of enlightened national interest,[28] resonating in the sensitivity attached to the family as an institution, which is recognised as a basic socio-economic cultural unit of the Indian system.[29]

Equally, analytical attentions are also not drawn on the sphere of security prevailing in most pre-colonial African states through their indigenous customary and formal institutions. The maintenance of peace within many African communities was based on four legal principles: deliberation and discussion-based dispute settlement, rather than force driven justice system; compensatory rectification of misconduct (except in severe crimes such as killing); assessment and adjudication by elders withstanding of impartiality; and fairness. In this context, the thirteenth century's Mande *Charter of West Africa* deserves proper notice. Its ruling ensured in Mali: (a) the prevalence of two inviolable principles guiding people's interrelationship: *sanankunya* (joking relation) and *tanamannyonya* (blood pact); (b) consequently establishing respect of the other and peaceful settlement of disputes as the rule; (c) significantly the absence of harm to foreigners and inviolability of foreign envoy's security.[30] Reflecting on the security setting in the Mali Empire, Ibn Battuta pertinently observed, "Among these qualities [of the Blacks] there is also the prevalence of peace in their country, the traveller is not afraid in it, nor is he who lives there in fear of the chief or of the robber by violence."[31]

The centuries-together people's linkages between Asia and Africa have yet to capture their due space in the analytical construct of the Liberal-Idealist strand of IR discourse. The pre-colonial interactions between India and the eastern seaboard of Africa were mainly economic and cultural. Trade was carried out between the two regions from very early times, some of it through intermediaries from the Persian or Arabian Gulf. India's cultural connectivity with East Africa extended to food and music. There is also evidence of Africa's long-standing connection with China and Indonesia.[32] Analytical inclusion of these varied cooperative behaviours and outlooks lying across the non-Western regions could have enhanced the cognitive expanse of the Liberal-Idealist narrative of the Anglo-Saxon dominated IR. Such a process has, however, failed to happen due to the inherent limitation of European Liberalism, which derives its genealogical motivation from monotheistic and Semitic theology that is anathema to the tradition of acceptance.[33] It is, therefore, necessary to explore non-European/ Western roots of Liberalism.

Conceptualising Ubuntu

The philosophy of Ubuntu remains deeply rooted in indigenous cultures of Africa, being interpreted by its many people, more specifically of Southern Africa, as a phenomenon of human interconnectedness.[34] Denoting a cultural worldview of trying to capture the essence of humanity, it is found in diverse forms in many societies throughout Africa, in particular among the Bantu languages of East, Central, and Southern Africa. Clearly articulated in Southern Africa's Nguni group of languages, it reflects the collectivist African philosophy of "I am human because I belong" in significant contrast to the individualistic Western philosophy of *Cogito, ergo sum* (I think, therefore I am).[35] Broadly defined as an African variant of humanism, the concept of Ubuntu accordingly places communitarian interests above those of the individual, with the premise that human existence is dependent upon interaction with others. Having a long tradition in Africa, its general meaning and spirit are mostly understood in common practice and parlance throughout much of the continent. [36] As a behavioural gift, Ubuntu is considered less an economy or even a philosophy, and more a lifestyle, a way of being, a way of seeing and acting. The gift is life itself and at the root of each society.[37]

Ramose sees the word 'Ubuntu' as 'two words in one', consisting of the prex 'ubu-' and the stem 'ntu-', evoking a dialectical relationship of being and becoming. In this sense, ubu- and ntu- are 'two aspects of being as oneness and wholeness'.[38] Desmond Tutu has described Ubuntu as "embracing hospitality, caring about others, being willing to go the extra mile for the sake of others....The solitary human is a contradiction in terms and therefore you seek the common good because your humanity comes into its community in belonging."[39] He has given one of the best definitions of the term in his book *No Future Without Forgiveness*, explaining the term thus:

> Ubuntu is very difficult to render into a Western language. It speaks to the very essence of being human. When you want to give high

> praise to someone we say, 'Yu, u nobuntu"; he or she has ubuntu. This means that they are generous, hospitable, friendly, caring and compassionate. They share what they have. It also means that my humanity is caught up, is inextricably bound up, in theirs. We belong in a bundle of life. We say, 'a person is a person through other people' (in Xhosa Ubuntu ungamntu ngabanye abantu and in Zulu Umuntu ngumuntu ngabanye). I am human because I belong, I participate, I share. A person with ubuntu is open and available to others, affirming of others, does not feel threatened that others are able and good; for he or she has a proper self-assurance that comes with knowing that he or she belongs in a greater whole and is diminished when others are humiliated or diminished when others are tortured or oppressed, or treated as if they were less than who they are.[40]

Desmond Tutu's reiteration of the indigenous concept of Ubuntu, conveying the profound truth of interconnectivity in human experiences (happiness or distress), resonates in the post-apartheid campaign of South Africa for promoting an African Renaissance. Nelson Mandela gave a similar reflection in his autobiography, *Long Walk to Freedom*,[41] explaining mutuality in human liberation. The ancient principles of 'respect and gifting; of social egalitarianism and normative nonviolence' are critical for constructing alternatives to the pursuit of hegemony and domination. Ubuntu stands out to be at the core of such new forms of political practices, putting forward an enlightening message of inextricably connected humanities and freedoms.[42] In its 1997 White Paper on Social Welfare, the South African government denes Ubuntu as "the principle of caring for each other's well-being...and a spirit of mutual support...Each individual's humanity is ideally expressed through his or her relationship with others and theirs in turn through a recognition of the individual's humanity." The White Paper adds, "Ubuntu means that people are people through other people. It also acknowledges both the rights and the responsibilities of every citizen in promoting individual and societal well-being." [43]

An interdependent consciousness in the social, economic and political behaviours reasonably emerges from the conception that existential mutuality underpins human interrelationships. Pertinently, the ancient ethic of Ubuntu offers a perceptual base for striving towards comprehensive peace and security in Africa. For instance, the Truth and Reconciliation Committee (TRC) in post-apartheid South Africa, a committee chaired by Desmond Tutu, is a remarkable experiment to reverse the systemically-inflicted dehumanisation. Timothy Murithi appropriately notes, "Even the supporters of apartheid were victims of the brutalizing system from which they benefited economically and politically: it distorted their view of their relationship with other human beings, which then impacted upon their sense of security and freedom from fear." Observing the correlation between Ubuntu and TRC, Murithi writes", The notion of Ubuntu sheds light on the importance of peacemaking through principles of reciprocity and a sense of shared destiny between peoples." He adds, "It provides a value system for giving and receiving forgiveness. It provides a rationale for sacrificing or letting go of the desire to take revenge for past wrongs." [44] Manifestly, the TRC experiment has gained traction as an innovative conflict resolution approach in many countries of Africa and beyond, signifying the relevance of Ubuntu, an African vision of humanism, for global endeavours of peace and security.

In conclusion, the idea of *Ubuntu* is located in African worldviews, which are underpinned by the non-Western pursuit of humanism, having substantial relevance for global efforts towards achieving peace, security, and harmony in a holistic sense. The Liberal-Idealism of the West that dominated global affairs discourse is an Anglo-Saxon version of eclecticism premised on the notions of individualistic economic freedom and Euro-centric cultural determinism, limiting its theoretical efficacy. The Liberal-Idealist tradition could, therefore, become global in scope and humane in substance, through the integration of the ancient collectivist ethos including the *Ubuntu* philosophy, into its analytical framework.

NOTES

1. Kant, Immanuel (1795), *Perpetual Peace: A Philosophical Sketch* (German: *Zum ewigen Frieden. Ein philosophischer Entwurf*), Königsberg: bey Friedrich Nicolovius.
2. Dan Reiter, "Democratic Peace Theory," *Oxford Bibliographies*, http://www. oxford bibliographies.com/view/document/obo-9780199756223/obo-9780199756223-0014.xml

3. President Obama: Libya aftermath 'worst mistake' of presidency, https://www.bbc.com/news/world-us-canada-36013703, 11 April 2016.
4. Robert O. Keohane, "Twenty Years of Institutional Liberalism", *International Relations,* 26(2), 2012, pp. 130-131.
5. "The U.S. denounces film's content", *The Hindu*, 15 September 2012, http://www.thehindu.com/todays-paper/tpinternational/article3899266.ece, Accessed on 16 September 2012.
6. "French agent shot Gaddafi on Sarkozy's orders", *Indian Express*, 02 October 2012, http://www.indianexpress.com/news/-french-agent-shot-gaddafi-on-sarkozy-s-orders-/1010552/2, Accessed on 03 October 2012.
7. Roberts, D. (2008), 'Hybrid Polities and Indigenous Pluralities: Advanced Lessons in Statebuilding in Cambodia', *Journal of Intervention and Statebuilding*, 2 (1), p. 64.
8. Darby, P. (2009), 'Rolling Back the Frontiers of Empire: Practising the Postcolonial', *International Peacekeeping*, 16 (5), pp. 699-716.
9. Ibid., p. 701.
10. Richmond, O. (2005), *The Transformation of Peace,* New York: Palgrave Macmillan, 2004.
11. Patrick Tom, "The Liberal Peace and Post-Conflict Peacebuilding In Africa: Sierra Leone", A Thesis Submitted for the Degree of Ph.D. at the University of St. Andrews 2011: http://hdl.handle.net/10023/2469, pp. 127-128.
12. Ibid., p. 131.
13. Donais, T. (2009), "Empowerment or Imposition? Dilemmas of Local Ownership in Post-conflict Peacebuilding Process", *Peace and Change*, 34 (1), p. 11; also see Lederach, J.P. (1997), *Building Peace: Sustainable Reconciliation in Divided Societies,* Washington D.C.: United States Institute of Peace Press.
14. R.J. Rummel (1997), *Death by Government: Genocide and Mass Murder Since 1900,* Routledge.
15. Hedley Bull (1977), *The Anarchical Society: A Study of Order in World Politics,* New York: Columbia University Press.
16. Sushanta K. Mishra and Kumar Kunal Kamal (2014), "Capitalism in the Indian Social Environment: An Ethnic Perspective", in Hamid Kazeroony and Agata Stachowicz-Stanusch, *Capitalism and the Social Relationship: An Organizational Perspective*, London: Palgrave Macmillan, p. 228.
17. Ibid.
18. G.W.F. Hegel (1956), *The Philosophy of History*, New York: Dover, p. 93.
19. Amitav Acharya, *Rethinking Power, Institutions, and Ideas in World Politics Whose IR?*, New York: Routledge, 2014, p. 3.
20. Amitav Acharya, Imagining Global IR out of India [Keynote Address to Annual International Studies Convention 2013, "Reimagining Global Orders: Perspectives from the South", 10-12 December 2013, Jawaharlal Nehru University, New Delhi, India].
21. Amitav Acharya, "Dialogue and Discovery: In Search of International Relations Theories Beyond the West", *Millennium: Journal of International Studies,* 39(3), p. 628.
22. Ibid.
23. Ibid, p. 637.

24. Swapna S. Prabhu1 & Niranjan Mohapatra, "Reconstructing India's Identity in World Politics: An Emerging Convergence between Public Diplomacy and Constructivism," *Sociology and Anthropology* 2(6): 230.
25. Karan Singh, "Vedanta in the Nuclear Age", *India International Centre Quarterly*, Vol. 28, No. 4, (Winter 2001/Spring 2002), pp. 148-149.
26. Ibid.
27. Nalini Kant Jha, "Cultural and Philosophical Roots of India's Foreign Policy," *International Studies* (New Delhi), Vol. 26, No. 1, January-March 1989, pp. 45-67.
28. Swapna S Prabhu1, & Niranjan Mohapatra, "Reconstructing India's Identity in World Politics: An Emerging Convergence between Public Diplomacy and Constructivism" *Sociology and Anthropology* 2(6): 230.
29. Bajrang Lal Gupta (2010), *A New Paradigm of Development: Sumangalam*, Delhi: Gyan Publishing House, pp. 174-176.
30. Guy Martin (2012), *African Political Thought*, New York: Palgrave Macmillan, pp. 17-18.
31. Said Hamdun and Noel King (1975), *Ibn Battuta in Black Africa*, Princeton, NJ: Markus Wiener Publishing, p. 58.
32. Ali A. Mazrui, *Africa's International Relations: The Diplomacy of Dependency and Change*, London: Heinemann, 1977, p. 114.
33. Prafulla Ketkar, "European Liberalism faces roadblock", Editorial, *Organiser*, Vol. 68, No. 49, June 4, 2017, p. 7.
34. Christian B. N. Gade (2012), What is Ubuntu? Different Interpretations among South Africans of African Descent, *South African Journal of Philosophy*, 31:3, 484-503,486-7
35. Birgit Brock-Utne, "Peace Research with a Diversity Perspective: A Look to Africa", *International Journal of Peace Studies*, Vol. 9, No. 2, (Autumn/Winter 2004), p. 114.
36. David A. McDonald (2010) Ubuntu bashing: the marketisation of 'African values' in *South Africa Review of African Political Economy*, 37:124, 139-152, 139-141.
37. Bernedette Muthien, "Egalitarianism and Nonviolence: Gifts of the Khoe-San", *Off Our Backs*, Vol. 38, No. 1 (2008), p. 57.
38. Ramose, M.B., 2002a. The philosophy of ubuntu and ubuntu as a philosophy. In: P.H. Coetzee and A.P.J. Roux, eds. *Philosophy from Africa*. 2nd ed. Cape Town: Oxford University Press, pp. 230–238. p. 230.
39. Tutu Foundation UK, http://www.tutufoundationuk.org/ubuntu.html [Accessed 15 September 2009].
40. Tutu, Desmond (1999), *No Future Without Forgiveness*, London: Rider, pp. 34-35.
41. Nelson Mandela (1995), *Long Walk to Freedom: The Autobiography of Nelson Mandela*, Boston: Back Bay Books.
42. Bernedette Muthien, "Egalitarianism and Nonviolence: Gifts of the Khoe-San", *Off Our Backs*, Vol. 38, No. 1 (2008), pp. 60-61.
43. Republic of South Africa [RSA] 1997, section 24.
44. Timothy Marathi, "Practical Peacemaking Wisdom from Africa: Reflections on Ubuntu", *The Journal of Pan African Studies*, Vol. 1, No. 4, June 2006, p. 29.

8

Bangladesh-China-India-Myanmar Sub-Regional Cooperation: Strategies for India's Northeast

Jajati K. Pattnaik

Bangladesh-China-India-Myanmar (BCIM) sub–regional cooperation thrusts are on growth and development across the neighbouring countries based on shared partnership. The borders which were earlier treated as barriers for cross-country development soon turned out to be the catalysts for cross-country collaboration/cooperation models. It became a new mode of interaction which entailed de-territorialized economic cooperation and free trade architecture thus making the spatial domain of territory secondary in the contemporary political economy of international relations.

India is cognizant that all the regions have tremendous potentialities in the geographical sense and perceives the geo-economic importance of Northeast India as the link between East and South East Asia in an era of increasing regional and global cooperation. Against this backdrop, the Look East Policy (LEP) envisioned Northeast India not as the periphery, but as the centre of a blooming and inclusive economic space that can link two vibrant regions with multiple networks interweaving the region. But in actuality, the LEP largely bypassed the Northeast region and the policy remained a mere rhetoric or cosmetic affair. In order to give a fillip to this, the Look East Policy was changed into Act East Policy (AEP) under the political dispensation spearheaded by Prime Minister Narendra Modi in 2014 who called for a robust and result-oriented diplomacy to attain India's national interest in its eastern neighbourhood. The piecemeal approach was replaced by a proactive one to steer the course with a renewed spirit to secure tangible results in a geo-economic perspective.

In this context, Prime Minister Modi focused upon the geographic significance of India's Northeast region as India's gateway to Asia in the 21st "Asian Century". He coined a new acronym for Northeast, i.e., Natural Economic Zone (NEZ) and focused upon the region's development through economic corridors to South and Southeast Asia. Conversely, the Chinese official establishment also found a compatible course with the recent overtures of the Modi Government and foresaw booming prospects of the Bangladesh-China-India-Myanmar corridor (Ramani 2015).

BCIM

Bangladesh, China, India & Myanmar (BCIM), previously called the Kunming Initiative in 1999, is at present a sub-regional cooperation forum between South-West China, India's Northeast, Myanmar and Bangladesh intending towards economic integration through trade, transport, industry, tourism, investment and other cooperative ventures to bring inclusive development in the region (Uberoi 2015). In fact, it was the brainchild of Professor Che Zhimin, the former Director of the Economic and Technological Research Centre of the Yunan Provincial Peoples Government, who scripted the trajectory of BCIM for the sub-regional cooperation. The several features of this sub-regional model posited by him are:

(i) BCIM can link the markets of China, South-East Asia and South Asia and can connect the two major markets of the world;
(ii) the region has abundant natural resources which could be harnessed for large-scale development in spite of its poor infrastructure and diverse topography;
(iii) the region is marked by relative poverty in the southwest of

China, the northeast of India and both Bangladesh and Myanmar;

(iv) the distribution of resources and different levels of economic development create space for complementarities of resources, product structures available in the region;

(v) it will 'enable rational planning and the optimal utilization of resources, as well as strengthen environmental protection';

(vi) it may also 'contribute to rooting out social evils such as drug production, drug trafficking and drug taking;'

(vii) it will facilitate the 'alleviation of poverty and promotion of social development';

(viii) the two big markets of India and China of this sub-regional cooperation 'will doubtlessly connect the unlinked markets of Asia and integrate the sparsely distributed economic strength of the continent;'

(ix) it will be 'the land bridge for connecting the Pacific Ocean , which had seen unprecedented growth before the Asian financial crisis with the Indian Ocean and the new focal point of world economic development'; and

(x) it will 'contribute to the establishment of the new multi-polar world order and to safeguard the peace and stability of Asia and the world' (Uberoi 2016:78-79).

Notwithstanding its potentialities, the BCIM forum did not take any institutional shape at the inter-governmental level. The terms 'growth zone,' 'growth polygon' and 'cooperation zone' were often used to delineate the scope of the BCIM regional/sub-regional forum. (Uberoi 2016). Beyond that, there was no further movement. However, the BCIM Car Rally of February-March 2013 from Kolkata to Kunming was a great turning point in bridging the gap between the two Asian giants. The Indo-China joint statement issued in May 2013 during the visit of Chinese Premier Li Keqiang to India lifted the BCIM from track I to track II forum. It mentioned: 'The two sides appreciated the progress made in promoting cooperation under the BCIM (Bangladesh, China, India and Myanmar) Regional Forum. Encouraged by the successful BCIM Car Rally of February 2013 between Kolkata and Kunming, the two sides agreed to consult the other parties with a view to establishing a Joint Study Group on strengthening connectivity in the BCIM region for closer economic, trade, and people-to-people linkages and to initiating the development of a BCIM Economic[1] Corridor' (MEA 2013). In recent times, the state governments in India have wooed foreign investors for infrastructural/industrial development.

The architecture of the free trade regime got a fresh impetus during Prime Minister Narendra Modi's visit to China in 2015 that thrust upon federalizing India's economic policy involving state. Both India and China agreed to institute a provincial partnership between Karnataka and Sichuan and sister-city contacts between Aurangabad and Dunhuang, Chennai and Chongqing and Hyderabad and Qingdao (*Strategic Digest* 2015). They also evoked the BCIM and the joint statement on Shaping the Regional and Global Agenda said: 'The two sides welcomed the progress made in promoting cooperation under the framework of the BCIM Economic Corridor. Both sides recalled the second meeting of the Joint Study Group of BCIM Economic Corridor, and agreed to continue their respective efforts to implement understandings reached at the meeting' (PIB 2015). Thus it is to be ascertained how such provincial/state-level partnership materializes in strengthening cross-border cooperation in terms of trade, investment, industry, agriculture, skill development, tourism and people-to-people exchanges both at the bilateral as well as multilateral forums like BCIM (Uberoi 2015).

India's Northeast

India's Northeast, consisting of Arunachal Pradesh, Assam, Manipur, Meghalaya, Mizoram, Nagaland and Sikkim share 98 per cent of its land boundary with Bangladesh, Bhutan, China, Nepal and Myanmar. The region is abundant with natural resources such as oil, natural gas, coal, limestone, rare herbs and medicinal plants. It is one of the hotspots of global biodiversity constituting near about half of the country's total bio-diversity (MDONER 2008). The region holds one fifth of the country's total hydrocarbon reserves and is highly affluent in hydropower reserves. Even the High Level Commission Report to the Prime Minister on 'Transforming the Northeast' observed that the resource-rich region of Northeast was a national asset. The hydroelectric, oil, gas, coal, bio-diversity and agro-silvicultural potentials held 'promise of national solutions through regional development' and would 'add immeasurably to national security in every respect' (Planning Commission, 1997).

Assessing its geo-economic potentials, the 'Northeastern vision 2020' was prepared to bring in development. The geo-political isolation of the region was redefined by innovating new policies in the areas of defence, foreign affairs, internal security and international trade. The vision document thrusts on:

(i) empowering 'the people by maximizing self-governance and participatory development through grass-roots planning';
(ii) emphasizing 'rural development with a focus on improving agricultural productivity and the creation of non-farm avocations and employment';
(iii) prioritizing 'development of sectors with comparative advantage in agro-processing industries, modernization and development of sericulture, investment in manufacturing units based on the resources available in the region';
(iv) utilizing 'large hydroelectric power generation potential and focus on developing services such as tourism to accelerate development and create productive employment opportunities';
(v) taking up 'capacity development to address the issue of imparting skills among the people to enhance their productivity and generating a class of entrepreneurs within the region willing to take risks';
(vi) strengthening 'infrastructure, including rail, road, inland water and air transportation to facilitate a two-way movement of people and goods within the region and outside, communication networks including broadband and wireless connectivity';
(vii) connecting 'NER with ASEAN to open up the sea route through the Chittagong port and the land routes through Bangladesh, Myanmar and China;' and
(viii) making 'adequate flow of resources for public investments in infrastructure, implementing framework for private participation in augmenting infrastructure and creating an enabling environment for the flow of investments to harness the physical resources of the region for the welfare of the people' (MDONER 2008).

In addition, the Look East Policy focused on border trade and connectivity to get benefits for the Northeast region demanding a qualitative change in the relationship with the neighbouring countries of Bangladesh, China and Myanmar. Experts working in this field opined that "considering the locational leverage of Northeast India, it emerges as a crucial land bridge connecting the South East and East Asia. Although the states of Northeast India are relatively marginalized, when looked at from a broader perspective, given their strategic significance amidst the major economic entities—China, India and ASEAN—they emerge as the central nodes of BCIM connectivity. Therefore, their development in terms of connectivity, especially physical connectivity, has potential economic implications" (BCIM–EC Framework Note). In this situation, the success of the BCIM corridor lies in realizing the following seven steps for the benefit of India's Northeast.

Step 1: Kolkata-Kunming Road Corridor

The Kolkata-Kunming corridor is an important segment of BCIM sub-regional cooperation. The corridor spanning around 2,766.5 kilometres (approximately) would link India's Northeast, Yunan province of China, Bangladesh and Myanmar by forging partnerships in trade, industry, energy, tourism, health and education for the benefit of all the stakeholders in the region. The corridor starts from Kolkata in West Bengal (India) and passes through Benapole-Jessore-Dhaka-Sylhet (Bangladesh), Agartala-Silchar-Imphal–Moreh (India), Tamu-Kalay-Mandalay (Mandalay) and Muse-Ruili (China) and reaches Kunming in Yunnan. Table 1 explains the road map for the Kolkata-Kunming corridor.

Table 1: Kolkata-Kunming Road Corridor

Origin	*Destination*	*Distance (2,766.5 km)*
Kolkata	Dhaka	316.8
Dhaka	Agartala	130.5
Agartala	Imphal	540.8
Imphal	Moreh	107.8
Moreh	Mandalay	473.6
Mandalay	Kunming	1197

Source: Author.

The BCIM watchers view a huge potentiality of the Kolkata-Kunming corridor crisscrossing development in multiple sectors. The simmering network of roadways, railways, airways, waterways, telecommunication linkages, transnational energy grids and hydrocarbon pipelines along the corridor would transform the geo-economic space of the region in myriad fields. It would also pave the way for the free trade architecture further pushing the region to have promising collaborations with ASEAN, ASEAN-China and ASEAN–India free trade zones (Bhatacharjee).

Map 1: Kolkata-Kunming Road Corridor

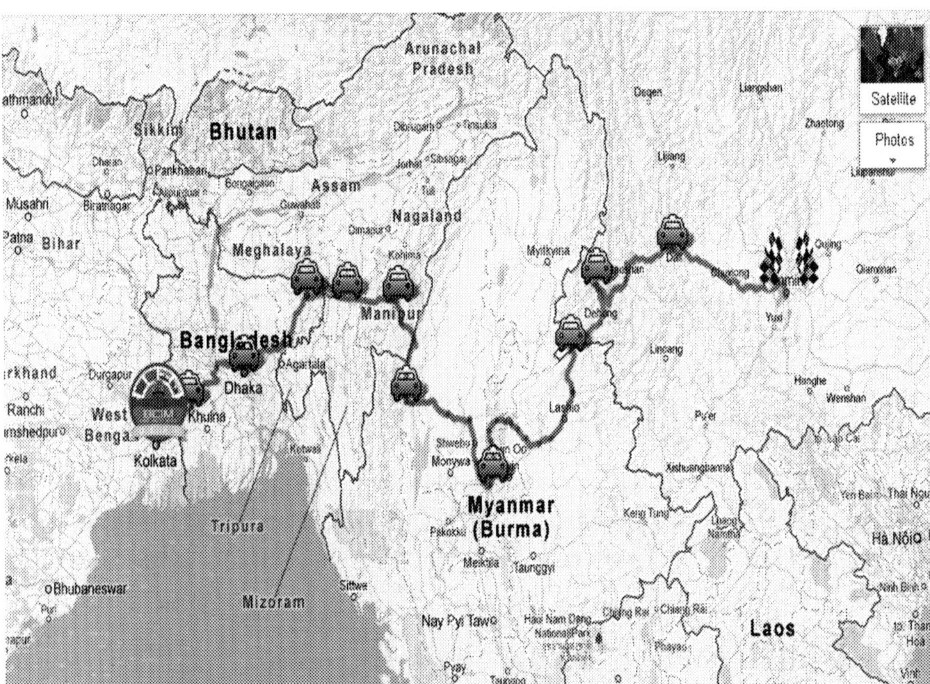

Source: BCIM Car Rally 2013, Google Maps.

Step 2: Kaladan Multi-Modal Corridor

The Kaladan multi-modal transport project is important for the success of BCIM sub-regional cooperation. This riverine road transport project seeks to provide maritime access to the landlocked North Eastern states of India to the Bay of Bengal linking it with the Indian ports on the Eastern seashore and Sittwe port in the western shore of Myanmar.

The passage covers a total distance of 907 km. As per the project, goods are to be transhipped from Kolkata port to Sittwe port (539 km) and from Sittwe to Paletwa by inland water transport (158 km) on Kaladan River and from Paletwa to the India-Myanmar border in Myanmar by road (110 km) and National Highway 54 Lawngtlai (Mizoram) in India by road (100 km) (MDONER 2014). Further, Lawngtlai would be connected by road with Silchar and Srirampur (Assam) all the way through Daboka, Nagaon and Guwahati (Assam). A relook of the project indicates that the Kaladan multimodal transport corridor, if implemented in time, would transform the geo-economic scenario of the region as well as end its maritime isolation. It would also give substantial advantage to the landlocked states of Northeast India to kick-start its trade with the BCIM and other regional groupings soon. Further, this riverine-road transport system would also augment the significance of the region from the perspective of the Act East Policy and transform it from a land locked to a land-linked region. This multi-modal transport corridor would also link the Northeast to Sittwe port in Myanmar and would pave the way for greater connectivity of the region with ASEAN as well. Table 2 explains the road map for the Northeast-Sittwe multi-modal corridor.

Table 2: Northeast-Sittwe Multi-modal Corridor

State	*Origin*	*Destination*	*Via NH/Distance in km*
Arunachal Pradesh	Itanagar	Sittwe (Myanmar)	NH 27 (1320.5)
Assam	Guwahati	Sittwe	NH 6 (1098.6)
Manipur	Imphal	Sittwe	NH 102B & 2 (983.3)
Meghalaya	Shillong	Sittwe	NH 6 (1005.6)
Mizoram	Aizawl	Sittwe	NH 2(615.6)
Nagaland	Kohima	Sittwe	NH 102B & 2 (1119.8)
Tripura	Agartala	Sittwe	NH 108 (955.5)

Source: Author.

At present, the project plans an integrated port and inland water transport (IWT) terminal at Sittwe, a smooth navigational channel from Sittwe to Paletwa and highway trans-shipment terminal at Paletwa. To make sure that it becomes an active pillar of the country's Act East Policy, the Government has approved the revised cost estimate of Rs.

2,904.04 crore for the early completion of this strategic port in the larger interest of India's Northeast. In the initial stage, the corridor would link the Northeast with Myanmar, but in the later stage, it would link the region with Phuket, Bangkok, Phnom Penh, Saigon and Ho Chi Minh and Singapore seaports in the free trade architecture.

Map 2: Northeast-Sittwe Multi-modal Corridor

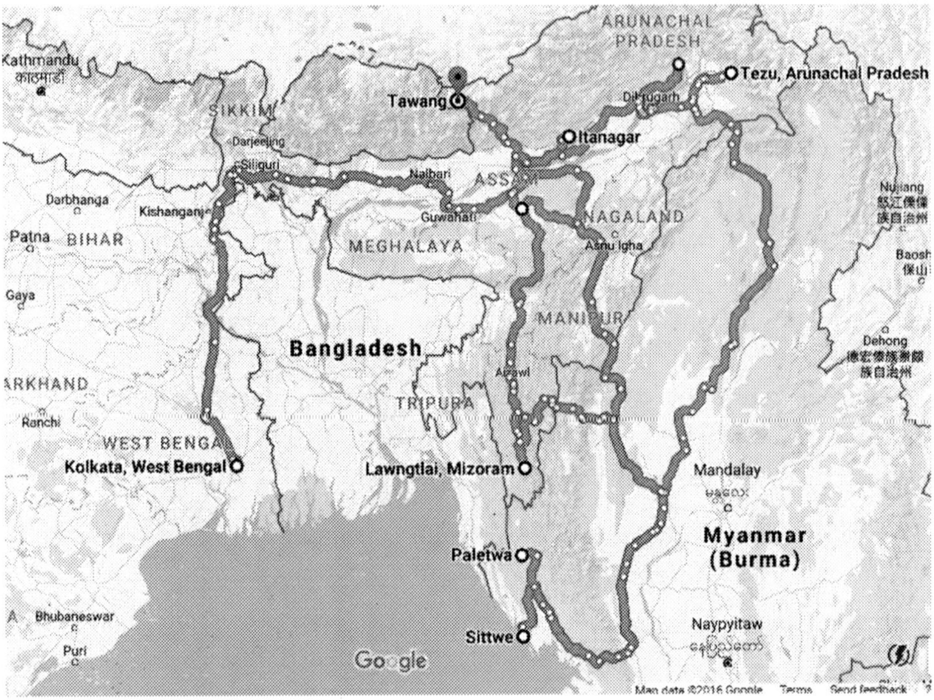

Source: Drawn by the Author, Google Maps

As External Affairs Minister Smt. Sushma Swaraj said at the inaugural session of Delhi Dialogue VIII: "We also have maritime boundaries with several ASEAN countries, and this is particularly important from a trade perspective. We have started negotiations on an ASEAN-India Maritime Transport Cooperation Agreement, and hope that it will be finalised by the end of the year. Likewise, work is in progress on the Kaladan Multimodal Transport Project which will provide a road and riverine link between Myanmar ad Mizoram as well as connect Indian ports to Sittwe port in Myanmar. Our experiment with a dedicated fortnightly freighter service with Myanmar has proven to be a commercial success. We plan to commission a study soon if this experiment can be replicated, both for cargo and passenger services, with other Southeast Asian countries. She further added: "we are simultaneously endeavouring to see how we can transform the corridors of connectivity into corridors of economic cooperation" (PIB 2015). Thus, with the change of regime in Myanmar, it has become quite easier on the part of New Delhi to deal with Yangon's democratic dispensation for closer economic cooperation, and remove the situational hurdle, if any, for the early completion of the project.

Step 3: Guwahati-Chittagong Corridor

The Guwahati-Chittagong corridor spanning over 752 km is significant for road, rail and sea connectivity within the BCIM. Recently, New Delhi has made a diplomatic breakthrough in securing Dhaka's consent

Map 3: Guwahati-Chittagong Corridor

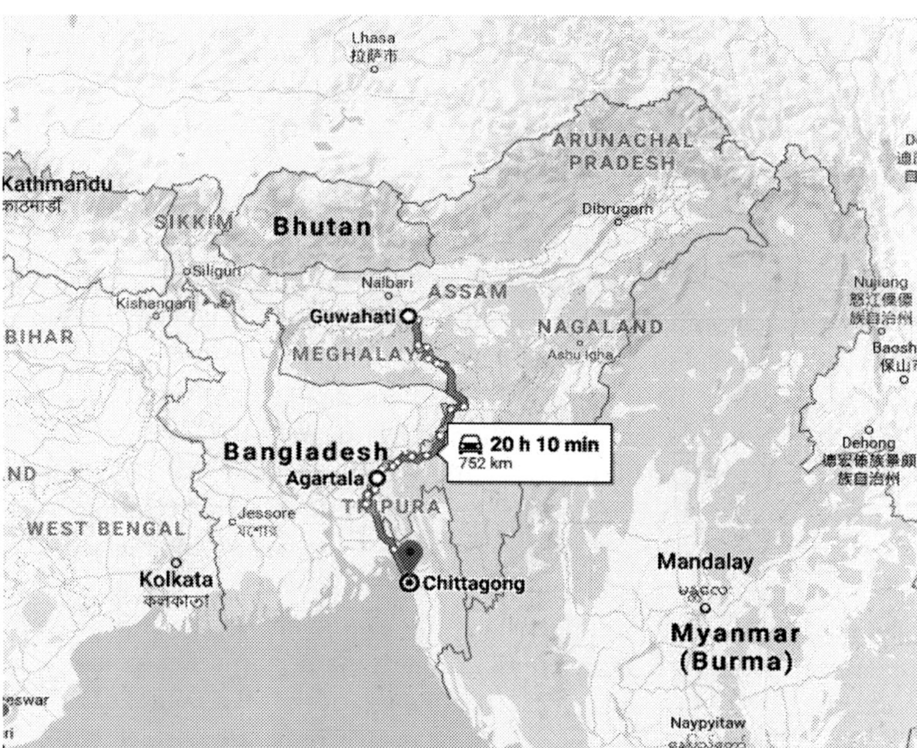

Source: Drawn by the Author, Google Maps.

to make use of Chittagong port, which is just 72 km from Seabrook, the southernmost border town of Tripura. India is building a 2.5 km bridge over the Feni river in Tripura to carry heavy machines and goods to the northeastern region through the Chittagong port of Bangladesh. The bridge with a cost estimate of Rs. 94 crore would provide transport connectivity to Chittagong through road and rail. The North Frontier Railway (NFR) is also constructing a 135 km railway line up to Sabroom in the border town of Southern Tripura and it is believed that the operationalisation of this railway link would provide a huge advantage to the Northeastern states in terms of connectivity to Chittagong port as well. Thus, once these railway projects are in place, they will help the region in breaking its geographical isolation and land-locked status (Patttnaik 2016).

Step 4: Augmenting Cross-Border Trade Synergies

Cross-border trade synergies are to be augmented by encouraging production and service sector links through movement of capital, technology and knowledge across the BCIM region. Border trade connotes the movement of 'goods and services across international land borders between countries' (Das 2006). It has a significant impact upon the economic structures of the bordering areas acting as a catalyst for regional development. The mere flow of goods and services across the borders only takes the form of transit trade; it does not indicate any trend of development for the people inhabiting the neighbouring areas of the borders. Transit trade may bring in infrastructural development in the bordering regions, but later it should be converted into growth-generating sectors linking it with resource bases and productive structures in order to develop 'dyadic and triadic linkages' (Das 2006). For instance, the nature of demand-supply requirements drives North Eastern Region (NER)–Bangladesh to secure mutual benefits through collaborative approaches. In this context, the resource-rich hill regions of the Northeast play a vital role for the resource-deficit plain regions of Bangladesh. It mainly exports coal, limestone and stone chips to Bangladesh, while it imports cement, readymade garments, plastic goods, processed food, drink, etc., from Bangladesh (MDONER 2011). However, NER-Bangladesh border trade is far from reality which has not brought any substantive or gainful effect in the region so far. Experts opine that the Bangladesh trade is not sustainable because it has only established a 'dyadic linkage' between the resource base and productive structures; it has not yet created any substantial 'triadic linkage' between the resource base, productive structure and trade except in setting up a few cement production enterprises. Similarly, NER-Myanmar trade has not brought any significant result in terms of cross-border collaboration and trading opportunities have neither been linked with local resources nor with the productive structures. As a result, it gave rise to poor 'dyadic and triadic linkages' (Das 2006:340-343). On the other hand, the NER-China border trade is only restricted to a few items. No such effort has been made to link the resource base and productive structure for cross-border synergy or create at least a dyadic linkage between them. Any kind of sub-regional cooperation would be successful when it intends towards creating growth zones integrating both hardware and software resources across the region. Thus, it is high time to identify the resource bases and develop cross-border projects for the benefit of all the stakeholders across the borders.

Step 5: Dealing with the Flooding of Cheap Chinese Goods

Economic concerns add to India's dilemma in unlocking the BCIM corridor. There is an insecurity prevailing that the opening of the economic corridors will pave the way for the flooding of cheap Chinese goods into the Northeast markets. This is true. The ground reality also speaks how of late 'foreign-made' goods have made strong inroads into Northeast India's markets at the cost of domestic products. The Customs officials also acknowledge such transactions (Rediff 1998). India thinks that in the event of the completion of the BCIM corridor, China would be the major gainer just like the OBOR (One Belt and One Road) initiative which covers 'a vast region stretching from China to Central Asia and beyond, under a strategic Chinese dominance'. Equally, Indian industry and business houses are quite worried about the BCIM corridor because of India's high trade deficit with China (Biswas, 2016).

So, this type of economic threat perception cannot be denied given the nature of easy overflowing of Chinese goods into the Northeast. Indian Commerce Minister Nirmala Sitharaman said "the Government is ready to give Indian businesses all help in rejuvenating and giving healthy competition to the neighbouring country. In my meeting with Indian industry, I raised my concern on why articles from pins to bathroom fittings to even the Lord Ganesha that we worship are being imported from China. We must look into areas where we have failed and why we have failed, and given an opportunity to Chinese (goods) to take over" (*Deccan Herald*, 2014).

On the other, India is the largest trading partner of China. A leading leather exporter says, 'By now, Indian buyers of Chinese goods understand very well the comparatively poorer quality of the cheaper Chinese products. Our home-grown goods are costlier, but they last longer.' He feels 'the challenge from China should make Indian goods even better quality-wise in the long run' (Biswas 2016). Thus, the need of the hour is to pool the complementary resources and adjust the balance of trade in India's favour by setting up quality-oriented manufacturing industries in Northeast India.

Step 6: Tackling the Influx of Drugs and Small Arms

There is an apprehension that the road corridors involving BCIM might lead to sneaking of drugs and small arms into the Northeastern region jeopardizing the peace and stability of the region. Myanmar, located in the opium-producing golden triangle, acts as the land bridge for such regional/sub-regional cooperation and in the event of cross-border trade, the Kolkata-Kunming corridor may be transformed into a potential drug corridor. It is reported that drug cartels use near about thirty trafficking routes and some of those marked by the Indian Narcotics Control Bureau (NCB) are: (i) Behiang-Singhat-Churachandpur-Imphal; (ii) Behiang-Singhat-Tipaimukh-Silchar; (iii) Mandalay-Tahang-Imphal; (iv) Tamu-Moreh-Imphal; (v) Homalin-Ukhrul-Jessami-Kohima; (vi) Mandalay-Tahang-Tiddim-Aizawl-Silchar; (vii) Homalin Khamjong-Shangshak Khullen–Ukhrul-Imphal; (viii) Myitkina-Maingkwan-Pangsau Pass–Nampong-Jairampur-Digboi; (ix) Putao-Pashighat-Tezpur-Guwahati; (x) Tamanthi-Noklak-Kohima-Dimapur; (xi) New Somtal-Sugnu-Churachandpur-Imphal-Kohima-Dimapur; (xii) Tahan-Tiddim-Melbuk-Champhai-Aizawl-Silchar; (xiii) Tohan-Vaphai-Khawlailung-Serchip-Aizawl; (xiv) Tahan–Falam–Ngarchhip-Khawlailung-Serchip-Aizawl; (xv) Falam-Dawn-

Thingsai-Hnahthial-Lunglei-Demagiri-Chittagong Hill Tracts-Chittagong; (xvi) Falam-Lungbun-Saitha-Chittagong Hill Tracts-Chittagong; (xvii) Churachandpur-Ngopa-Aizawl-Phuldungsei-Jampui Hills–Agartala-Chittagong (Bhaumik 2015:193-194). In this context, the potential threats emerging out of these drug corridors cannot be easily overlooked.

It is also pertinent to mention that the State-run Chinese arms manufacturing company, i.e., China North Industries Corporation (Norinco) of Yunan which shares its border with the Indian states of Arunachal Pradesh, Nagaland and Manipur supplies unlawful weapons to 'buyers ranging from African dictators to the Asian rebels' (Uninathan 2011). Hence, any kind of illegal arms smuggling from across the border would pose a serious challenge to the peace and stability of Northeast India. Subir Bhaumik observed: 'It is however hard to believe that Norinco and other Chinese ordnance establishments can sell weapons on a large scale to non-state actors without at least the tacit approval of the Chinese government. It is still harder to believe that these weapons would easily pass through military-ruled Burma, unhindered and unchecked, to the rebel groups based in the jungles of Sagaing enroute Northeast India. There is growing evidence of connivance between Chinese Intelligence and ordnance establishments, as well as evidence of paybacks to Burmese military commanders who allow the weapons to pass through Burmese territory from Yunan to Northeast India' (Bhaumik 2015:189). Unless this unlawful smuggling of arms is stopped, it would be quite difficult to materialize any sub-regional cooperation or cross-border synergy involving the BCIM. Yet, this problem can be can be addressed specifically by India and Myanmar by reinforcing joint surveillance mechanisms through information and communication-induced technology and intensifying border patrolling to check illegal entry of drugs and small arms. No doubt, the Memorandum of Understanding (MOU) signed between India and Myanmar for sharing Intelligence information, synchronizing patrolling across the international border, exchanging information to combat insurgency, arms smuggling and drug trafficking and initiating measures to foil illegal cross-border movements, if implemented in the true spirit, would ensure 'peace, stability and security' across the international border (MEA 2014). On the other, China has to lend a hand to India and Myanmar to curb the influx of drugs and small arms into the region for the eventual success of BCIM regional/sub regional cooperation.

Conclusively, it is suggested that India must weigh its benefits as well as challenges before joining BCIM cooperation. Moreover, the doctrine of 'enlightened national interest' pursued by the Modi Government towards regional/sub-regional issues could be tested in case of the BCIM to secure our national interest in India's immediate/ extended neighbourhood. Moreover, an Indic approach to International Relations—*Vasudhaiva Kutumbakam* (the world is one family) as compared to the Chinese hierarchical approach to international relations—Tianxia (all under heaven)—could be an effective alternate strategy to ensure equity, growth and all-round development for the success of any kind of sub-regional/regional cooperation in the days ahead.

NOTES

1. Economic corridors 'serve as blueprint for enhanced connectivity, increased competitiveness, and greater sense of community in a region'. They strengthen 'national and regional connectivity by making it faster, cheaper, and easier for people and goods to move within and across borders'; decreases 'the cost of trade, enhancing the competitiveness of national and regional production networks and promoting greater investment; upholds greater regional and global integration and faster economic growth'; facilitates in 'reducing poverty by improving poor people's access to economic opportunities, lowering the cost of goods and services they consume, and providing better access to essential infrastructure services'; lessening 'narrow development gaps among regional economies by providing small, poor, land-locked and remote countries and areas with better access to regional markets and production networks, thereby stimulating investment, trade and economic growth in those areas' and props up 'greener technologies and a more efficient use of regional resources, such as gas reserves and rivers with hydroelectric potential by developing cross-border projects that permit regional energy trade' (BCIM-EC Framework Note, De and Iyengar, 2014).

REFERENCES

BCIM-EC Background Note (2014), Paper circulated at Consultative Workshop, Guwahati, 18-19 July.

Bhaumik, Subir (2015), *Troubled Periphery: Crisis of India's Northeast*, New Delhi: Sage Publications.

Bhattacharjee, Rupak (2016), 'Bangladesh, China, India and Myanmar-Economic Corridor: Ushering a New Era of Interconnectedness', *Indian Defence Review* &

South Asia Monitor, 18 September, http://www.indiandefencereview.com/spotlights/bangladesh-china-india-and-myanmar-economic-corridor-ushering-a-new-era-of-interconnectedness/ (accessed on 14 May 2019).

Biswas, Ashis (2016), 'India Failing to Meet Beijing Challenge,' *The Shillong Times*, 16 October, http://www.theshillongtimes.com/2016/10/20/india-failing-to-meet-beijing-challenge/ (accessed on 15 January 2019).

Das, Gurudas (2006), 'Border Trade in India's Northeast: Theory and Practice,' in David et al (eds.), *Challenges of Development in Northeast India*, New Delhi: Regency Publications, pp. 332-343.

De, Prabir and Iyengar, Kavita (2014), *Developing Economic Corridors in South Asia*, Asian Development Bank, Manila.

Deccan Herald (2014), 'India Raises Issue of Cheap Chinese Goods Flooding Indian Market', 7 August.

Ministry of Development of Northeastern Region, Government of India (2008), 'Northeastern Region Vision 2020', pp. 1-4, http://www.MDONER.gov.in/sites/default/files/silo2_content/ner_vision/Vision_2020.pdf (accessed on 14 January 2019).

______ (2011), 'Look East Policy and the Northeastern States', http://www.mdoner.gov.in/sites/default/files/silo2_content/Look%20East%20Policy/Aspects%20of%20 Look%20East%20Policy.pdf (accessed on 18 March 2019).

______ (2014), 'Kaladan multi Modal Transit Transport Project,' https://mdoner.gov.in/infrastructure/kaladan-multi-modal-transit-transport-project-inland (accessed on 17 March 2019).

Ministry of External Affairs, Government of India (2013), "Joint Statement on the State Visit of Chinese Premier Li Keqiang to India", http://mea.gov.in/bilateral-documents.htm?dtl/21723/Joint+Statement+on+the+State+Visit+of+ Chinese+ +Li+Keqiang+to+India (accessed on 15 January 2019).

______ (2014), 'India and Myanmar Sign Memorandum of Understanding on Border Cooperation', http://www.mea.gov.in/press-releases.htm?dtl/23315/India+ and+ Myanmar+sign+Memorandum+of+Understanding+on+Border+Cooperation (accessed on 20 February 2019).

Pattnaik, Jajati K. (2016), 'Look East policy and India's North Eastern Region: Status of Cross Border Trade and Connectivity', in Gurudas Das and C. Joshua Thomas (eds.), *Look East to Act East Policy: Implications for India's Northeast*, London: Routledge, pp. 213-228.

Planning Commission, Government of India (1997), 'Transforming the Northeast, High Level Commission Report to the Prime Minister', http://planningcommission.nic.in/reports/genrep/ne_exe.pdf (accessed on 11 September 2018).

Press Information Bureau (2015), 'Joint Statement between India and China during Prime Minister's visit to China', 15 May, http://pib.nic.in/newsite/PrintRelease.aspx?relid=121755 (accessed on 18 June 2018).

Ramani, Srinivasan (2015), 'Bridging Ties with the New Silk Road,' *The Hindu*, 29 June.

Rediff.com (1998), 'Chinese Goods Swamp Northeast India', http://www.rediff.com/business/1998/aug/04negood.htm (accessed on 24 October 2014).

Strategic Digest (2015), "Joint Statement between the India and China at Beijing", p. 625.

Uberoi, Patricia (2015), 'Prospects of the Bangladesh-China–India-Myanmar (BCIM) Economic Corridor,' IPRI Conference, pp. 1-25.

______ (2016), 'The BCIM Forum: Is it Sustainable?' in Gurudas Das and C. Joshua Thomas, *Look East to Act East Policy: Implications for India's Northeast*, London: Routledge, pp. 78-79.

Uninathan, Sandeep (2011), 'Gunrunners of Northeast', *India Today*, 6 June, http://indiatoday.intoday.in/story/chinese-agents-smuggle-arms-to-spread-militancy-in-Northeast/1/139538.html (accessed on 21 February 2018).

9

Acting Resurgent on 'Look East' : Rebooting 'Soft Power' Strategy

Sourabh Jyoti Sharma

Introduction

> *"Historically India has had an enormous influence on Southeast Asia; economically and culturally too. The Ramayana story is present all over Southeast Asia in different versions....The civilisations in the region were really Indian in origin..."*[1]
>
> —**Lee Kuan Yew**, former Prime Minister of Singapore and currently its Minister Mentor

> *"We are of Asia and the peoples of Asia are nearer and closer to us than others. India is so situated that she is the pivot of Western, Southern and Southeast Asia. In the past, her culture flowed to all these countries and they came to her in many ways. Those contacts are being renewed and the future is bound to see a closer union between India and Southeast Asia..."*.[2]
>
> —**Pt Jawaharlal Nehru,** India's first Prime Minister and Foreign Minister at the 'Asian Relations Conference' in New Delhi in 1947.

India is an old civilisation of sun worshippers. It has, therefore, always been looking east.[3] one of the most overlooked yet promising relationships in Asia is between Southeast Asia and India. This is despite the fact that both parties, in addition to sharing cultural and civilisational links that stretch back to millennia, are major players in the global economy, important contributors to the future development of Asian regionalism, and partners who have significant common interests in various fields. The Indo-Pacific region as a whole would also benefit from a closer partnership between ASEAN and India, since it helps create a more open, peaceful and stable Asia which is in the interest of both India and the ASEAN member-countries.

Southeast Asia and India are by no means strangers but civilisational *natural* allies. Civilisational and cultural links date back thousands of years, perhaps even well into the prehistoric period. However, ideological differences precluded close political ties from developing after Indian independence from the British in 1947 and throughout most of the Cold War. However, things began to change after the end of the Cold War when India found itself completely isolated in its 'near abroad' in the eastern flank. India's balance of payment crisis and subsequent economic liberalization, coupled with the collapse of the USSR and ASEAN's success as a model for regional cooperation in contrast to the stagnated South Asian Association for Regional Cooperation (SAARC), forced a rethink and pulled New Delhi's attention toward Southeast Asia via its 'Look East' Policy (LEP) under the then Indian Prime Minister, Narasimha Rao, whose strategic foresightedness must be applauded.

Over the years India-ASEAN relations have made great strides in many fields of their common interests but here the argument is that India can achieve much more if it can maximise on its 'soft power' natural advantages which India has not used as vigorously to the hilt as it should right from the onset of the LEP. The importance of Soft Power has increased in the context of globalisation and the growing disquiet over the use of military power for achieving foreign policy objectives.

If we look carefully, India, in spite remaining aloof from the Southeast Asian states since the formation of ASEAN in 1967, nevertheless, made relatively efficacious interaction with them in the last two decades under the aegis of LEP which is largely based on India's 'soft power' of attraction rather than the hard power of coercion.

Hence, here the proposition is, if India wants to reap rich dividends in translating its foreign policy's 'core objectives' into realities, it must give all its attention onto the fullest utilisation of its huge 'soft power' potentials in the region. It can also serve India in its subtle but effective containment of a 'rising' China which is based on 'countering without confronting' in the Southeast Asia.

What is 'Soft Power'?

The international system of the twenty-first century is characterized by diverging trends. On the one hand, the economic benefits of globalization have increased national State power and have strengthened the idea of a multi-polar world. On the other hand, non-State actors challenge state authority and global institutions exert increasing influence on State behaviour via international regimes and regulations.

Under the conditions of growing, political and economic interdependence of a non-polar world will, therefore, be a much more likely scenario than a multi-polar order. In such constellations, traditional concepts of hard power will no longer be sufficient to pursue national interests. The concept of 'soft power' has extended the scope to include more aspects into the analysis of international politics.

The term which is now widely used in international politics by strategic analysts, statesmen and researchers alike was coined by Prof Joseph S. Nye Jr. of Harvard University in a 1990 book, 'Bound to Lead: The Changing Nature of American Power.' He further developed the concept in his 2004 book, '*Soft Power: The Means to Success in World Politics.*'

'Soft power' is "the ability to obtain what you want through attraction rather than coercion or payments."[4] It arises due to the attractiveness of a country's culture, political ideals, and policies, that is, through elements which are 'real but intangible'.[5]

It can be contrasted with 'hard power', that is the use of coercion and payment. In contrast to military and economic power, 'soft power' differs in its behaviours, primary currencies and government policies. 'Soft power' behaviour is characterized by attraction and agenda setting, the primary currencies being values, culture, policies, institutions and government policies being shaped mainly by public diplomacy, bilateral and multilateral diplomacy. 'Soft power' can be wielded not just by States, but also by all actors in international politics, such as NGOs or international institutions.

Hard and 'soft power' can be regarded as two extremities on a continuum of power.[6] They involve different ideas, interactions and institutions for foreign policy whether in the areas of security, politics or economics. Ideally, hard power strategies focus on military intervention, coercive diplomacy, and economic sanctions in order to enforce national interests resulting in confrontational policies vis-à-vis neighbouring countries while 'soft power' strategies stress on common political values, peaceful means for conflict management, and economic co-operation in order to achieve common solutions.

Though 'soft power' cannot produce results as fast as hard power, its effects are more long-lasting and it is less expensive. The importance of 'soft power' is due to its ability to influence others unobtrusively and unconsciously. It is, thus, an indirect way to get what you want and hence has been termed by Nye as the 'second face of power'.[7]

Power is becoming less fungible, less coercive and less concrete today. Co-optive behavioural power and 'soft power' resources are not new. However, recent trends and changes in political issues have made them more significant. Today's major powers are not as able to use their traditional power resources to achieve their purposes as in the past. Private actors and small States have become more powerful on many issues. At least five trends have contributed to this diffusion of power: economic interdependence, transnational actors, rise of nationalism in weak states, the spread of technology and changing political issues.[8]

According to Nye, in the information age, three kinds of countries are in a good position to gain 'soft power':[9]

(1) 'those whose dominant culture and ideas are closer to prevailing global norms' (which now emphasise liberalism, pluralism, and autonomy),
(2) 'those with the most access to multiple channels of communication and thus more influence over how issues are framed', and

(3) 'those whose credibility is enhanced by their domestic and international performance'.

The 'soft power' of a country rests mainly on three resources: 'its culture (in places where it is attractive to others); its political values (when it lives up to them at home and abroad); and its foreign policies (when they are seen as legitimate and having moral authority).'[10]

Strategic Significance of 'Soft Power' in Foreign Policy Formulation across the Globe

But why is 'soft power' so important? Is not hard power equally important? Renowned Italian political scientist Giulio M. Gallarotti has this answer: "hard power exhibits a greater conflict of interests relative to 'soft power."[11] Moreover, contemporary factors in international affairs such as globalization and interdependence, spread of nuclear weapons, emergence of advanced technology, decline of "warrior ethics", spread of democracy, and growth in regimes and international organisations have contributed to the elevation of soft power's importance.[12] As Gallarotti writes, "The exclusive use of hard power is risky and often self-defeating."[13] Also, as Colin S. Gray said, "The use of force is more costly today than was the case in the past." [14]

But hard power and 'soft power' are not mutually conflicting but mutually complementary in nature, i.e., soft power also reinforces hard power and vice versa. 'Soft power', like hard power, is a form of power. Nye, who coined and popularised the concept argues that it should be defined both in terms of resources and behaviour.[15] In terms of resources; hard power of coercion is based on military and economic power resources. Military and economic resources can contribute to 'soft power' behaviour which is also based on attractive culture, political values and foreign policy.[16] In behavioural terms, 'soft power' is the ability to get the preferred results by the power of attraction and hard power is the ability to wield influence by coercion (also by sanction and inducement).

Any type of resource can contribute to 'soft power' behaviour, but any kind of behaviour is not 'soft power' behaviour.[17] There is a clear distinction between coercion and attraction. However, the beauty and benefits of using 'soft power' over hard power lies, as Uma

Purushothaman said, in the fact that "A nation with a large amount of 'soft power' and the goodwill so won can inspire other countries to acculturate, thus avoiding the need for expensive hard power expenditures."[18]

'Soft power', as Nye said, is only one facet of the three powers that he has put forward. To quote Nye, "Power is the ability to alter the behaviour of others to get what you want, and there are basically three ways to do that: coercion (sticks), payment (carrots) and attraction (soft power)"[19]

The importance of 'soft power' in the contemporary world can be seen if we look at why China pulled out all the stops to hold a successful Olympics in 2008. Hence, India cannot afford to lag behind on this front. It is the ultimate *mantra* of winning without waging war.

A Relook at India's 'Look East' Foreign Policy

India and Southeast Asia both share a common civilisational and cultural ancestry of historical memories. If there were drift between them in the past, it was never due to any misunderstanding but negative spin-offs of Cold War propaganda politics when the world was divided between 'us' or 'them'. This is what kept India apart when ASEAN came into being in 1967. But we must never forget how India's first Prime Minister Pt. Jawaharlal Nehru viewed the Southeast Asian nations by referring to them as 'Greater India'.[20]

Nehru's vision of a "closer union with the East was shaped by the strength of India's geographical proximity, similarity of historical experiences, cultural identity, economic interests and common strategic concerns in relation to the countries of the East. The vast stretch of the Indian Ocean and its economic and strategic significance in links with its eastern neighbours was not lost on Nehru and his associates."[21]

However, it was the malicious politicking of the Cold War that marred India's dream of resurgent East Asian solidarity towards peace, progress and prosperity. But India did not completely give up on its eastward orientation. It played a very constructive role in working for peace and stability in the Indo-China region, under UN auspices and as Chairman of the International Control Commission, following the

Geneva Agreement of 1954. This difficult assignment delivered by India with passion and perseverance for peace is still appreciated and fondly remembered in Vietnam, Kampuchea (then Cambodia) and Laos. The goodwill earned by India in this region is and can be harnessed even today. Prior to this, India was also involved in the Korean Armistice in 1953 and played a constructive role between China and the West.[22]

Very few people know or remember that India under Indira Gandhi also associated itself with the process of the formation of ASEAN (Association of Southeast Asian Nations) during 1966-67. It worked intensely for evolving a broad-based regional organisation of cooperation, which did not identify itself with any of the superpowers strategic and Cold War oriented-interests. This however, was not acceptable to the powers involved in establishing ASEAN against a strategic backdrop of the messy Vietnam war. The result was an ASEAN representing an ideologically and strategically divided Southeast Asia in which India had no place.[23]

But the decade of the Eighties saw a sudden spurt in Indo-ASEAN bilateral dialogues with prime ministers from Indira Gandhi to Rajiv Gandhi and others visiting many ASEAN member-states to rekindle the old ties lost in narrow cold war politicking reminding India's age-old ties with these nations since time immemorial.

India's LEP, introduced in 1992, was officially defined and articulated in September 1994, by the then Indian Prime Minister Narasimha Rao at a lecture in Singapore. He had stressed the point that India's historical and cultural relations were very old and strong and there was nothing new in India looking towards reinforcing cooperative linkages with its eastern neighbours. He emphasised on building a strong economic and security relationship between India and its eastern neighbours.[24]

There are three main crucial factors behind the launching of LEP by India:

- The growing political and economic importance of ASEAN in the Indo-Pacific region,
- The emerging potential of ASEAN as a regional trading bloc with Regional Trading Arrangement (RTA), Preferential Trading Arrangement (PTA) with huge source of Foreign Direct

Investment (FDI) and prospects of being a formidable trade partner, and

- Above all, the need to play a balancing role in countering the growing clout of a rising Communist China in the South-East Asian region.

After almost a decade, the policy assumed a more pronounced strategic flavour and expanded to countries other than ASEAN members like Australia, Japan and Korea. India's then Foreign Minister Yashwant Sinha heralded the second phase of the LEP in 2003, by saying:

> "The first phase of India's Look East policy was ASEAN-centred and focused primarily on trade and investment linkages. The new phase of this policy is characterised by an expanded definition of "East", extending from Australia to East Asia, with ASEAN at its core. The new phase also marks a shift from trade to wider economic and security issues including joint efforts to protect the sea lanes and coordinate counterterrorism activities." [25]

Enhancing relations with ASEAN has been central to India's LEP and there has been steady progress in the ASEAN-India relations since the policy was initiated in the early Nineties. (see Figure 1).

Figure 1: Timeline of Milestones in India-ASEAN Relations

Year	*Event/Agreement*
1992	Sectoral Dialogue Partnership of ASEAN
1995	Full Dialogue Partnership of ASEAN
1996	Membership in ASEAN Regional Forum
1997	Establishment of BIMSTEC
2000	Mekong Ganga Cooperation Initiative begins
2002	First India-ASEAN Summit and India-ASEAN Business Summit
2003	Framework Agreement on Comprehensive Economic Cooperation
2003	India signs Treaty of Amity and Cooperation
2003	ASEAN India Joint Declaration for Cooperation to Combat International Terrorism
2004	ASEAN-India Partnership for Peace, Progress and Shared Prosperity
2005	India becomes member of East Asian Summit
2009	Signing of the ASEAN-India Free Trade Agreement (AIFTA)
[2010 – FTA in Goods; 2012 – ASEAN Strategic Partner and 2015 – FTA in Services.]	

The year 2012 marked twenty fruitful years of the ASEAN-India dialogue partnership and the 10th anniversary of ASEAN-India Summit-level partnership. To celebrate these historic occasions, India hosted the ASEAN-India Commemorative Summit in New Delhi in December, 2012. The theme of the summit was 'ASEAN-India Partnership for Peace and Shared Prosperity' as a roadmap for further enhancing the relations in the future. Both sides reiterated their common desire to boost Track II (people-to-people) diplomacy and to celebrate the occasion in both India and the ten ASEAN member-nations from 2012 to 2013 with pomp and gaiety.

If we look at India-ASEAN economic ties, the volume of bilateral trade has been increased. (see Figure 2).

Figure 2: Recent India-ASEAN Bilateral Trade (2016-2018)

	TOTAL EXPORT		*TOTAL IMPORT*	
Country	*2016-17*	*2017-18 (Apr-Oct)*	*2016-17*	*2017-18 (Apr-Oct)*
Brunei	42.88	29.88	627.85	286.56
Cambodia	105.06	64.15	36.10	29.68
Indonesia	3488.12	1982.48	13,427.99	9,402.25
Laos	25.72	11.24	207.38	125.27
Malaysia	5,244.86	2,788.34	8,93359	5,211.17
Myanmar	1,107.89	511.19	1,067.25	540.28
Philippines	1,482.52	900.85	494.62	465.15
Singapore	9,564.48	5,623.90	7,08657	4,038.78
Thailand	3,133.44	1,978.47	5,415.40	3,916.55
Vietnam	6,786.56	4,236.23	3,320.56	2,373.23
Total	30,961	18,126.72	40,617.31	26,588.92
India's Total	275,851.71	166,469.58	384,355.55	257,527.60
% share	11.22	10.88	10.56	10.32

All figures in $ million

Source: Surojit Gupta, "Indo-Asean trade rises 10% to $72bn in FY17, but is long way off potential", *Times of India*, January 26, 2018.

Also, over the years India's trade with Asian countries has increased manifold in terms of both export and imports. (see Figure 3).

Figure 3: Foreign Direct Investment (FDI) Flows between India and ASEAN in USD billion from 2010-2015

	2010	*2011*	*2012*	*2013*	*2014*	*2015*
FDI Inflows into ASEAN from India	3.80	-1.96	6.63	2.10	0.61	1.25
FDI Outflows from ASEAN into India	3.02	1.76	5.29	2.59	6.14	6.96

Note: FDI Outflows from ASEAN into India only include data points for a few Southeast Asian countries namely Indonesia, Singapore, Philippines, Malaysia, Thailand, Myanmar and Vietnam. For others, no data is available.

Source: ASEAN Investment Report, 2916; FDI Statistics for different years from DIPP website.

India's 'Soft Power' Potentials in LEP vis-à-vis China: A Comparative Analysis

India is being touted in many recent publications as a rising power in Asia—and has the potential to become one of the great powers in the world.[25] It has the world's second largest population, after China, fourth largest economy on purchasing power parity terms, second largest army, fourth largest air force, fifth largest navy and the second most dominant navy in the Indian Ocean (after the USA), bordering some of the world's key shipping lanes, especially for energy. The 1998 nuclear tests and the recent U.S.-India civilian nuclear agreement are further elements in India's emergence as a power to reckon with in today's complex polycentric world order. But India's efforts to increase its power and expand its sphere of influence are not based exclusively on the traditional tools of economic or military power or hard power but equally on projecting the country's 'soft power'. Over the years, Indian policy-makers have been actively trying to promote India's image in the world and increase the attractiveness of its society, government, economy, and culture in order to bring other countries into closer relationships with India.

A democratic India, inheritor of Mahatma Gandhi's world-acclaimed philosophy of non-violence and the birthplace of Buddhism—all these prominent inbuilt ingredients have already made India a potent 'soft power' by default.

U.S. President Barack Obama had the following words to say while addressing the joint session of the Indian Parliament in 2010: "I might not be standing before you today, as President of U.S., had it not been for Gandhi and the message he shared with the U.S. and the world." [26]

Perception matters in both politics and international power politics where India by default has an edge over a Communist China in the 'soft power' arena. Elaborating on India's historic sphere of influence or cultural-cum-civilisational footprints ('soft power' quotient) over the countries comprising this geo-strategically important region, Graver said:

> "At the core of modern India's nationalist narrative is the notion that India is a great nation whose radiant influence moulded a wide swath of the world beyond its boundaries.... The geographic scope of India's traditional sphere of influence was neatly presented by a series of exhibitions set up at the First Asian Relations Conference in New Delhi in March-April 1947....The exhibition...identified Burma, Siam (Thailand), Malaya, Cambodia, Champa, Sumatra, Java, and Bali as regions of Southeast Asia which had received 'strong influences from India in the domain of religion, language, art, and architecture."[27]

India can pride itself in many areas that naturally (without any impetus from the Indian State) give it more leverage over China which is very weak or vulnerable in this front. Bollywood as a quasi-global dream fabric, and India's long engagement in multilateral institutions are indicators that seem to qualify India as one of the leading soft powers of the twenty-first century. Moreover, the high economic growth rates post the 1991 liberalization, notwithstanding the current temporary declining slide, have increased the country's international attractiveness.

China may be 'rising', but it has hardly any bearing in increasing what Joshua Kurlantzick has called the 'charm offensive'.[28] Chinese policy makers since 1949 have been suffering from 'strategic blindness' with regard to the Southeast Asian region. But of late, seeing India's rapid strides with its ties with ASEAN via its LEP, China too has increased its attention towards this region, mainly to contain India's growing clout in its backyard. Knowing its limitations on the cultural and image fronts, China being the second largest economy in the world, has increased its infamous 'no strings attached' aid diplomacy with the ASEAN countries in a bid to win them over. But, territorial disputes in the South China Sea and the "China Threat" alarm have raised a suspicion among Southeast Asian countries about China's strategic intentions.[29] The issue of overseas Chinese also complicates China's relationship with Southeast Asian countries.[30] In terms of regional economic integration, the fear of a-China dominated East Asia has provoked measures to hedge against China, such as the East Asia Summit that brought in India, Russia, and Australia.[31] Because of India's democratic experience, its rise (unlike China) has been perceived as complementing rather than challenging the existing Asian and international orders.

Furthermore, there seems to be a broad maritime continental divide splitting Southeast Asian attitudes towards China, with Continental Southeast Asia having regional strategic outlooks that are dominated by the role of China, and Maritime Southeast Asia enjoying more room for manoeuvre because of geographical distance and the strategic attraction of the U.S.[32]

As a result of these findings, it appears China is still trudging an uphill road in projecting 'soft power' in Southeast Asia. India, however, must take serious note of Beijing's efforts to increase its 'soft power' in the region and therefore, must not be complacent.

Sources of India's 'Soft Power' Charm Offensive: Towards a 'Soft Powered' LEP

'Soft power' has now become an active element of India's diplomacy in parallel with the development of its hard power resources. India has progressively understood that these two dimensions of power should not be placed in opposition to one another, especially for an aspiring global power. India's political and economic appeal would not be possible if it had not developed robust political institutions over the last 65 years and sustained high economic growth rates over the last two decades. Similarly, as India's hard power capabilities, notably in the economic and military realms, have increased over the last decade, it became important to develop in conjunction a 'soft power' strategy to give legitimacy and credibility to India's leadership role in the world and continuing with its 'advantage India' image vis-à-vis the ASEAN nations.

India has many sources of 'soft power' that lead to increase its attractiveness in the Southeast Asian region. Here, let us briefly discuss the major ones.

Pluralist, Secular and Multicultural 'Soft Power' of Indian Culture

India's cultural influences on East and Southeast Asia, as well as some countries of the Asia Pacific region, have been extensive. Hinduism and Buddhism spread throughout Asia from India, initially along trading routes. While Hinduism found its way across much of Indonesia, Malaysia and Thailand, Buddhism reached Japan and Vietnam through China and Korea, and also flourished in countries closer to India, such as Burma, Cambodia and Thailand.

As Indian trading patterns expanded and religious ties spread throughout Asia, so did cultural elements including language (particularly Sanskrit), social customs, styles of art and architecture. Great Indianised kingdoms arose over the centuries throughout Asia and particularly in Southeast Asia.[32] Aside from the solitary instance of invasion of the Srivijaya kingdom in Sumatra by the Indian king, Rajendra Chola, in the eleventh century AD to protect Indian commercial interests; India did not show any imperialist ambitions in Southeast Asia.[33]

Three of the largest Indianised and Hindu kingdoms in the mainland of Southeast Asia were Funan (Cambodia), Kambuja (which succeeded Funan) and Champa (modern Vietnam), which existed roughly between the first to sixth centuries AD, sixth to fifteenth centuries AD, and the seventh to eighteenth centuries AD, respectively.[34] Indianisation also included the alphabetical basis of Southeast Asian scripts, the incorporation of Sanskrit in vocabularies along with the adoption of Hindu-Buddhist religious beliefs and the Indian concept of royalty.[35] Moreover, the renowned maritime Southeast Asian dynasty of Sailendra, which became the dominant maritime and land power in Malaysia by the eighth century,[36] is believed to have originated in the Indian state of Odisha. The last Hindu kingdom in the Southeast Asian region was Majapahit, which flourished between the thirteenth and fifteenth centuries in Java.[37]

The popularity of the *Ramayana* (with varying nuances from one country to another) in the Buddhist heartland of Southeast Asia may be seen as an unmistakable imprint of this synthesis. It is no wonder that the images of *Ganesha, Garuda, Shiva, Parvati, Rama* and *Sita* are adored and worshipped in many parts of Southeast Asia, along with those of Buddha. This imprint is also visible in languages, where Pali and Sanskrit provide the texture and base of many Southeast Asian languages. The cultural synthesis is also reflected in the names of the people and places, lifestyles and festivities and patterns of old architecture and temples of this region.

Countries in Southeast Asia still have remnants of Indian traditions: the Angor Vat temple in Cambodia, temples and pagodas in Thailand and Myanmar as well as the presence of several Sanskrit words in languages like Bhasha (Indonesia) prove the influence of Indian culture on these countries.

India's continuing 'soft power' in the Indo-Pacific can be seen in the ongoing multination project of building Nalanda University in Bihar as a noble endeavour to revive the once world famous varsity in partnership with China, Japan, South Korea and Singapore. This initiative is an example of the convergence of the 'soft power' agendas of five different countries.

The 'Soft Power' of Indian Diaspora in Southeast Asia

The Indian Diaspora is a crucial actor in India's influence in Asia. Southeast Asia alone accounts for an estimated 6.7 million people of Indian origin.[38] Noted geo-strategist C. Raja Mohan argued that "India could always count itself among the few nations with strong cards in the arena of soft power", asserting that India's biggest "instrument" of 'soft power' was its Diaspora."[39]

India's Diaspora is a huge 'soft power' asset. There are millions of Indian Diaspora spread across countries as far as Fiji, Guyana, Malaysia, Mauritius, Surinam, South Africa, Sri Lanka and Trinidad. While Indians were taken as indentured labours to far-flung parts of the British Empire in the nineteenth-century, the professional elite from this expatriate community has found its way to the USA, Canada, Australia, and other nations of the West in the twentieth century. They have contributed immensely to the countries they have settled in and command influence and respect in these countries. Countries like Fiji and Mauritius have large Indian communities with People of Indian Origin (PIOs) holding important political positions.

Beginning in the 1990s, it became clear that the overseas Chinese community was contributing to China's economic development. In reaction, India began outreach efforts to wealthier expatriates who were well situated to play a vital role in strengthening ties between India and other countries. The government established in 2000 a High-Level Committee on Indian Diaspora to review the status of PIOs and Non-Resident Indians (NRIs) in the context of constitutional provisions, laws and rules applicable to them both in India and countries of their residence. By studying the characteristics, strengths and weaknesses of this community, which represents twenty million people worldwide, this committee aimed to study the role that PIOs and NRIs may play in the economic, social and technological development of India. The holding of the annual *Pravasi Bharatiya Diwas* to unite the Indian Diaspora is a right step in the right direction.

A well-cultivated Diaspora community can be translated into a major instrument and an extended arm of a country's foreign policy framework, e.g., how the Indian NRI community played a crucial role via lobbying through the influential U.S. India Political Action Committee (USINPAC) and India Caucus in helping the historic Indo-US Nuclear Agreement passed by the U.S. Congress.

There exists a vast number of PIOs in ASEAN countries. They, like their U.S. counterpart, can play a great role towards building more closer and robust Indo-ASEAN relations in the 21st century.

The 'Soft Power' of India's Democratic, Liberal Values, Politically Empowered Civil Society and Independent Judiciary

As the world's largest democracy, with a vibrant free press, active and independent judiciary as well as a politically empowered civil society armed with the Right to Information (RTI) Act, India has important 'soft power' advantages over the other rising power in the region, Communist China. The bottom line: States can increase their 'soft power' capacity if they live up to their political values at home and abroad.

Although India had been regarded as a democratic model vis-à-vis Communist China already in the 1950s and 1960s, her democratic credentials, despite the blot of the short-lived Emergency period, came to be appreciated fully only after the end of the Cold War or 'end of history' (Fukuyama). The new international consensus on democracy, human rights and market-oriented economic reforms brought about a reassessment of India's political achievements.

Democracy in India has not only survived but thrived in spite of many prominent Western doomsayers, notwithstanding the existence of many 'killer of democracy' factors (or paradoxes?) like widespread poverty, high illiteracy rates, multi-ethnic society and a high level of violence, which over the years have declined but nevertheless still exist.

Moreover, India's balanced and pragmatic policy of 'non-alignment' as part of its larger foreign policy objectives during the heightened Cold War bloc politicking and support for restoration of democracy in Bangladesh, Maldives, Nepal and Bhutan has been seen in the most positive light. Above all, its refusal to let its territory, men and machines to be used in the Cold War games in Vietnam, Cambodia and Korea earned high appreciation from all of its ASEAN neighbours after the end of the Cold War.

The 'new social movement' ushered in the era of a vibrant civil society in India since the early Nineties and played a very effective role in reforming the existing political system making it more responsive, accountable, transparent and, above all, pro-people. The historic 'Right to Information Act, 2005' in making Indian democracy truly democratic in nature is a gift of Indian civil society to the common citizens of India whose relentless campaign made the government to finally enact it.

The active and independent Indian judiciary also plays the 'guardian role' bestowed to it by the Constitution of India in effective 'checks and balances' in safeguarding the 'basic structures' of Indian democracy. As the 'final interpreter' of the Constitution, its role has to be enabling hope among the common citizens of India in curbing criminal, feudal and anti-democratic elements and practices.

In short, India has taught the world that the road to *consensual agreement* goes via the upheaval bumpy road of *contested disagreements*; peaceful and non-violent.

The 'Soft Power' of India's Spirituality, Music, Bollywood, Food and Information Technology

India's spirituality is much needed in these days of conflict and strife. India's age-old legacy of tolerance for different religions and cultures is now a global legend. After all, this is the land which has preached *'Vasudhaiva Kutumbakam'* (the world is but one family) and *Loka Samastha Sukhino Bhavanthu* (let all people have happiness in the world).

India's message of secularism which actually means different religions co-existing in harmony with each other, rather than the Western concept of separation of religion and the State is a valuable lesson in these days when there is so much strife in the name of religion.

One of India's most successful and enduring exports—*yoga*—is practised all over the world both as a form of exercise and as a stress-buster by millions of people. Yoga is already a global phenomenon and is rapidly becoming part of mainstream culture, particularly in the West, and Southeast Asian nations.

The power of music can bridge borders and bring people closer. Indian music and movies have a large international market and have become increasingly popular abroad, particularly in Asia, Europe, Africa and West Asia. Even in countries like Russia, Syria and Senegal, Indian films, particularly Hindi (Bollywood, which is the most important movie industry in the world after Hollywood) movies, have a following. Indian movies are popular and watched not only in South Asian countries like Bangladesh, Nepal, Pakistan, Afghanistan and Sri Lanka due to their close proximity with India and due to certain similar cultural outlooks present in the movies but also in Europe, Africa, the Middle East, the Asia Pacific and increasingly started in East Asia also. Wax statues of several actors from the Indian film industry at Madame Tussaud's in London bear testimony to the influence of Indian cinema and India's soft power.

Indian cuisines with its subtle use of spices and herbs grown across the Indian subcontinent are also becoming popular across the globe, especially where there is a large Indian Diaspora. Indian foods like *samosa, dosa, poha, jalebi, mithais,* egg-curry, butter chicken, lemon rice, etc, have also gained popularity in the Southeast Asian countries and there are many Indian restaurants in the large cities of Thailand, Indonesia, Malaysia and Vietnam.

The success of Indian companies like Infosys Technologies and Wipro Technologies in the Information Technology (IT) sector; the success of other multinational companies like Tata Group and Reliance Group; and the worldwide recognition of the academic excellence of the Indian Institute of Management (IIMs) and Indian Institute of Technology (IITs)—the centres of excellence for higher training, research and development in science, engineering and technology in India—have contributed to the new image of India as a country with English-educated, enterprising people. India's 'software' needed to be married with ASEAN's 'hardware' to become the global No. 1 in their respective fields.

The 'Soft Power' of India's Public Diplomacy, Humanitarian Assistance and Peace Building

In international relations, public diplomacy or people's diplomacy, broadly speaking, is the communication with foreign publics to establish a dialogue designed to inform and influence.

Coined by Edmund A. Gullion, then Dean at Fletcher School, Tufts University, in 1965 who defined it as

> "the one that deals with the influence of public attitudes on the formation and execution of foreign policies. It encompasses dimensions of international relations beyond traditional diplomacy; the cultivation by governments of public opinion in other countries; the interaction of private groups and interests in one country with those of another; the reporting of foreign affairs and its impact on policy; communication between those whose job is communication, as between diplomats and foreign correspondents; and the processes of inter-cultural communications."[40]

Public diplomacy is centred on 'people' since people, not just states, are of global importance in a world where technology and migration increasingly face everyone; an entire new door of policy is opened. India, too, needs to invest heavily in this arena that will it give its 'soft power' the much needed thrust in the Southeast Asian region via making more people-to-people contacts (Track II diplomacy), scholarships to students, cultural exchanges, celebration of Indian festivals like *Diwali, Holi,* etc., by organisations like Indian embassies and the Indian Council for Cultural Relations (ICCR) to create a India-friendly constituency in this region in the future with a long term objective.

Humanitarian assistance too is crucial to generating public goodwill towards India that transcends beyond borders. The way the Indian Navy helped in 'Operation *Sadbhavana*' and 'Operation *Sahayata*' in the post-tsunami and post-Lebanon crises in 2004-05 and 2006, respectively, earned the goodwill of the people of East Asia and PIOs of Lebanon. Its swift and daring 'Operation Cactus' in 1988 to restore democracy in Maldives and prevent attempts to stage a *coup* by rogue elements also gave India's 'soft-power' a much needed boost. Further, India must use its 'good offices' and influences in building peace in the region, especially in the volatile South China Sea that has several disputed islands, more so now to protect India's strategic energy interests there.

Factors Eroding India's 'Soft Power' Advantage Edge

There are many factors that can blunt India's sharp edge of 'soft power' attraction that it enjoys today amongst ASEAN nations and the world at large. A few crucial factors are:

- growing cases of gross human rights violations in fighting cross-border terrorism in J&K, North East and anti-Naxal or Left-Wing Extremism (LWE) in Chhattisgarh and other states,
- dismal show in UNDP-conducted Human Development Index (HDI) and other global indices,
- burgeoning corruption that erodes not only its global image but also impedes its rapid economic development towards the dream of a "developed" India by 2020,
- hunger on the rise with rising "unchecked" population growth,
- failure to get a permanent seat at the UN Security Council (UNSC) in spite of its vigorous efforts,
- "soft stand" against "rogue" States like Iran, Sudan, North Korea, etc. India's "supportive" role gave them their much-needed "legitimacy" by claiming to be backed by the world's largest democracy,

- insignificant show in the medal tally of various sporting events across the globe (especially in the Olympics) together with the lacklustre hosting of Commonwealth Games in 2010,
- failure to host the Olympics even once ever since it began while China successfully organized it in 2008,
- unresolved disputes with its immediate neighbours also affect India's soft power potential,
- unresolved disputes within India, like the ones in Kashmir and the North-East also affect India's 'soft power'. The very fact that these disputes are continuing despite 65 years of democratic governance are proof that the benefits of democracy and development have not reached the people in these regions.

Conclusion

'Soft power' cuts in many ways. There is an attractiveness and repulsiveness in 'soft power' as well as a nexus between what 'you do' and 'what you are'. On the one hand, attractiveness is enhanced when India acts in a manner that is consistent with its stated ideals and values. On the other hand, repulsiveness is intensified by inherent contradictions.

Many have misgivings on 'soft power' thinking that 'soft power' means being a 'soft State' (Gunnar Myrdal) too, which is not true. Also, holding 'soft power' does not mean discarding hard power. As Shashi Tharoor said, "Hard power without soft power stirs up resentments and enmities; soft power without hard power is a confession of weakness."[41]

There exists a mutually beneficial and symbiotic cultural-cum-civilisational ties between India and the East Asian nations throughout history but unfortunately, many in the Indian Right (the proponents of *Hindutva* or Hindu nationalists) try to project the nations as India's "cultural colonies"[42] overly exaggerating India's 'early Hindu influences' in the region which as C. Raja Mohan,[43] said can be detrimental to India's 'soft power' edge in future as no nation likes to see itself under the age-old 'cultural subjugation' of another nation, howsoever 'great' the 'subjugating' nation might be.

To increase its international clout, notably in its growing

competition with China over which power tells the 'better story', India will have to use its 'soft power' in a more systematic and planned manner. For India to continue to be an attractive power, and most importantly, for it to present a more compelling development model than China, it will also need to continue to improve its internal economic performance; most importantly it must immediately arrest the current economic slump and sluggish growth rate. Since 'soft power' has a fluctuating value, India will need to resolve its lack of social and economic equality by adopting a 'zero tolerance' approach on combating the growing menace of corruption if it wants to retain its soft power edge in the East Asian region and the world.

India must not rest on its laurels on the 'soft power' front of the past because the future possibilities of a 'soft powered' LEP can exceed our present expectations. India must aspire to be such a State with which everybody wants to be a friend with and nobody wants to mess with. Also, as ASEAN has expanded and might expand more in the future, it can become India's flagship foreign policy tool in building closer ties with countries beyond East Asia, viz., the USA, Russia, the UK, European Union nations, etc.

To increase India's 'soft power' in the region, India must take note of the factors that are eroding it and envisage actionable corrective measures with a long term perspective plan. The role of states in projecting India's soft power is under-leveraged. States like Bihar with Bodhgaya have the potential to attract Buddhist followers from South East Asia. States like Assam, Arunachal Pradesh, Sikkim having prominent Buddhist sacred places of great religious significance in particular and the rest of the states of the North East region (NER), supported by the respective governments as well as by the Ministry of Development of the North Eastern Region (DONER) have huge potentials to develop a 'Buddhist Circuit' with the ASEAN nations, including Japan and Korea. In short, cultural, socio-religious and ethnic affinity of the people of the NER with that of the ASEAN and the Far East region should be utilised to the hilt for the success of leapfrogging from 'Look East' to the 'Act East' grand-strategy now under PM Modi. To conclude, India's 'soft power' strategy in its LEP can go beyond its present role, promising great possibilities and rich dividends in the future. But is India ready to act *hard* on 'soft power'?

NOTES

1. Datta-Ray, Sunanda K. (2009), "*Looking East to Look West: Lee Kuan Yew's Mission India*" New Delhi: Penguin Books India, p. 13.
2. Asian Relations, Report of the Proceedings and Documentations of the First Asian Relations Conference, New Delhi, March 1947. For further reading see also, Jawaharlal Nehru, Speeches, Vol. 1 (1946-49) and Vol. 2 (1949-53), Publications Division, Government of India, Delhi.
3. Muni, S.D., "India's 'Look East' Policy: The Strategic Dimension", *ISAS Working Paper* No. 121, 1 February 2011, p. 2.
4. Nye Jr, Joseph S. (1990), "*Bound to Lead: The Changing Nature of American Power*", New York: Basic Books, Inc., Publishers, p. 188.
5. Mohan, C. Raja, "Indian Diaspora and 'Soft Power", *The Hindu*, January 6, 2003, New Delhi.
6. Wagner, Christian, "From Hard Power to Soft Power? Ideas, Interaction, Institutions, and Images in India's South Asia Policy", *Working Paper* No 26, March 2005, http://archiv.ub.uniheidelberg.de/volltextserver/volltexte/2005/5436/pdf/hpsa cp26.pdf. (accessed on November 18, 2013).
7. Nye Jr, Joseph S. (1990), "Soft Power", *Foreign Policy*, No. 80, Fall 1990, pp. 153–170, cited in Raghavan, 'After the Unipolar Moment: Asia and Regional and Global Order', *Working Paper*, The Stanley Foundation's Conference: May 31, 2007 http://www.stanleyfoundation.org/publications/working_papers/RAGHAVAN_working_paper_May_conference_FINAL.doc (accessed on November 18, 2013).
8. Ibid.
9. Nye Jr, Joseph S. (2002), "*The Paradox of American Power: Why the World's only Superpower Can't Go It Alone*", Oxford: Oxford University Press, p. 14.
10. Ibid.
11. Giulio M. Gallarotti, "Soft Power: what it is, why it's important, and the conditions for its effective use", *Journal of Political Power*, Vol. 4, No. 1 (2011), p. 28.
12. Ibid.
13. Gallarotti, Giulio M. (2010), "Cosmopolitan Power in International Relations: A Synthesis of Realism, Neo liberalism and Constructivism", New York: Cambridge University Press, p. 5.
14. Gray, Colin S., "Hard Power and Soft Power: The utility of Military Force as an Instrument of Policy in the 21st century", *Strategic Studies Institute Monograph*, April 2011, p. 21.
15. Nye, Joseph S., "Power and Foreign Policy", *Journal of Political Power*, Vol. 4, No. 1(2011), p. 10.
16. For detailed discussion, see Joseph S. Nye, "The Future of Power" (New York: Public Affairs, 2011), pp. 3–109.
17. Ibid.
18. Purushothaman, Uma, "Shifting Perceptions of Power: Soft Power and India's Foreign Policy", *Journal of Peace Studies*, Vol. 17, Issues 2 & 3, April-September, 2010, p. 2.
19. Nye, Joseph, "Think Again: Soft Power", *Foreign Policy*, 23 February, 2006 (http://www.foreignpolicy.com/articles/2006/02/22/think_again_soft) (accessed on

November 18, 2013).

20. Nehru, Jawaharlal (2004), *"The Discovery of India"*, New Delhi: Penguin Books, p. 213.
21. See K.M. Panikkar, "The Strategic Problems of the Indian Ocean" (Allahabad, 1944); K.M. Panikkar, *"India and the Indian Ocean: An Essay on the influence of Sea Power on Indian History"* (London: George Allen & Unwin, 1945); and Werner Levi, "Free India in Asia" (Minneapolis: University of Minneapolis Press, 1952).
22. For details of India s role see, Eric Gonsalves, Oral History, "Resolving the Korean Crisis", *Indian Foreign Affairs Journal*, Vol. 2, No. 2 (New Delhi: Cambridge University Press-India, April-June 2007).
23. Sridharan, Kripa (1996), "The ASEAN Region in India's Foreign Policy", USA: Dartmouth Publishing Co. Also see "India-ASEAN Relations: Evolution, Growth and Prospects", in Chandran Jeshurun (ed.) (1993), "China, India, Japan and the Security of Southeast Asia" Singapore: Institute of Southeast Asian Studies.
24. See the text of Prime Minister Narasimha Rao's speech at the Institute of Southeast Asian Studies (ISAS), National University of Singapore in 1994. (Website: www.isas.nus.edu.sg).
25. See Yevgeny Bendersky. "India as a Rising Power," *Asia Times*, August 20, 2004; Stephen P. Cohen (2001). "India: Emerging Power", Washington, D.C.: Brookings Institution Press; Baldev Raj Nayar & T. V. Paul (2003), *"India in the World Order: Searching for Major-Power Status."* Cambridge, U.K.: Cambridge University Press, or Volume 85, Number 4 (July/August 2006) of *Foreign Affairs* on "The Rise of India."
26. http://uscpublicdiplomacy.org/index.php/about/bio_detail/Abhay_K. (accessed on November 18, 2013).
27. John Garver. Protracted Contest: pp. 11-12. Original sources, For India, Asian Relations, Being Report of the Proceedings and Documentation of the First Asian Relations Conference, New Delhi, March-April 1947 (New Delhi, India: Asian Relations Organization, 1948), pp. 302-310.
28. Kurlantzick, Joshua, (2007), *"Charm Offensive: How China's Soft Power Is Transforming the World,"* Yale: Yale University Press.
29. Wang, Zhengxu and Yang, Ying, "Is China's Soft Power Dominating Southeast Asia?: Views From the Citizens", *Briefing Series* - Issue 44, China Policy Institute, The University of Nottingham, October 2008, p. 1.
30. See Garth Alexander (1974), *"The Invisible China: The Overseas Chinese and the Politics of Southeast Asia"*, New York, Macmillan; Leo Suryadinata (2007), "Understanding the Ethnic Chinese in Southeast Asia", Singapore: Institute of Southeast Asia Studies.
31. For the East Asian Summit, see Malik, Mohan, "The East Asia Summit: More Discord than Accord", *Yale Global*, December 20, 2005.
32. See Coedès, G., "The Indianized States of Southeast Asia", Walter F. Vella (ed.), Translated by Susan Brown Cowing, Honolulu: East-West Centre Press, 1968.
33. Sardesai, D.R. (2010), *"Southeast Asia: Past and Present"* (6th ed.) (Boulder CO, Westview Press, 2010), p. 17.
34. Pandya, Archana and Malone, David M, "India's Asia Policy: A Late Look East", *ISAS Special Report*, No. 02, 25, August 2010, p. 3.
35. See Coedès. G 32.

36. See Nehru 20, p. 216.
37. See Sardesai 33, pp. 53-54.
38. Sridharan, Kripa (1996), "*The ASEAN Region in India's Foreign Policy*" Aldershot, UK: Dartmouth Publishing, pp. 79-80.
39. See Mohan 5.
40. http://fletcher.tufts.edu/Murrow/what is public diplomacy/Tufts Fletcher School.htm (accessed on November 18, 2013).
41 Tharoor, Shashi, "Indian Strategic Power: Soft", *Global Brief*, May 13, 2009 (http://globalbrief.ca/blog/2009/05/13/soft-is-the-word/) (accessed on November 18, 2013).
42. See Jaffrelot, Christophe, "India's Look East Policy: An Asianist Strategy in Perspective, *India Review*, Volume 2, Issue 2, 2003.
43. Mohan, C. Raja, "Soft Power, Hard Facts", *The Indian Express*, November 19 2007. (New Delhi Edition).

10

Soft Power Diplomacy in India-Vietnam Relations

Chau Khahn Tam

Introduction

'Soft power' is an important concept in modern international relations. This term was first coined by American scholar Joseph Nye in his book *Bound to Lead* which was published in 1990. According to him, soft power is "the ability to get what you want through attraction rather than coercion or payment. It arises from the attractiveness of a country's culture, political ideals, and policies."[1] The USA is a successful story of soft power. For example, we cannot help remembering "the impact of Franklin Roosevelt's Four Freedoms in Europe at the end of World War II; of young people behind the Iron Curtain listening to American music and news on Radio Free Europe; of Chinese students symbolizing their protests in Tiananmen Square by creating a replica of the Statue of Liberty; of newly-liberated Afghans in 2001 asking for a copy of the Bill of Rights; of young Iranians today surreptitiously watching banned American videos and satellite television broadcasts in the privacy of their homes."[2]

Different from hard power which focuses on politics, economic and military power, soft power mainly concentrates on culture, goodwill and co-operation. With hard power, countries use political, economic and military forces to create pressure on their rivals. However, these measures seem to create hatred and resentment in the minds of other countries. The Second World War happened partly due to such resentment. After World War I, Germany was devastated and humiliated by the Allied Powers. Its resources and army were reduced by the terms of the Versailles Treaty. As a result of the harsh terms imposed by the Treaty, the German people were incited and easily influenced by the fascist and dictator, Adolf Hitler.

In contrast, a country applying soft power aims to produce good and friendly relationships with other countries. For example, the influence of India in Afghanistan is not only caused by India's economic aid to Afghanistan but also by the spread of Bollywood movies and songs in this country. Thanks to the Bollywood industry, India can exert positive influence in Afghanistan and many Afghans can understand and speak the Hindi language. Because of realizing the benefits of soft power, many states in the world have had wielded this kind of power to attract more allies and avoid rivals. China, Britain, France, South Korea, etc., have utilized their political ideals, culture and other values to create new bonds with others.

India is in a process of becoming a superpower, and it has been trying to apply soft power in its foreign policy in the past two decades. Its rich cultural and spiritual heritage (Buddhism and Hinduism), political and ethical inheritance (Gandhian concepts like non-violence and non-cooperation), film industry, the prosperous Diaspora and the Indian Council for Cultural Relations (ICCR) have been deployed to boost India's image at the global sphere. Recently, "the presence of Indian businesses in different parts of the world has also emerged as one of India's sources of Soft Power".[3]

Vietnam, a country in South East Asia, has been influenced by India's soft power. India and Vietnam have had historical, religious, and cultural links in the past, which in the present times, have been strengthened more and more. The ties between India and Vietnam "go back to the ancient Cham civilization when people from Orissa travelled to Vietnam and found a hospitable home there, mingling cultures, customs, language, and beliefs"[4]. India's Buddhism, Yoga,

Bollywood movies, and the Indian Council for Cultural Relations (ICCR) have contributed to enhancing the relationship between these two countries. Thus, the topic "India's Soft Power and Its Manifestations in Vietnam" is very important for exploring the links of soft power between India and Vietnam.

The Definition of Soft Power

Since the term "soft power" was coined by American scholar Joseph Nye in the book *Bound to Lead* in 1990, it has been used by various political leaders, writers, journalists, etc. According to him, "soft power is the ability to get what you want through attraction rather than coercion or payment. It arises from the attractiveness of a country's culture, political ideals, and policies. When our policies are seen as legitimate in the eyes of others, our soft power is enhanced".[5] In other words, "soft power describes the ability to influence the actions of others by virtue of one's culture, values and policies rather than by force. Soft power works through attraction and cooptation instead of coercion rather than military or economic power".[6]

Shashi Tharoor, an Indian politician, diplomat-cum-writer, states that "a country's soft power, to me, emerges from the world's perceptions of what that country is all about. The associations and attitudes conjured up in the global imagination by the mere mention of a country's name is often a more accurate gauge of its soft power than a dispassionate analysis of its foreign policies. In my view, hard power is exercised; soft power is evoked."[7] Joseph Nye observes, "When you can get others to admire your ideals and to want what you want, you do not have to spend as much on sticks and carrots to move them in your direction. Seduction is always more effective than coercion, and many values like democracy, human rights, and individual opportunities are deeply seductive."[8]

When a country's power is seen as legitimate, it may encounter less resistance to its desires and aims. For instance, "if a country's culture and ideology are attractive, others more willingly follow. If a country can shape international rules that are consistent with its interests and values, its actions will more likely appear legitimate in the eyes of others. If it uses institutions and follows rules that encourage other countries to channel or limit their activities in ways it prefers, it will not need many costly carrots and sticks."[9]

Soft power permits political and religious leaders to lessen the use of sticks and carrots to realize their aims. For example, "loyal Catholics may follow the Pope's teaching on capital punishment not because of a threat of excommunication, but out of respect for his moral authority. Some radical Muslims are attracted to support Osama bin Laden's actions not because of payments or threats, but because they believe in the legitimacy of his objectives. Even after bin Laden's organization was disrupted by the U.S. military presence in Afghanistan, many terrorist groups around the world organized themselves in his image."[10] Soft power "uses a different currency (not force, not money) to engender cooperation. It can rest on a sense of attraction, love, or duty in a relationship, and appeal to values about the justness of contributing to those shared values and purposes."[11]

In International Politics, "the resources that produce soft power arise in large part from the values an organization or country expresses in its culture, in the examples it sets by its internal practices and policies, and in the way it handles its relations with others".[12] It is not always easy for governments of countries to control and implement soft power, but the role of the government in the enhancement of the country's soft power should not be underestimated.

Soft power is not equal to influence because soft power is only one source of influence. In fact, "influence can also rest on the hard power of threats or payments. Nor is soft power just persuasion or the ability to move people by argument, though that is an important part of it. It is also the ability to entice and attract. Attraction often leads to acquiescence. In behavioural terms, soft power is attractive power. In terms of resources, soft power resources are the assets—tangible and intangible—that produce such attraction".[13] And "whether a particular asset is a soft-power resource that produces attraction can be measured by asking people through polls or focus groups. Whether that attraction in turn produces desired policy outcomes has to be judged in particular cases. Attraction does not always determine the preferences of others, but this gap between power measured as resources and power judged as the outcomes of behaviour is not unique to soft power. It occurs with all forms of power. Before the fall of France in 1940, Britain and France had more tanks than Germany, but that advantage in military power resources did not accurately predict the outcome of the battle."[14]

Some people claim that soft power is a manifestation of weakness. However, Joseph Nye disagrees by saying "...soft power is not weakness. It is a form of power, and the failure to incorporate it in our national strategy is a serious mistake".[15] He assumes that "those who deny the importance of soft power are like people who do not understand the power of seduction."[16]

After the Cold War, the role of soft power in International Relations and Diplomacy has been extending. With the emergence of the phenomenon of globalization and the unprecedented interconnectedness among countries, the use of violence and warfare is less and less accepted in International Politics. Countries with huge arsenals and large sums of money may not afford to obtain their aims. Indeed, "in this information age, with free movement of people, capital and ideas, perceptions matter more than ever".[17] Since the concept "soft power" was coined in 1990, it has enjoyed a spectacular international career. Although "originally designed for the USA, as the sole superpower, soft power has been gradually 'de-Americanized' and incorporated into the foreign policy strategies of many countries."[18]

India's Sources of Soft Power

India is a civilizational state with a diverse culture and long history. It can be said that India is one of the most culturally diverse countries in the world. It is the birthplace of a number of religions like Hinduism and Buddhism and is the converging point of various cultures and beliefs. In terms of culture, India is a very rich country.

India has various sources of soft power which include political values, cultural and spiritual heritage, foreign policy, the vigorous and successful community of a Diaspora, and economic success. These factors have helped India built its soft power over the last recent years. India's cultural and spiritual heritage includes Hinduism and Buddhism and their influence in Asia and beyond, the tradition of Yoga, Indian cuisine, Indian film industry, Indian classical arts and music, Indian literature and scriptures, etc. India's political values that can act as India's soft power sources include India's democratic values of federalism, secularism, pluralism as well as Gandhian concepts of non-violence and non-cooperation. India's peaceful and co-operative and legitimate foreign policy can also contribute to this country's soft power. Particular foreign policy initiatives and practices like the establishment of the Non-Aligned Movement and the support for the United Nations peace-keeping operations are only some of the legitimate foreign strategies of India. And these policies have promoted India's image abroad. India is not considered as an aggressive state but a responsible and peace-loving country.

Manifestations of India's Soft Power in Vietnam

The Spread of Buddhism in Vietnam

Buddhism is one of the most popular and widespread religions in Vietnam. This religion entered Vietnam a long time ago indirectly from China and directly from India. Because of Vietnam's geographical location, it "has been exposed to two main forms of Buddhism. The Mahayana form predominates in the north, where the Chinese influence is strongest, and the Theravada school has a presence in certain parts of the south near the Cambodia-Vietnam border, which has stronger links to the Buddhism of South-east Asia."[19]

In the past, Buddhism had a significant influence on Vietnam's feudal dynasties. For example, "by the time Vietnam achieved independence from China in the tenth century, Buddhism had been an integral part of the cultural landscape for over eight hundred years. The first emperor of independent Vietnam, Dinh Bo Linh, put together a system of hierarchical ranks for government officials, Buddhist monks, and Taoist priests after ascending to power in 968 C.E. Thereafter, Buddhist monks were part of the national administration, serving the ruler as advisors, rallying the people in times of crisis, and attending to the spiritual needs of the masses."[20]

After that, in the Lý Dynasty (1010–1225), Buddhism became "more widely disseminated among the common people, as monks came into villages and 'converted' local deities, ancestors, and cultural heroes to their religion and now declared them 'protectors of the *Dharma*'. This move worked to unify the disparate local cults under the Buddhist umbrella, and aided the unification of the country. In return, the Lý kings supported Buddhism lavishly: giving stipends to eminent monks, erecting and refurbishing temples, and sending envoys to China in search of scriptures."[21]

Then, many emperors of the Tran dynasty (1225–1400) "abdicated and retired to Mount Yan Tu to practice Buddhism full-time after Confucian careers as national rulers. Tran rulers also sponsored the establishment of the first actual 'schools' of Buddhism in Vietnam, beginning with the Truc Lam (Bamboo Grove) Chan school founded by the third Tran king. Missionary monks also arrived continuously from China, bringing both the Linji and Caodong schools into Vietnam, and they found a ready audience among the Tran aristocracy."[22]

In the present time, Buddhism is "arguably the most visible religion in Vietnam, although it is estimated that fewer than 10 per cent of the Vietnamese actively practice."[23] Buddhism in Vietnam "has a considerable contribution to the cultural community, the perception of the world, the society and the people, especially the promotion of the responsibility of every individual and the whole nation as well throughout history".[24]

Buddhism in Vietnam has been developing in the last few years. In fact, the number of Buddhist pagodas, festivals and followers has increased significantly. Furthermore, "the enhancement of the awareness of Buddhology for monks and nuns is implemented through the organization of workshops on Buddhism. The strong development of Buddhism in Vietnam is now beyond the national scope, which is shown by the fact that the Vietnamese Buddhism has been widely disseminated in many countries around the world by Buddhist monks. It can be said that the role and the position of Buddhism in the society has been constantly promoted."[25]

The Buddhist Sangha is "very involved in the community and temples often run schools, orphanages, medical clinics, and homes for the disabled. Lay people play an important role in religious life."[26]

Most monks and nuns enter the Buddhist temples at a young age and are encouraged to pursue higher education. In reality, "most Vietnamese Sangha go to university, and now some hold jobs as teachers, doctors, lawyers and journalists. Many are also proficient in foreign languages, especially Chinese and English."[27]

The main Buddhist festivals in Vietnam include Vesak (*Buddha's Birthday*) and Vulan (*Ullambana*). The Vietnamese people "traditionally visit the temple on the fifteenth day of the lunar month (in Vietnamese, it is called *Ram*), and also in the various festival days of the Mahayana Buddha's and Bodhisattvas. Committed lay people go through a formal ceremony of 'taking refuge', where they are given a Buddhist name. They wear a traditional grey costume over their normal clothes when they go to the temple, to signify their status as serious Buddhists."[28]

There is "great equality among monks and nuns, as there is between men and women throughout Vietnamese society. Monks are addressed as 'Thay' (Teacher), nuns as 'Su Co' (Sister). All Sangha take the name 'Thich' to signify that they have left their worldly family, and have joined the family of the Buddha. Buddhists greet each other by placing their palms together at chest level and saying, 'Mo Phat' (Praise Buddha). An alternative form of greeting is to recite the name of Amitabha Buddha."[29]

Vietnam organized the United Nations (UN) Day of Vesak 2019 from May 12–14 in the northern province of Ha Nam, attracting over 10,000 participants. According to the Vietnam Buddhist Sangha, "this is the third time the event is held in Vietnam. Earlier, the UN Day of Vesak was successfully organized in Hanoi in 2008 and in the northern province of Ninh Binh in 2014."[30] With the theme "Buddhist Approach to Global Leadership and Shared Responsibility for Sustainable Society", the UN Day of Vesak 2019 will "see the participation of 1,500 leaders of Buddhist organizations; professors, doctors, researchers and scholars of Buddhism, as well as Buddhist followers coming from some 90-100 countries and territories around the world, as well as 10,000 Vietnamese Buddhist followers and people".[31]

Nowadays, many Vietnamese Buddhist followers visit the Buddhist pilgrimage sites in India. They mostly visit Body Gaya, where the Buddha attained Enlightenment; Sarnath, where the Buddha "delivered his first sermon in the deer park";[32] Shravasti, where the Buddha delivered many important sermons and performed miracles;

Kushinagar, where the Buddha entered Nirvana; Sanchi, where many Buddhist stupas are located.

Moreover, there are many Vietnamese monks and nuns who come to India for Buddhist studies. They study in various Indian universities like Delhi University, Gautam Buddha University, Nalanda University, Sanchi University of Buddhist-Indic Studies, Pune University, etc.

International Day of Yoga in Vietnam

Yoga is regarded as "one of the most effective methods of establishing a connection between the body and mind by Indian sages since time immemorial. It is a type of exercise that is performed through diet, breathing and physical posture for the relaxation of body and mind. This ancient form of holistic healing got formal recognition by the United Nations General Assembly on December 11, 2014. The UN General Assembly formally recognized 21 June as World Yoga Day. The resolution, led by India, was adopted without vote by 177 out of the 193 countries that constitute the UN. It had 175 co-sponsors, the highest ever for any such resolution in the UN General Assembly."[33]

Indian Prime Minister Narendra Modi "first called for the adoption of June 21 as International Yoga Day while addressing the UN General Assembly on September 27, 2014. The resolution accomplishing this soon followed".[34] "Yoga is an invaluable gift of Indian ancient tradition. It embodies unity of mind and body, thought and action, restraint and fulfilment, harmony between man and nature, a holistic approach to health and well-being,"[35] Modi said.

"Yoga is harmony between yin and yang, man and nature, and male and female. Vietnamese people are clearly aware of this harmony," Indian Ambassador to Vietnam Parvathaneni Harish said. "I have visited many places in the world. But Vi t Nam is the only place where young and old, male and female, wake up at 5 A.M. to do morning exercises. The people always practise out in the open, close to nature. So I think that International Yoga Day, initiated by Indian people, will be warmly welcomed by Vietnamese people."[36]

On June 21 2015, the "first International Yoga Day was celebrated in different parts of the world. The main action was centred on the Indian capital of New Delhi, where a record number of 35,985 people from 84 different nations practiced yoga on Rajpath for 35 minutes. It was a world record in itself. It is estimated that around 200 million people worldwide practice yoga. The number stands at 20 million in the USA alone."[37] Vietnam was one of the first countries to co-sponsor the resolution.

Vietnam was also among the countries that organized the first International Yoga Day. In fact, "nearly 2,000 people gathered at a stadium in Hồ Chi Minh City on Sunday (June 21, 2015) to set a national record for the largest gathering in a yoga event. The event, which was also held in Hanoi, was to mark International Yoga Day, which was jointly organised by the Ministry of Sports, Culture and Tourism and the Indian Embassy in Vietnam. Singers Ho Ngoc Ha and Nguyen Phi Hung participated in the event in Ho Chi Minh City as ambassadors".[38] Mrs. Smita Pant, Indian Consul General in Ho Chi Minh City, said "the event aimed to promote yoga benefits and bilateral relations between India and Vietnam. She also called for yoga centres and clubs to open free classes at least once a month."[39]

Since 2015, cities in Vietnam have been organizing the International Yoga Day. The latest event was organized on June 16, 2018 in Hanoi: "More than 1,200 people joined a yoga protocol performance at Hanoi's Indoor Athletics Palace on June 16, 2018 in response to International Day of Yoga".[40]

Speaking at the ceremony, Indian Ambassador to Vietnam Parvathaneni Harish said that "Yoga has been even more popular worldwide since the United Nations General Assembly chose June 21 as the International Yoga Day following the proposal of Indian Prime Minister Narendra Modi".[41] Yoga has been a "key element contributing to the friendship and solidarity between Vietnam and India", he said, adding that "he has witnessed the popularity of yoga in Vietnam in the past two years living there. Yoga is India's gift to humanity," he stressed", given that Yoga helps people balance their bodies, mind and soul".[42]

Indian Restaurants in Vietnam

Thanks to the globalization process and the immigration of Indians to Vietnam, there are more and more Indian restaurants located in the big cities of Vietnam. A number of websites such as *Tripadvisor* and *atevietnam.com* have listed the names and addresses of the best or most famous Indian restaurants in Vietnam.

According to website *atevietnam.com,*[43] the best Indian restaurants in Ho Chi Minh City—the largest city in Vietnam, include:

1. Tandoor: Tandoor has always been one of the iconic Indian restaurants in Ho Chi Minh City. This restaurant serves both north and south Indian specialties. Also, it comes with both veg and non-veg favourites. Another outlet is situated in the centre of Saigon, it offers a favourable accessibility and an upscale environment. For those who have searched for good Indian restaurants in Hanoi, the name Tandoor has no longer been a strange thing.. The best thing about this brand name is that it maintains uniformity in the flavour and quality of service. The chefs are all Indians, ensuring the authenticity of the dishes.

2. Ganesh: Along with Tandoor, Ganesh has long claimed itself as one of the good Indian restaurants in Ho Chi Minh City with a long-lasting reputation. Ganesh has been slowly developing into a chain of restaurants and you can enjoy Ganesh dishes in either Saigon, Phu Quoc, or Nha Trang . The name Ganesh takes its origin from the name of a god in India—a symbol of wisdom, success and good luck. Unlike Tandoor, Ganesh offers a more dynamic atmosphere. People come, enjoy the dishes and lively discussions. So if you want something more like a casual restaurant in India, this one should be a good choice.

3. Baba's Kitchen: Ask Trip Advisor for the best Indian restaurants in Saigon, and you will always get its name. Baba's Kitchen is favoured by both local and foreign travellers. This place, despite not being a fancy-looking restaurant, is a place where people feel like home. The service is what makes it really stand out in any competition.

Baba's Kitchen is also known as an excellent restaurant with great generosity. It always includes freebies like a side dish or a sweet, offering guests an over-deliver concept. And more importantly, the pricing at this restaurant is a great pulling factor that attracts many travellers to come and enjoy the meals.

4. Namaste: Namaste is just a few doors away from Baba's Kitchen, but their flavours have never shared any similarity. If Baba's Kitchen gives the natives a feeling of home, Namaste is the perfect harmony of the Indian and Vietnamese atmosphere. In other words, it is where you can taste Indian dishes in a local manner.

The target of Namaste is backpackers as it offers an active and friendly atmosphere. This restaurant is where you can come and enjoy all three meals in a day. The diversity of the dishes in the menu will never let you down; they come with their own distinctiveness in their flavours and arrangement.

5. Saigon Indian: The list of best Indian restaurants in Saigon will never miss this name. Saigon Indian is the first Indian restaurant in HCM City that wins the award for outstanding food and service quality. This place provides a supreme authenticity of the dishes and a high-class quality of service.

The place is filled with a warm décor and a broad variety of mouth-watering Indian cuisine. Many travellers coming to Saigon have marked this place as a determining factor that made their trip so memorable. Saigon Indian is also favoured as one of the highest quality vegetarian restaurants in Saigon. The menu is compatible with both non-veg and veg gourmets.

6. Taj Mahal: Its space is tiny yet cosy, and if you want something hipster, Taj Mahal is a top recommendation. And even though this place is not a classy restaurant, it claimed a slot in the list of the best Indian restaurants in Saigon with its uniqueness of flavour. Muhammad Zaman opened Taj Mahal about ten years ago, and the reputation of this restaurant has risen ever since.

The menu comes with extensive dishes from lamb and chicken, to seafood and beef. Also, it offers a superior affordability, attracting most budget travellers and backpackers. Taj Mahal, in short, is an ideal and cost-effective place to escape from other usual Vietnamese local dishes.

7. Ganges: The Ganges is a place where you can customize your meals based on your spice quotient. It also gives a very welcoming ambiance, emphasizing on the friendly and customer-focused concept. The food is authentic, yet still has scope for guests to make it more fit to their specific taste.

The Ganges is thus a place where you can return many times

without the feeling of abundance. Every time you come back, the same dish you tried earlier can be different in the way you want it. This place is for those who always want to try something new but do not want to ruin the authentic flavour.

Vietnam and the Non-Aligned Movement

After being established in September 1961, the Non-Aligned Movement (NAM) "has become a leading multilateral forum for promoting international cooperation and dialogue, as well as protecting the legitimate rights of developing countries".[44]

Vietnam officially became a member of the Non-Aligned Movement in 1976. Since then, Vietnam "has increasingly cooperated with other members to strengthen the solidarity and promote peace, national independence, democracy, and social progress."[45]

Vietnam has made "active contributions to NAM's development through its struggle against foreign invaders for national independence. It attended the Asian-African conference, a precursor of NAM, in Indonesia in 1955 during which it helped strengthen solidarity among the newly-independent countries and formulate the basic principles of the movement."[46]

In the 1960s and 1970s, "Vietnam made great contributions to the struggle for national independence of NAM member countries and for eradication of colonialism and imperialism in the world. Since 1976, Vietnam has coordinated with other members to strengthen the solidarity in the common struggle for peace, national independence, democracy, social progress and development. Following the foreign policy guideline of independent diplomacy, self-reliance, multi-lateralisation and diversification of relationship, and global integration, set by the 11th National Party Congress, Vietnam will contribute more actively to the movement. Vietnam will work closely with other member-countries to maintain international peace and security and create a favourable environment for the development of each member-country by promoting dialogue to settle disputes and conflicts in compliance with the UN chapter and the basic principles of international law."[47]

Vietnam always upholds the Non-Aligned Movement's

foundational "principles and goals in respect to peace, stability, and national sovereignty. In addition, it has made practical contributions for the benefit of all members and for regional and international stability. As a non-permanent member of the United Nations Security Council (UNSC) in 2008-2009, Vietnam put forth many initiatives to gather opinions for the annual report on the UNSC operation which was highly appreciated at the 15th NAM summit in Egypt in 2009."[48]

According to Le Luong Minh, Vietnam's Deputy Minister of Foreign Affairs, Vietnam will "do its best to boost the movement's solidarity, persist in its operational principles, promote South-South cooperation, and deal with global issues such as the economic crisis, climate change, food and energy security. Vietnam will join efforts with other member countries to help reform the UN and other multilateral institutions and deal with the crisis more effectively."[49]

Angola Foreign Minister Manuel Domingo praised Vietnam's role as an active member of NAM: "With its political stability and economic growth, Vietnam will continue to play more actively in the movement".[50] Myanmar Foreign Minister Myo Mint said Vietnam plays a leading role in ASEAN and its economy is growing well. "I believe that Vietnam will improve its status and make more contributions to NAM",[51] Minister Mint added.

Indian Movies and TV Series in Vietnam

In recent years, Indian soap operas have been very popular in Vietnam. They are dubbed in Vietnamese language and broadcast in Vietnam's national and local television channels.

Balika Vadhu is an outstanding example. It an Indian soap opera that was aired on Vietnam's Today TV channel. The story, "which is set in rural Rajasthan, traces the arduous journey of a child bride from the brink of childhood to womanhood. The first season focuses on the life of Anandi and Jagdish, who were married in childhood. The second season reflects the lives of Anandi's daughter Nandini who was also a child bride. It has been credited as the first Indian show to surpass 2,000 episodes. When the blockbuster was introduced in Vietnam, it attracted a huge audience of different ages."[52]

In Vietnam, the drama began airing under the title *Cô Dâu 8 Tu i*

(8-Year-Old Bride) from 11 November 2014 and ended on 11 February 2017. It "has enjoyed immense popularity in Vietnam and during its run had been the number one show in the country since its premiere. The show's popularity resulted in the show's actress, Avika Gor, receiving an award from the channel head of Today TV. Gor also visited Vietnam on a two-day trip to the country to celebrate the success of the show; other cast members including Avinash Mukherjee and Smita Bansal also visited the country. The show was the ninth most searched item in 2015 in Vietnam on Google as confirmed by the annual Google Trends end-of-year report. The popularity of Balika Vadhu is part of a wider interest in Asian dramas in Vietnam, which experts say have a 'cultural edge over their Western counterparts' due to cultural similarities that are found in soap operas imported from South Asia, Southeast Asia and East Asia."[53]

Apart from soap operas and TV series which are available on Vietnam's TV channels, Indian movies are available on various websites. In these websites, Indian movies are subtitled in Vietnamese. One such website is https://phim3s.pw. In this website, we can see various new Indian movies such as *Uri: The Surgical Strike, Rajma Chawal, Thugs of Hindustan, October, Sonu Ke Titu Ki Sweety, Rocky Handsome, The Vision of Bharat, Stree, Baaghi, Raazi, Hichki, Padmavaat, Secret Superstar, Tiger Zinda Hai, Commando, Baahubali, Shivaay, Lion, Ae Dil Hai Mushkil, Kapoor and Sons, Rudhramadevi, Drishyam, Bajrangi Bhaijaan, Mary Kom,* etc

On December 18, 2015, the first ever Indian Film Festival-Vietnam kick-started in Ho Chi Minh City: "Organized by the Indian Embassy in Vietnam and the Directorate of Film Festivals, Ministry of I&B, Government of India, the six-day event was attended by award-winning film makers including Rakeysh Omprakash Mehra, Umesh Shukla and Bollywood producer Rahul Mitra".[54]

The program was initiated by "Smt. Preeti Saran, the Indian Ambassador to Vietnam, who feels this would be an ideal way to introduce Indian Cinema to the Vietnamese audience. Aimed at developing a deeper understanding and appreciation of Indian cinema and culture in Vietnam, this film festival will showcase big recent Bollywood hits like *'Bhaag Milkha Bhaag'*, *'Oh My God'*, *'Jodha Akbar'*,

'Taare Zameen Par', *'Wake Up Sid'*, *'Paheli'*, *'3 Idiots'*, *'Dil Chahta Hai'* and *'Maqbool'*. It will also offer the Vietnamese film industry a unique opportunity to learn about India's multi-faceted culture and long history of film making."[55] The festival will be "a great platform for the new generation of Indian producers and directors who are now seeking to re-launch Indian cinema on big screens in Vietnam. These film makers will attend a seminar titled "Vietnam – India Cinema Cooperation and its role in Promotion of Tourism" with a view to make films in Vietnamese locations."[56]

Hindi Day in Vietnam

Hindi is the fourth most spoken language of the world. In India, "Hindi is spoken as a first language by nearly 425 million people and as a second language by some 120 million more".[57] Thus, it is the most widely spoken language in India. The "first World Hindi Conference was held under the auspices of Rashtra Bhasha Prachar Samiti, Wardha, in Nagpur on 10 January 1975. In a meeting of the Follow-up Committee on the World Hindi Conference held on June 8, 2005 under the chairmanship of the then Minister of State for External Affairs, Rao Inderjit Singh, it was decided to commemorate 10 January as World Hindi Day every year. Accordingly, World Hindi Day was celebrated for the first time on 10 January 2006."[58]

The first World Hindi Day "was celebrated on 10 January 2006 by former Prime Minister Dr. Manmohan Singh. Since then, World Hindi Day is celebrated on 10 January every year".[59] It should be noted that "World Hindi Day is the promotion of the language at the global stage".[60]

Hindi has been taught "as part of Bachelor of Arts in Department of Indian Studies under Faculty of Oriental Studies at the University of Social Sciences and Humanities since 2000. Hindi is getting more and more popular in view of the widespread admiration for Indian TV serials, Bollywood films and songs in Vietnam with the result that an increasing number of people are keen on learning the language."[61]

Since 2007, "World Hindi Day has been celebrated in Vietnam, with most of the events held at the Ho Chi Minh City University of Social Sciences and Humanities, and at Tra Vinh University and An Giang University".[62]

A ceremony to mark World Hindi Day (January 10, 2012) "took place on Tuesday night at the residence of the Indian Consul General in Ho Chi Minh City's District 3. The event attracted around 100 people including teachers and students of the Ho Chi Minh City University of Social Sciences and Humanities, media organizations and other invited guests".[63] Participants had the opportunity to "listen to a letter by Indian Prime Minister Manmohan Singh to welcome World Hindi Day and students reciting poems and delivering speeches in Hindi language".[64] "Hindi is not only a language but an integral part of our civilization and culture. The Hindi language is poised to play a significant and valuable role in the progress of India, a country which is moving dynamically on the path of economic development," said former Prime Minister Manmohan Singh in the letter sent to the Indian Consulate General in Ho Chi Minh City. "We seek and expect your kind support in our efforts to achieve the status of an important world language for Hindi".[65]

On January 10, the Ho Chi Minh City University of Social Sciences and Humanities and the Consulate General of India in Ho Chi Minh City "successfully co-hosted World Hindi Day 2018 in celebration of Hindi winning recognition as the official language of India. The World Hindi Day 2018 welcomed distinguished delegates and international partners. On the host side, Prof. Dr. Vo Van Sen, USSH's President; Dr. Ho Minh Quang, Dean of Faculty of Oriental Studies and representatives from other departments and faculties attended the event. Joining the celebration, there were also international guests, including Dr. K. Srikar, Consul General of India in Ho Chi Minh City; Mr. Jasem MaMa Abomazouq, Second Secretary of the Consulate General of the State of Kuwait; Mr. Huynh Minh Thien, President of HCM City Union of Friendship Organizations; Mr. Nguyen Van Manh, Vice President-cum-General Secretary of HCM City Union of Friendship Organizations and more than 200 students".[66]

Prof. Dr. Vo Van Sen, President of the Ho Chi Minh City University of Social Sciences and Humanities presented the importance of Hindi in the world culture: "Hindi symbolizes for globalization while not only reinforcing the specific features of Indian culture but also simultaneously spreading its values to the world. Rooting from India-Aryan of Europe-India's language branch, Hindi has developed and connected closely to history of India Peninsula, absorbed and reserved the unique Indian culture. Hindi has also been enriched by values of the other cultures and civilizations. The Hindi speakers, therefore, can suitably adapt the language in various cultural and geographical spheres".[67] Moreover, he emphasized the role of the World Hindi Day in enhancing mutual understanding between India and other countries, including Vietnam.

Hindi seems to become an important language of the future due to India's emerging economic influence and population. Realizing Hindi's potential, the Indian Government has been making efforts to promote this language in many countries. Vietnam is not an exception to this trend. Thanks to Hindi classes and World Hindi Day, it is hopeful that the relationship between India will be more and more enhanced and strengthened.

Conclusion

Soft power is an increasingly important concept in international relations and diplomacy. A country's soft power is its ability to influence other countries by way of attraction. A country's soft power acts like a magnet pulling other countries towards it. In the present time, the role of soft power is becoming more and more crucial. It does not mean that hard power and its tools are no longer relevant or effective. Soft power can supplement hard power but cannot completely replace hard power.

Vietnam is a country in South East Asia. In the past and in the present, Vietnam has been influenced by India's cultural, spiritual and foreign policy legacies. India's soft power is visible in Vietnam. It is one of the first countries in South East Asia to adopt Buddhism. Meanwhile, the kingdoms located in modern Vietnam's territory adopted Hinduism as their national religion. We can still see the remnants of these buildings as well as cultural legacies in Central and Southern Vietnam. India's yoga is a global phenomenon and has spread to various countries in the world. And Vietnam is not an exception. One can easily find yoga centres in big cities of Vietnam like Hanoi and Ho Chi Minh City and Danang City. Moreover, Vietnam is one of the first countries to organize the International Day of Yoga.

Vietnam's big cities, especially Ho Chi Minh City, are home to Indian communities. These communities bring with them their cuisine and culture and festivals. As a result, in the last few years, dozens of Indian restaurants have been opened in a number of Vietnam's cities and attract many Vietnamese customers. Moreover, the Indian film industry is no longer alien in Vietnam. Bollywood hit movies such as *Three Idiots* and *PK*, and soap operas such as *Balika Vadhu* have been welcomed in Vietnam. And it is likely that in the future, Vietnam's film industry and Bollywood of India may join hands to produce movies together. Last but not least, India's masterpiece of foreign policy, the Non-Aligned Movement, has attracted Vietnam for the last decades. Vietnam joined the Non-Aligned Movement in 1976 and since then it has been contributing to its operation and activities.

It is obvious that India's soft power initiatives and efforts have promoted India's image in Vietnam. More Vietnamese people know about Indian culture and the spiritual legacies through movies and restaurants and cultural centres. However, India's image abroad is significantly shaped by its domestic policies and situations. India's domestic issues of sexual assault, gender inequality, pollution, sanitation, poverty, etc., have damaged India's reputation and brand abroad. Thus, India needs to make more efforts to improve its domestic issues before wielding soft power abroad.

NOTES

1. Joseph S. Nye, Jr., *Soft Power: The Means to Success in World Politics* (New York: Public Affairs, 2004), p. x.
2. Ibid.
3. Tridivesh Singh Maini, "Can Soft Power Facilitate India's Foreign Policy Goals", *The Hindu Centre for Politics and Public Policy*, https://www.thehinducentre.com/the-arena/current-issues/article8943319.ece, published on August 5, 2016.
4. Manish Chand, "India & Vietnam: Old Friends, New Vistas", https://www.mea.gov.in/in-focus-article.htm?23947/India+amp+Vietnam+ Old+ Friends+ New+Vistas, August 24, 2014.
5. Joseph S. Nye, Jr., *Soft Power: The Means to Success in World Politics* (New York: Public Affairs, 2004), p. x.
6. Patryk Kugiel, *India's Soft Power: A New Foreign Policy Strategy* (New Delhi: KW Publishers Pvt. Ltd., 2016), p. vii.
7. Shashi Tharoor, "Indian Strategic Power: Soft", https://www.huffpost.com/entry/indian-strategic-power-so_b_207785, May 25, 2011.

8. Joseph S. Nye, Jr., *Soft Power: The Means to Success in World Politics* (New York: Public Affairs, 2004), p. x.
9. Ibid, pp. 10-11.
10. Joseph S. Nye Jr., *The Powers to Lead* (New York: Oxford University Press, 2008), pp. 30 – 31.
11. Ibid, p. 31.
12. Joseph S. Nye, Jr., *Soft Power: The Means to Success in World Politics* (New York: Public Affairs, 2004), p. 8.
13. Joseph S. Nye Jr., *The Powers to Lead* (New York: Oxford University Press, 2008), p. 31.
14. Joseph S. Nye, Jr., *Soft Power: The Means to Success in World Politics* (New York: Public Affairs, 2004), p. 6.
15. Ibid, p. x.
16. Ibid, p. 8.
17. Patryk Kugiel, *India's Soft Power: A New Foreign Policy Strategy* (New Delhi: KW Publishers Pvt. Ltd., 2016), p. viii.
18. Ibid.
19. Charles S. Prebish & Damien Keown, *Introducing Buddhism (Second Edition)* (London and New York: Routledge, 2010), p. 158.
20. Ibid, p. 159.
21. Charles S. Prebish & Damien Keown, *Introducing Buddhism (Second Edition)* (London and New York: Routledge, 2010), pp. 159-160.
22. Ibid, p. 160.
23. Barbara O'Brien, "History of Buddhism in Vietnam", https://www.learn religions.com/buddhism-in-vietnam-450145
24. "Buddhism in Vietnam Culture in present", https://www.vietnamtravel.co/news/ buddhism-vietnam-culture-in-present.html
25. Ibid.
26. "Buddhism in Vietnam", https://www.buddhanet.net/e-learning/buddhist world/vietnam-txt.htm
27. "Buddhism in Vietnam", https://www.buddhanet.net/e-learning/ buddhistworld/vietnam-txt.htm
28. Ibid.
29. Ibid.
30. "Over 10,000 people to join UN Day of Vesak 2019 in Vietnam", http:// en.dangcongsan.vn/social-affairs/over-10-000-people-to-join-un-day-of-vesak-2019-in-vietnam-501211.html
31. Ibid.
32. "Top Buddhist Pilgrimage Sites in India", https://www.indiapilgrimtours.com/ articles/top-buddhist-pilgrimage-sites-india/, November 29, 2013.
33. "International Day of Yoga", http://www.yogadaycelebration.com/international-day-of-yoga.html
34. "Cities to celebrate International Yoga Day", https://vietnamnews.vn/life-style/ 298126/cities-to-celebrate-international-yoga-day.html#GULsj4I9FFHhKV52.97, June, 14/2016.

35. Ibid.
36. "Cities to celebrate International Yoga Day", https://vietnamnews.vn/life-style/298126/cities-to-celebrate-international-yoga-day.html#GULsj4I9FFHhKV52.97, June, 14/2016.
37. "International Day of Yoga", http://www.yogadaycelebration.com/international-day-of-yoga.html
38. Thien Kim, "Vietnam marks 1st International Yoga Day with national record", thanhniennews.com, http://www.thanhniennews.com/health/vietnam-marks-1st-international-yoga-day-with-national-record-46973.html, Monday, June 22, 2015.
39. Ibid.
40. "Fourth International Day of Yoga observed in Hanoi", https://en.vietnamplus.vn/fourth-international-day-of-yoga-observed-in-hanoi/133025.vnp, Sunday, June 17, 2018.
41. Ibid.
42. "Fourth International Day of Yoga observed in Hanoi", https://en.vietnamplus.vn/fourth-international-day-of-yoga-observed-in-hanoi/133025.vnp, Sunday, June 17, 2018.
43. "Best Indian Restaurant in Ho Chi Minh City", http://atevietnam.com/best-indian-restaurant-in-ho-chi-minh-city/
44. "Vietnam – an active member of the Non-Aligned Movement", https://english.vov.vn/politics/vietnam-an-active-member-of-the-nonaligned-movement-225484.vov, Thursday, 09/01/2011
45. Ibid.
46. "Vietnam – an active member of the Non-Aligned Movement", https://english.vov.vn/politics/vietnam-an-active-member-of-the-nonaligned-movement-225484.vov, Thursday, 09/01/2011
47. Ibid.
48. "Vietnam – a model in Non-Aligned Movement (NAM)", https://english.vov.vn/politics/vietnam-a-model-in-nonaligned-movement-nam-234327.vov, Tuesday, 09/06/2011.
49. "Vietnam – an active member of the Non-Aligned Movement", https://english.vov.vn/politics/vietnam-an-active-member-of-the-nonaligned-movement-225484.vov, Thursday, 09/01/2011.
50. "Vietnam – a model in Non-Aligned Movement (NAM)", https://english.vov.vn/politics/vietnam-a-model-in-nonaligned-movement-nam-234327.vov, Tuesday, 09/06/2011.
51. Ibid.
52. "Indian blockbuster actors visited Vietnam", https://english.vietnamnet.vn/fms/art-entertainment/160642/indian-blockbuster-actors-visit-vietnam.html, July 18, 2016.
53. https://en.wikipedia.org/wiki/Balika_Vadhu
54. Ambika Choudhary Mahajan, "Vietnam hosts first Indian Film Festival, will screen '3 Idiots', 'Jodha Akbar'", https://indianexpress.com/article/entertainment/bollywood/vietnam-hosts-first-indian-film-festival-will-screen-3-idiots-jodha-akbar/, December 19, 2015

55. Ibid.
56. Ibid.
57. "Hindi Language", https://www.britannica.com/topic/Hindi-language
58. University of Social Sciences and Humanities, Vietnam National University – Ho Chi Minh City, http://en.hcmussh.edu.vn/?ArticleId=4a238d05-b5d7-45db-a432-e3bf0092182d
59. "World Hindi Day 2019: Its Significance and How it is Different from Hindi Diwas", https://www.news18.com/news/india/world-hindi-day-2019-its-significance-and-how-it-is-different-from-hindi-diwas-1997425.html, January 10, 2019.
60. Ibid.
61. Indian Business Chamber in Vietnam, "World Hindi Day", http://www.incham.vn/en/events-cohost/past-events/world-hindi-day/
62. Kieu Giang, "World Hindi Day celebrated in town", https://english.thesaigontimes.vn/21385/World-Hindi-Day-celebrated-in-town.html, Thursday, Jan 12, 2012.
63. Kieu Giang, "World Hindi Day celebrated in town", https://english.thesaigontimes.vn/21385/World-Hindi-Day-celebrated-in-town.html, Thursday, Jan 12, 2012.
64. Ibid.
65. Ibid.
66. University of Social Sciences and Humanities, Vietnam National University – Ho Chi Minh City, http://en.hcmussh.edu.vn/?ArticleId=4a238d05-b5d7-45db-a432-e3bf0092182d
67. University of Social Sciences and Humanities, Vietnam National University – Ho Chi Minh City, http://en.hcmussh.edu.vn/?ArticleId=4a238d05-b5d7-45db-a432-e3bf0092182d

11

Buddhist Heritage and India's Soft Power Diplomacy: A Tool to Revitalize International Image

Arvind Kumar Singh

Mr. Narendra Modi, the Prime Minister of India,[1] once stated that India would emerge as a *Vishwa Guru* not only to give direction to the world but also to proect our own heritage. The idea is to highlight how India straddles ancient history and modernity. *"India is the world's youngest country and its most ancient"* and its ancient and modern cultures revitalize our international image. India's cultural heritage (Buddhist) is a source of inspiration to people everywhere. Its cultural exchanges with Buddhist countries are centuries old and continue to inspire people-to-people relationships. There is a visible impact of the Indian Buddhist heritage on the scriptures and the way of life of the people of those regions. There is a deep conviction about the Buddhist traits of humility, gentleness, justice and charity. There are many similarities in languages of the region with Sanskrit. The *Mahabharata*, the *Ramayana*, the *Panchatantra*, and the *Jataka Tales* are narrated with great enthusiasm and are a part of the folklore of these countries which are indicative enough of India's ancient connections in these countries and are well reflected in our relationship in present days.

In recent years, soft power has become an important component of foreign policy globally. There is no one definition that can truly encapsulate such a broad concept as Soft Power. The most commonly accepted definition of Soft Power was given by Joseph Nye:[2] *"The ability to get what you want through attraction rather than coercion or payment."* India, too, has been giving greater importance to Soft Power in the past two decades, ever since its economic status has risen. The Narendra Modi Government has made it an important tool in its foreign policy, yet a number of issues such as domestic politics and insufficient financial resources are proving to be major obstacles. This article aims to provide an overview of Indian Soft Power, the efforts being made by the current government for promotion of the same, and highlight some of the key drawbacks in the current strategy.[3]

Rich Buddhist Heritage of India and its Ancient Connections

The Modi-led government is placing a strong accent on the use of soft power in India's foreign diplomacy. India's Soft Power can be classified under a number of categories. One of the first and foremost is India's cultural and spiritual heritage that has played a key role in building links with other regions including East Asia and South East Asia. In the last decade or so, the aspiring global power began engaging in what has come to be called *'Buddhist diplomacy'* in its outreach to countries in the South, East and Southeast Asia. The Indian Government is diligently pursuing India's *'Buddhist agenda'* and taking it beyond its borders with an emphasis on the Indian and Hindu links with Buddhism. One of the more novel manifestations of these initiatives has been engagement in Buddhist diplomacy. The Buddhist faith, due to its emphasis on peaceful co-existence and its wide pan-Asian presence, lends itself well to soft-power diplomacy.

India has the advantage of being the historical founder the Buddha who was born in *Bharata Varsha* (Ancient India) and it was at Bodh Gaya (Ancient Name: Uruvela) that he obtained enlightenment, thereby gaining the title of the Buddha, the "Enlightened One." It was in India at Isipattana/Migadava at modern Sarnath that the Buddha delivered his first sermon; it was in India that he continued to teach the *Dharma*, and it was in India that he set up a continuing community: the Sangha.[4] Finally, it was in India at Kushinagara that he died. These sites have been linked together in the "Buddhist Circuit" by the Indian Government, organized domestically by the Ministry for Tourism but also used externally in Indian diplomacy. Their wider importance has been noted by government figures, who have acknowledged that it is very useful to focus on the Buddhist Circuit as well because that is one of the more important linkages that we have with Southeast Asian countries.[5]

Pranab Mukherjee has already laid claim to the Buddha's mantle (Buddhist heritage) for India and says that we can rightfully be proud that India is the *janma-bhoomi* ["land of birth"] and *karma-bhoomi* ["place of work"] of this great son of India. It is also a matter of pride for all Indians that it is we who nurtured and developed the Buddha's teachings and spiritual traditions at Nalanda, Vikramshila and other Buddhist centres after his *parinirvana*.[6] In addition, Mukherjee invoked Buddhist missionaries from India, going on to say that "his [the Buddha's] message of peace and tolerance was carried abroad by Indians".[7] The geographic range was broad, including Mahinda, the son of Emperor Ashoka, [carrying the message] to Sri Lanka, [...] Padmasambhava to Tibet, [...] Kashyapa Matanga and Bodhidharma to China, and [...] countless others to the vast swathe of our world from Central Asia to the islands of Japan.[8]

On the diplomatic benefits of invoking the Buddhist Heritage, Mukherjee already argued that "the renewed interest in Asia's Buddhist heritage will rekindle ancient links between East and South Asia and will help us come closer together".[9] Narendra Modi has taken a particularly strong lead in invoking the Buddha and Buddhism, a lead that represents *"an amalgamation of cultural and faith-based diplomacy"*.[10] Previously, as Chief Minister of Gujarat, Modi took a personal interest in the rediscovery of ancient Buddhist sites. He also made a point of visiting Buddhist events. At the Buddhist Heritage Seminar organized in Gujarat in January 2010, he celebrated the modern "relevance" of Buddhism and, irritatingly for China, went on to praise the "authority" of the Dalai Lama.[11] Currently, as Prime Minister, Modi has made highly positive comments about the figure of the Buddha, tweeting, *"On Buddha Purnima, we bow to the venerable Lord Buddha, whose teachings have guided the entire humanity for centuries"*.[12] He continued to make a point of attending important Buddhist-related events, being chief guest at the International Buddha Poornima Diwas celebrations (Vesak) in May 2015, organised by the International Buddhist Confederation. Modi has publicly embraced the Buddha as a reformer whose message has been re-absorbed into Hinduism.

Of course, this devalues the independent development of Buddhism as a religious tradition, but it enables Modi to use the Buddha to portray Hinduism in a better light and to shape a more Indian focus for Buddhism. Modi played a particularly prominent role at the Global Hindu-Buddhist Initiative on Conflict Avoidance and Environment Consciousness held in New Delhi in September 2015. He welcomed the delegates with domestic but also external nuances: "You are visiting a nation that is extremely proud of its Buddhist heritage [...which] draw pilgrims from ASEAN nations, as also from China, Korea, Japan, Mongolia, and Russia [...]. My government is doing everything possible to give an impetus to this Buddhist heritage across India, and India is taking the lead in boosting the Buddhist heritage across Asia."[13] On the third day, Modi joined the delegates for a trip to Bodh Gaya, leading a formal meditation session underneath the sacred Bodhi tree where the Buddha was supposed to have achieved enlightenment. Modi cited Vivekananda's earlier incorporation[14] of the Buddha into Hinduism and went on to assert, "I would personally call India "Buddhist India" as it has imbibed all the values and virtues of the teachings of Buddha by their [i.e., Hindu] religious scholars incorporating them in their literature."[15]

In effect, Modi made the Buddha into a national asset by incorporating his life into a Hindu context: "Buddha is the crown jewel of the Indian nation [...]. So, Hinduism after the Buddha's advent became Buddhist Hinduism or Hindu Buddhism"[16]. Furthermore, the holy sites of the Buddha's ministry were deployed as an international asset: I recognise how Buddhists all over the world revere Bodh Gaya as a place of pilgrimage. We in India would like to develop Bodh Gaya so that it can become the spiritual capital and civilisational bond between India and the Buddhist world. The Government of India would like to provide all possible support that its Buddhist cousin nations need for the satisfaction of their spiritual needs from this holiest of holy places for them.[17] In contrast, because of the nature of the Chinese political system and its underpinning ideology, Xi Jinping is unable to make such overtly "spiritual" use of Buddhism towards Chinese "political" ends. Alongside this official domestic embrace and further use of Buddhism within India, there has been a noticeable external invocation of the Buddha and of Buddhism within Indian diplomacy under Modi.[18] It is quite clear that the Modi government is *"keen on drawing up a Buddhist connect as part of its Look East, Act East policy,"* and to add further that *"Mr. Modi is well aware of the connections that Buddhism has in the entire region, and who better to string it together than India, the home of the Buddha"*.[19] India's soft-power bridge of Buddhism was invoked at length during Modi's visits to Mongolia, Sri Lanka, Vietnam and Japan, whereas Xi Jinping's visits to those countries had no similar Buddhist invocations. This is not to suggest that Buddhism is the most important feature in India's relationship with those countries. Rather, the geo-cultural invocation of Buddhism facilitates the geo-political advantages of drawing Sri Lanka and Myanmar out of China's orbit and strengthening security cooperation with Mongolia, Vietnam and, above all, Japan, who have similar concerns about a rising China. Soft-power linkages thereby feed into the hard power–balancing behaviour that IR realism theory would expect.[20]

India has been reaching out to East Asian and South East Asian countries through Buddhism in the past. During his visits to Sri Lanka, Japan, Mongolia and China, Prime Minister Modi sought to draw upon India's Buddhist links with these countries and visited important shrines like the Sri Mahabodhi Temple in Anuradhaprua in Sri Lanka, Toji and Kinkakuji Buddhist Temples in Japan and the Wild Goose Pagoda in Xian, China, dedicated to the famous Buddhist pilgrim, Hieun Tsang.[21] Interestingly, Xian also happens to be the Chinese President Xi Jinping's hometown and was Modi's first stop during his China visit. Modi also inaugurated the Buddha Poornima Diwas celebrations in New Delhi in 2015 stating, 'Without Buddha, this century cannot be Asia's.[22]

Why Buddhist Heritage as Soft Power Diplomacy

Buddhism's potential utility in foreign policy is derived to a large extent from the manner in which the faith was revived in the aftermath of the Second World War. The revival of the faith had a decidedly internationalist outlook to it, and focused on transgressing extant sectarian and geographical boundaries. This was facilitated by the foundation of a number of organizations and the convening of numerous councils and conferences in the decades after the war that emphasized on transnational cooperation amongst various sects of Buddhism.[23] This began with a conference organized in newly independent Sri Lanka, where the World Fellowship of Buddhists was founded.[24] In 1952, in Pt. Jawaharlal Nehru's time, India hosted the International Buddhist Conference in Sanchi which was attended by over 3,000 Buddhist nuns, monks, scholars and followers. At that time, it was one of the largest gatherings of Buddhist preachers and followers in the world.[25] In 1954, the Sixth Buddhist Council[26] was convened in Burma. In the decades since, the tradition of holding conferences and convening councils has continued, strengthening the global network of Buddhism.

In East Asia, Japan and South Korea began embracing their Buddhist heritage as they recovered in the decades following the end of the Second World War, as did a number of former members of the Soviet Union after the Cold War.[27] Today, 97 per cent of the world's Buddhist population lives in the Asian continent, and a number of countries such as Bhutan, Myanmar, Thailand, and Sri Lanka conceive of Buddhism as intrinsic to their national values and identity.[28] It is within this context that one can understand the efforts of the Indian Government at incorporating the Buddhist heritage in order to form a basis for further diplomatic, economic, cultural, and strategic associations within its foreign policy. The established transnational network for Buddhism, and the important role played by the faith in the lives of millions across the world, is what allows it to possess the potential for Indian foreign policy. The pan-Asian presence of the religion and its importance for national identities in the region, coupled with its image as a peaceful religion makes it ideal for soft power diplomacy, with its focus on non-coercive power.[29]

Recent Developments in Soft Power Diplomacy

The present Indian Government's interest under Prime Minister Modi in India's indulgence[30] in Buddhism is not a religious exercise but a cultural one; the Prime Minister has in fact taken an audacious approach in linking Buddhism and Hinduism, while attempting to build on India's soft power and providing an impetus to his government's *Look East, Act East* policy through the promotion of Buddhism. For instance, Buddhist and Hindu influences have helped in building strong links with South East Asia. If one were to examine the efforts by the current Government to promote soft power, its focus has been on Ayurveda, Yoga, and Buddhism, besides reaching out pro-actively to the Indian Diaspora. A major success in this regard is the international recognition accorded to Yoga. In 2015, on the Indian Prime Minister's appeal, the United Nations General Assembly (UNGA) declared June 21 as International Yoga Day. Since then, the day has been celebrated with mass yoga practice, not just by overseas Indians and staff of Indian embassies but also by people of other nationalities.[31]

Viewing the recent developments, it seems that India was rather late in realizing the potential of its Buddhist legacy relative to China which has taken a remarkable interest in developing the few Buddhist sites on its territory and is also reaching out to SAARC, ASEAN, BIMSTEC, etc. The development of Buddhist sacred and academic sites in India should remain high on the priority list of government authorities. Meanwhile, the Public Diplomacy Division of the Ministry of External Affairs (MEA) can play an important role in helping India assert its Buddhist links by encouraging transnational academic exchanges and collaborations.

Documentaries and films elucidating India's rich past and Buddhist connection can also aid India in enhancing its soft power. Apart from academic collaboration, there is also enormous potential for partnership in the development sector. Though there have been such involvements, India can further encourage and call for foreign investments to develop its Buddhist sites. Such collaboration will not only benefit India but also enable its investing neighbour to gain goodwill among the Buddhists back home.

The plan to encourage Buddhist tourism by developing a *Buddhist Circuit* is an important initiative of the Ministry of Tourism along with the Bihar and Uttar Pradesh tourism departments and International Finance Corporation (World Bank Group). The planned circuit will be connecting Buddha's birthplace, Lumbini in Nepal, to Varanasi,

Shravasti and Kushinagar in Uttar Pradesh; and Bodh Gaya, Vaishali and Rajgir in Bihar. In the next phase, the Buddhist Tourist Circuit will cover 17 states, including Madhya Pradesh, Maharashtra, and Odisha. The Government of India has taken constructive steps in the direction of promoting India's Buddhist heritage.[32] During the Prime Minister's visit to China, a Memorandum of Understanding was signed between the Indian Council for Cultural Relations and Fudan University on starting a Centre for Gandhian and Indian Studies which would also focus on research on Buddhism and ancient India-China contacts.[33] While Modi might be aware of the possibility of stepping on China's toes when furthering India's Buddhist diplomacy in Asia, he has constructively employed India's Buddhist heritage to connect with China as well. In September 2014, ahead of Chinese President Xi Jinping's visit to India, Narendra Modi stressed that Buddhism is a very strong bond between China and India.[34] He emphasised the same links in China in May 2015, while acknowledging that the relationship has been complex in recent decades and stated that "we have a historic responsibility to turn this relationship into a source of strength for each other and a force of good for the world."[35]

In spite of Modi's enthusiasm and the progressive steps he has taken, there are limitations and challenges that the Prime Minister faces in furthering his Buddhist diplomacy. As Modi highlighted in Bodh Gaya, in India Buddhism is often considered merely a derivative of Hinduism, and Gautam Buddha, a part of the Hindu pantheon. This was not the case, however, when Buddhism was founded in India. While Gautam Buddha was indeed Hindu and a prince, he opposed a number of Hindu practices and found little good in traditional Hinduism. Some evidence suggests that during the reign of King Ashoka and the Gupta dynasty there was a struggle between Hinduism and Buddhism to gain control of India.[36] In September 2015, in Bodh Gaya, Modi mentioned that the Buddha played an important role in the *enlightenment* of Hinduism.[37] Belonging to a party based on Hindu nationalist principles, Modi treads carefully so as to not relegate Hinduism to second-fiddle while exalting Buddhism.

Analysts point out that given his party's alliances and inclinations, overtly pushing a religion could have domestic political repercussions.[38] The domestic debate on secularism will also be brought up if the Prime

Minister is perceived to be overstepping certain religious lines. While Modi runs the risk of overdoing and upsetting domestic constituencies, conversely there is also the debate about sustaining the Government's interest in the topic. It has been argued that the Buddhist constituency in India is of no political significance, to begin with, and the *pressure* to pursue any form of Buddhist diplomacy emanates only from outside the country. The lack of emotional commitment to the cause has also been cited to explain India's neglect of Buddhist diplomacy.[39]

Discussing the role of soft power in Indian foreign policy, David M. Malone has spoken of the time when India's cultural diplomacy was perceived as gauche. Laden with ideas of cultural superiority, it seemed to put forward the notion that some Southeast Asian countries were India's cultural colonies.[40] While integrating Buddhism into a national soft power strategy, Narendra Modi will have to bear in mind the precedents, limitations and challenges posed by such endeavours. Though Modi understands fairly well that religion can be connected to foreign policy, he must comprehend that his initiative has cultural as well as faith-based underpinnings and needs to be handled with the utmost political care and diplomatic competence.

A Way Forward for Buddhist Heritage and Soft Power Diplomacy

The entire Thai landscape in tourist havens such as Bangkok, Chiang Mai and Authiyya (Ayodhya) is lit up with Buddhist shrines. Likewise, in Cambodia, the magnificent and 12th- century Hindu temple in Angkor Wat is respected, preserved and cherished, like Buddhist shrines elsewhere in the country. In Myanmar, the gold-plated pagodas in Yangon, Mandalay and elsewhere and the 2,200 Buddhist temples and shrines constructed between the 9th and 12th centuries in Pagan are preserved with pride. These traditions are also observed meticulously in Japan, South Korea and Taiwan. There are today an estimated 600 million Buddhists in the world. A serious effort will have to be mounted by the Indian Government to develop India as the Asian epicentre for Buddhist Tourism and Studies. Connectivity has to be established and improved through road, rail and air, linking Buddhist sites starting from Lumbini on the Indo-Nepal border, and heritage sites such as Bodh Gaya, Bharhut, Amaravati, Shravasti, Sankasya,

Nalanda and Rajgir, together with other commemorative monuments in Sanchi, Amaravati, Ajanta, Ellora, Kanheri and Karli. Developing India as the epicentre of Buddhist heritage will receive external funding and support if the countries of East and Southeast Asia are associated as partners. There would be substantial interest if foreign investment in heritage infra-structure were combined with offers by India for the governments of Buddhist countries to construct temples and pagodas portraying their distinct national architectural styles, in select Buddhist heritage sites in India. This is an issue which should be discussed individually and collectively with ASEAN members, and even raised at the East Asia Summit. All this will require an imaginative effort by the Government, in partnership with the domestic tourism industry and its foreign counterparts.

In these circumstances, India's Act East policies will receive a boost if it acts imaginatively in building infrastructure and promoting Buddhism not only in India but abroad as well through its embassies, consulates, SVCCs, etc., which will serve as a catalyst for increasing Buddhist tourism, and promoting academic and other exchanges on the life and message of the Buddha. Such initiatives will create a pro-India environment in Buddhist countries which in turn will be beneficially from the diplomatic point of view or International Relations. With Nalanda University focusing, according to its former chancellor, on "secular" education, the University for Buddhist and Indic Studies in Sanchi needs to step in expeditiously as the country's premier institution for Buddhist Studies. Recently, the International Buddhist Confederation (IBC) has started to grant scholarship to those foreign nationals who are interested in studying Buddhism in India. This is going to be a major boost for soft power diplomacy through the Buddhist Heritage.

Under the banner of India's 'Act East' policy, the Indian Government has used culture to appeal to the peoples of Asia through Buddhism and hosted the *International Buddha Poornima Diwas*, a global celebration of Buddha's birth, enlightenment and passing. The decision to host this event in India was initiated by PM Modi who stated *"Without the Buddha this century cannot be Asia's century"*. Thus, the Government is trying to promote India as the spiritual birthplace of Buddhism and the home of the Buddha. The utilization of Buddhism does not necessarily contradict Hindutva ideology, which seeks to protect and promote all that is deemed Indian heritage, including Buddhism, Jainism and Sikhism. One of India's aims with Buddhism is to neutralize any Chinese soft power advantage. China's foreign ministry has recently sought to elevate Buddhism's role as a foreign policy tool. Beijing has the benefit and cache of having the world's largest Buddhist population and is said to be undergoing a Buddhist renaissance under President Xi Jinping. India has only a small number of Buddhists, many from poorer sections of society.[41]

While China has been helping build and preserve monasteries in Burma, Thailand, and Cambodia, Modi visited Buddhist monasteries during his trips to Japan, South Korea and Mongolia where, like for other Asian countries, he gifted a sapling of the sacred Bodhi tree. India can compete through highlighting not only Buddhism, but also Hinduism and Sanskrit as its ancient ties to the region. The largest and most influential ASEAN member, Indonesia, has a language influenced by Sanskrit, a coat of arms containing the 'Garuda' a bird from Hindu mythology, and boasts notable Buddhist and Hindu temples. Cultural diplomacy was also deployed in India's own neighbourhood. Buddhism was used to appeal to Bhutan and Nepal. Modi's efforts perhaps yielded most significant results in Sri Lanka, one of the oldest Buddhist countries. If geopolitical history and strategic and economic interests were the sole determiners of India's reputation in the island, India would lag behind China. Modi has managed to reduce this gap in part through appealing to ancient Indo-Lankan Buddhist ties, dating back to the Mauryan Empire under Ashoka.

Conclusion

There is a general feeling among the people of Buddhist countries that "India does not have to worry about its connection with powerful countries of the world because it may go to any other countries for weapons and support, but for salvation we are bound to go to India especially Bodh Gaya." Yet India does not truly value this extraordinary legacy, let alone taking pride on it.

India gave the world one of its most precious resources, the Buddha. Yet India does not truly value this extraordinary legacy, let alone take pride in it." Buddhist scholars note that the even the historic Nalanda

University, which attracted scholars from Tibet, China, Korea and Central Asia for centuries before being razed to the ground by Bakhtiyar Khilji in 1193, has adopted a syllabus that virtually excludes teachings on the Buddhist heritage. In marked contrast, China, which endeavoured to discard its religious heritage during the Mao era, opened up in the 1970s. There are now emerging signs of a Buddhist revival, although under strict state control. China today boasts of the richest collection of Buddhist heritage sites, viz., Mogador Caves, Longmen Grottoes, Dazu rock carvings, the Leshan Giant Buddha, etc.

Culturally, India is in a good position in South East Asia with common bonds of Buddhism and Hinduism. Cultural diplomacy can thrive because many Indian symbols are accepted. For a real appreciation of Indian culture, scholarly exchanges are necessary. The ICCR centres need to be considered as investments for cultural dissemination. India has strong institutions for the dissemination of culture, language and art forms. I hope the Modi Government will create more opportunities and facilities to receive artists, journalists and tourists.

NOTES

1. Martin, Peter, "Yoga Diplomacy - Narendra Modi's Soft Power Strategy", *Foreign Affairs*, May 2015.
2. Nye, Jr., Joseph. "Soft Power: The Means to Success in World Politics" New York: Public Affairs, (2004). p. 10.
3. Maini, Tridivesh Singh, 'Can Soft Power Facilitate India's Foreign Policy Goals?' published in *The Hindu Centre for Politics and Public Policy* on August 5, 2016.
4. Scott, David (2016), 'Buddhism in Current China–India Diplomacy', in *Journal of Current Chinese Affairs*, 45, 3, published by GIGA German Institute of Global and Area Studies, Institute of Asian Studies and Hamburg University Press, 2016: 139–174. ISSN: 1868-4874 (online), www.CurrentChineseAffairs.org
5. Akbaruddin, Syed (2014), *Media Briefing by Secretary (East) on the Coming ASEAN and East Asia Summits*, 8 November, online: http://mea.gov.in/media-briefings.htm?dtl/24213 (10 July 2016).
6. Mukherjee, Pranab (2008), *Speech by Shri Pranab Mukherjee, Hon'ble Minister for External Affairs at 8th Buddha Mahotsava, Tawang*, 9 November, online: http://mea.gov.in/Speeches-Statements.htm?dtl/1759 (10 July 2016).
7. Ibid.
8. Ibid.
9. Mukherjee, Pranab (2007), *Statement by External Affairs Minister Shri Pranab Mukherjee at the EAS Foreign Minister's Lunch*, 31 July, online: www.mea.gov.in/press-releases.htm?dtl/2478/ (10 September 2016).

10. Chauhan, Rishika, *Modi and Buddhism: Between Cultural and Faith-Based Diplomacy*, ORF Occasional Paper, 77, 30 November, 2015: 2 online: www.orfonline.org/wp-content/uploads/2015/12/OP_77.pdf (10 July 2016).
11. Modi, Narendra (2010), *Shri Narendra Modi's Speech in Buddhist Heritage Seminar*, 15 January, online: www.youtube.com/watch?feature=player_embedded &v=DTW5wZJXpQ8 (10 July 2016).
12. Modi, Narendra (2014a), *Tweet*, 13 May, online: https://twitter. com/ narendramodi/status/466468362240135168/photo/1 (10 July 2016).
13. Modi, Narendra (2015e), *Text of PM's Address at "Samvad" – Global Hindu –Buddhist Initiative on Conflict Avoidance and Environment Consciousness*, 3 September, online: http://pib.nic.in/newsite/PrintRelease. aspx?relid=126588 (10 July 2016).
14. Long, Jeffery (2005), Claiming the Buddha for Hinduism: Swami Vivekananda and the Rediscovery of Buddhism in India, in: Sukalyan Sengupta (ed.), *The Cyclonic Swami: Vivekananda in the West*, New Delhi: Samvad India, 113–120.
15. Modi, Narendra (2015f), *Text of PM's Address at Mahabodhi Temple in Bodh Gaya*, 9 September, online: http://pmindia.gov.in/en/news_updates/text-of-pms-address-at-mahabodhi-temple-in-bodhgaya/ (10 July 2016).
16. Modi, Narendra (2015e), *Text of PM's Address at "Samvad" – Global Hindu –Buddhist Initiative on Conflict Avoidance and Environment Consciousness*, 3 September, online: http://pib.nic.in/newsite/PrintRelease.aspx?relid=126588 (10 July 2016).
17. Modi, Narendra (2015e), *Text of PM's Address at "Samvad" – Global Hindu –Buddhist Initiative on Conflict Avoidance and Environment Consciousness*, 3 September, online: http://pib.nic.in/newsite/PrintRelease.aspx?relid=126588 (10 July 2016).
18. Mohan, Raja C. (2015), Faith and Diplomacy, in: *Indian Express*, 1 September, online: http://indianexpress.com/article/opinion/columns/faith-and-diplomacy/ (10 July 2016); Mohan, Raja C. (2014), Modi's Buddhism, in: *Indian Express*, 3 December, online: http://indianexpress.com/article/opinion/editorials/chinesetakeaway-modis-buddhism/ (10 July 2016).
19. Haidar, Suhasini (2015), Buddha Link High on PM's Eastern Foray, in: *The Hindu*, 3 April, www.thehindu.com/news/national/buddha-link-high-on-narendra-modis-look-east-act-east- policy/article7062839.ece (10 July 2016).
20. Scott, David (2016), 'Buddhism in Current China–India Diplomacy', in *Journal of Current Chinese Affairs*, 45, 3, published by GIGA German Institute of Global and Area Studies, Institute of Asian Studies and Hamburg University Press, 2016: 139–174. ISSN: 1868-4874 (online), www.CurrentChineseAffairs.org
21. Kasturi, C.S., 'Modi govt plans Buddhism blitz in cultural diplomacy refocus', *The Telegraph*, August 31, 2015. Last accessed August 4, 2016.
22. Maini, Tridivesh Singh, op. cit.
23. Kishwar, Shantanu, The Rising Role of Buddhism in India's Soft Power Strategy, published in ORF Issue Brief No. 228, 1 February 2018.
24. Juyan Zhang, 'Revival of Buddhism after the WWII' published in *Buddhist Diplomacy: History and Status Quo*, Los Angeles: Figueroa Press, 2012: 23.
25. Sharma, Suresh K. and Sharma, Usha, 'The Great Sanchi Congregation' published in *Cultural and Religious Heritage of India: Buddhism*, New Delhi: Mittal Publications, 2004: 287.

26. Juyan Zhang, 'Revival of Buddhism after the WWII', published in *Buddhist Diplomacy: History and Status Quo*, Los Angeles: Figueroa Press, 2012: 23.
27. Juyan Zhang, 'Revival of Buddhism after the WWII'. published in *Buddhist Diplomacy: History and Status Quo*, Los Angeles: Figueroa Press, 2012: 23.
28. Stobdan, P., 'As China Pushes for a Buddhist Globalisation, India Isn't Making the Most of Its Legacy', in *The Wire*, May 15, 2017. https://thewire.in/133670/india-china-buddhist/
29. Kishwar, Shantanu, The Rising Role of Buddhism in India's Soft Power Strategy, published in ORF Issue Brief No. 228, 1 February 2018.
30. Suhasini Haider, 'Buddha link high on PM's eastern foray', in *The Hindu*, April 3, 2015.
31. Ibid.
32. Annual Report, 2013-2014, Ministry of Tourism, Government of India, available at http://tourism.gov.in/writereaddata/Uploaded/Tender/081220141131463.pdf Accessed May 27, 2015
33. List of Agreements signed during the visit of Prime Minister Narendra Modi to China, Ministry of External Affairs, Government of India, May 15, 2015, available at http://www.mea.gov.in/bilateral- documents.htm?dtl/25260/List+of+Agreements+signed+during+the+visit+of+Prime+Minister+to+China+May+15+2015. Accessed May 20, 2015.
34. Narendra Modi, "Buddhism a very strong bond between China and India", September 15, 2014, available at http://www.narendramodi.in/pm-buddhism-isa-very-strong-bond-between-china-and-india Accessed May 27, 2015
35. Prime Minister's Media Statement in Beijing during his visit to China, May 15, 2015, available at http://www.mea.gov.in/outoging-visit-detail.htm?25239/Prime+Ministers+Media+Statement+in+Beijing+during+his+visit+to+China+May+15+2015. Accessed May 27, 2015
36. Sheen Vincent, The Buddhism that was India, in *Foreign Affairs*, Vol. 29, Issue 2, January 1951: 289.
37. Prime Minister Modi's speech at Bodh Gaya, https://www.youtube.com/watch?v=frpjW6oPUBM Accessed on September 8, 2015.
38. Waghamode, Vishwas, 'India was a Buddhist country: Maharashtra OBCs plan 'ghar wapsi' from Hinduism', *First Post*, December 30, 2014, available at http://www.0rstpost.com/india/india-was-a-buddhist-country-maharashtraobcs- plan-ghar-wapsi-from-hinduism-2021943.html. Accessed on June 1, 2015
39. Sepala Weliwitigoda, "India's Buddhist Soft Power Diplomacy", *Pulse: Linkedin*, March 31, 2015 https://www.linkedin.com/pulse/indias-buddhist-soft-powerdiplomacy-sepala-weliwitigoda. Accessed on June 1, 2015.
40. David M. Malone, 'Soft Power in Indian Foreign Policy', *Economic and Political Weekly*, Vol. 46, No. 36, September 3, 2011.
41. Pethiyagoda, Kadira, *Modi Deploys His Culture Skills in Asia.*

12

The Significance of Buddhism in Buryatia (Federal Republic of Russia)

Amit Kumar

The influence of Central Asian culture and Buddhism is vital in terms of the identity formation of Buryats. Buddhism has been existing in Buryatia since the seventeenth century and it penetrated from Mongolia and Tibet. From then onwards, especially its Eastern part, has ceaselessly been under the influence of Mongolian Buddhism. The influence of Christianity is more visible in the Western part. Somehow, Buddhism managed to survive during the socio-economic and cultural breakdown fostered by the communist regime under Soviet rule. The genuine revival of Buddhism began with the introduction of *Perestroika* which granted religious freedom. Apart from this, Yeltsin's move to grant maximum sovereignty to regions in the post-Soviet period also created cultural revivalism in regions like Buryatia and by striking at the Buryats' Pan-Mongolian[1] identity, the intellectuals of this school touched upon their Mongolian origin and gave them adequate reason to integrate. This Pan-Mongolism was also used for political benefits, and, as a consequence, in 1992, a non-governmental political organisation 'Negedel' was formed. This organisation was blamed for propagating the secession of Buryatia from Russia and championed to create a Central Asian Confederation. Thus, against this background, the present paper attempts to study the significance of Buddhism in preserving the Buryats' distinct identity along with underlining the penetration of Mongolian Buddhism to the region since the seventeenth century and its recent politicization in the post-Soviet period. Apart from this, this research paper also strives to study the spread of the Tantric creed of Buddhism from India to Tibet, and then to Buryatia. Particularly, the last theme of this paper shall focus on the Indian connection with special reference to Tantric Buddhism and its penetration in Buryatia.

Historical Context

The Republic of Buryatia is a subject of the Russian Federation and it is part of the Far Eastern Federal District. It is located in the southern part of Eastern Siberia, to the South and to the East of Lake Baikal (The Republic of Buryatia Official Portal 2019). Thirty per cent population of the Republic is ethnic Buryats while 66.1 per cent comprises ethnic Russians. The ethno-federal basis of the federal power division under the Soviet rule accorded the status of a Republic to this region. 'Buryats', shares ancestral lineage with the ancient Mongolians and their forefathers were the early inhabitants of the Lake Baikal region. They are the northern-most Mongol-speaking people, occupying the steppe and riversides to the east, south, and west of Lake Baikal. Lake Baikal located in southern Siberia has a long history of human habitation (Krader 1954: 322).

The forefathers of the Buryat and Yakut ethnic groups, known as *Kurykan*, were the early tribe who inhabited the Lake Baikal region. Buryats are descendent of Mongol and their origin can be traced from the Mongol civilisation. This has been the reason for identical cultural practices shared by the Buryats with that of Mongolic tradition. Similarly, Lake Baikal finds special mention in the development of Buryat society near it. The Buryat people have traditionally been pastoral nomadic with mastery over hunting. Their herds consist of cattle, sheep, goats, horses and camels (Ibid.).

However, this traditional occupation started to recede during the course of the nineteenth century. The Buryats came in contact with the Russians and gradually developed sedentary agriculture. Nonetheless, the Buryats became stable at one place; inevitably they completely lost their traditional occupation of hunting for livelihood and pastoralism (Ibid.). The Buryats are a sparsely populated community. As per the 2010 census, the total population of Buryatia was 972,021 with a population density was 2.8 people per square kilometre square (The Official Census of the Russian Federation 2010). At present, Buryats are scattered in the Russian Federation, Mongolia and China; however, their highest number lives in the republic of Buryatia (Hurelbaatar 2000: 73).

The Shamanistic tradition of Buryatia is derived from the Mongols and this is widely practised by them especially by the elder populations. Shamanism is based on their belief in extra-mundane affairs, a kind of belief that the everyday happenings of their life are somehow connected to the spirit world. Contextually, the Shaman is key link of this practice—a person who can establish connection with the spirit world and can explain the present condition of an individual in relation to the spirit world. In the Buryat tradition, the Shaman is a very powerful person; he not only can cure any ill person, but can rather also extend life by a few years (Krader 1975: 105-144). Every aspect of Buryat life, i.e., from birth to death, is guided by Shamanistic practices. Nevertheless, being key values of Buryat life, Shamanism has been abandoned in past and only its private aspect is surviving today. It is present in the cities as well as in the countryside. The present form of Shamanism is divinatory as well as therapeutical, which means that on the one hand it is related to human health while on the other it relates to luck, love, fertility, success and achievement in business. Shamanistic practices are not present in a fixed text form. It totally depends upon the competency and skill of the individual Shaman. Each Shaman has his own way of doing things and dealing with individual cases. The efficacy of Shamanic practices depends upon the individual capacity of the Shaman (Hamayon 1998: 52-57).

The penetration of Tibetan Buddhism in Buryatia became apparent from the eighteenth century especially among the Buryats of Trans-Baikalia. It came from Mongolia and Buddhist doctrine made inroads into Buryat soil with the use of the native language. It also used indigenous proselytes (newcomers), who themselves were from Mongolia, to spread Buddhism among the tribes. Primarily, there were two important factors responsible for the rapid spread of Buddhism in Buryatia; first, the clergy of Buryatia, in order to use it for their own use in terms of their own obscure foreign origin, quickly transformed this into a dynamic of hierarchical centralisation. Since they were relying on strong wealthy organizations, therefore, they soon opened monasteries that became centres of attraction for the nomads. Second, Buddhism in Buryatia was encouraged by the Russian Empire itself. It was invited to Trans-Baikalia by the request of the Tsarist government to effectively highlight the frontier settlement with China fixed by the Treaty of Burinsk of 1728 (Ibid: 55).

Buddhism therefore, became a significant political instrument in Russia, and its political use continued in the beginning of the Communist regime in Russia. In particular, the clergy used it for organising literary classes in Mongolian. Buddhism that experienced remarkable expansion in the early period of the Soviet rule. However, during the Russification campaign of the 1930s, the number of lamas came down from 16,000 in 1917 to 900 in 1936. Most of the monasteries were either closed or destroyed (Ibid.).

There were two attempts to establish a Buddhist state in Siberia; the great Mongolia attempt in 1919 and another attempt was made by a well–known Buryat yogi, Sandan Tsydenov, in the same period. Apart from this, the actual destruction of Buddhism started after the end of the civil war in 1923 with the final blow coming with the announcement of the 'collectivisation programme' in 1929. This led to a total breakdown of the social, economic and cultural life (Terentyel 1996: 63-64).

After the end of the Second World War, Stalin accepted a very limited revival of Buddhism in Buryatia by allowing them to re-open two small monasteries there. The limited freedom kept the scope of Buddhism alive until the onset of the *Perestroika* period when actual religious freedom was allowed. Within the short period of 1988-1991, nineteen datsan were built in the Buryat republic. To study Buddhism, students were sent to Tibet and Mongolia. In the later phase, a school was opened in the Ivolginsky Datsan which, after a year of its establishment, was accorded the recognition of a state university for higher learning (Ibid: 64-66).

There were serious attempts to revive the Tantric tradition of

Buddhism in 1972-73 by a famous Buryat Buddhist known as Dandaron. The revival of the Tantric tradition began in Tibet in the eighth and ninth centuries and it was practised by only a small circle of people in Buryatia. The first attempt to revive this tradition was in the twentieth century and was led by the Buryat lama Samdan Tsydenov and the Tibetan Dzhayaksa Gegen. However, in that period, the official Buddhist institutions and the secular authorities were against this. Samdan Tsydenov was jailed thrice and he died in 1922. Then, his disciple tried to follow his path and he was found guilty of violating Article 247, part 1 and Article 147, part 3 of the Criminal Code of the RSFSR "for organizing a Buddhist sect". He was sentenced to five years of deprivation of freedom in a general regime corrective labour colony. He died under suspicious circumstances in 1974 (Zhukovskaia 2000: 30-31).

Another attempt towards revival was made by Agvan Dorzhiev and his activism was strongly manifested at the end of the nineteenth and first third of the twentieth century. His actions were unique and brought new ideas to the Russian soil, like the reform of Buddhism on a renewalist basis, the construction of Buddhist temple in St. Petersburg in 1910-15 and opening of several datsans in the east of the Lake Baikal region. He was also the one of the seven mentor-teachers of the Thirteenth Dalai Lama (Ibid: 32).

Post-Soviet Trend

The post-Soviet period witnessed a phase of intermixing of culture in general and for Buryatia in particular. Language, custom and tradition, inter-ethnic marriages, etc., played a vital role in the intermingling of different cultures. Apart from this, the Law "On Freedom of Religion" of RSFSR was adopted on 25 October 1990. This resulted in a dramatic change in the ethno-confessional condition of Buryatia. From mere eight religious organisations and associations in 1990, the number rose to 190 on 1 January 2007 (Buraeva 2011: 288-295).

The present Constitution of the Russian Federation, in chapter two, that is Rights and Freedoms of Man and Citizen in Article 28, clearly states that "Everyone shall be guaranteed the freedom of conscience, the freedom of religion, including the right to profess individuality or together with other any religion or to profess no religion at all, to freely choose, possess and disseminate religious and other views and act according to them" (The 1993 Constitution of the Russian Federation).

The post-Soviet period has also been the phase of 'cultural revivalism' as well as of the politicisation of religion. The social and political organisations aspired to bring the ethnic factors into politics. Various cultural as well as political organisations were established; for example, in 1990, the national cultural society was formed, and on the basis of this the Buryat Mongolian Peoples' Party was established. Similarly, in 1992, the national unity movement "Negedel" and in 1996 the Congress of the Buryat People were formed. The All Buryat Association for the Development of Culture was established in February 1991 with the focus on solving the problems of the cultural revival of the Buryats (Ibid: 290-291).

The post-Soviet cultural revivalism was also fostered by Yeltsin's move of granting enough sovereignty to the regions. In a way, Yeltsin's move became problematic for Russia as it fostered cultural revivalism in regions like Buryatia. By striking at the 'Pan- Mongolian' identity of the Buryats, the intellectuals of this school touched upon their Mongolian origin and gave them adequate reason to integrate. Pan-Mongolism was also used for political benefit, as an outcome in 1992 when a non-governmental political organisation "Negedel" was created that attempted to propagate secession of Buryatia from Russia. It tried to consolidate the Mongolian people and create a Central Asian confederation that would include Buryatia, Mongolia, Tyva, Kalmykia and two autonomous regions of China (Baldano 2011: 330-331).

Indian Connection

The religious and philosophical origin of Buddhism can be traced back to the mid sixth and mid fourth centuries BCE. It arose from the teachings of the Buddha who lived in north India. During this period, Buddhism spread to Central and South East Asia, China, Korea, and Japan and in the twentieth century it spread to the West.

After attaining enlightenment in 528 BC in Bodh Gaya, Buddha went to Sarnath (Varanasi) from where he formally began his teachings. He renounced the luxury of his palace in the search for ultimate truth and followed the extreme path of asceticism. Experiencing the two extremes of life from a monarchic existence to asceticism, he arrived at the conclusion that life exists in the middle. This means avoiding extremes and following the middle way. Buddha considers the middle way of moderation as the most conducive to search for the ultimate truth (Verdu 1995: 1).

So, any form of Buddhism being practised across the countries does have an Indian connection in general and Tantric Buddhism, which is widely practised among the Buryats, also has Indian roots in particular. Tantric Buddhism is basically characterised by an abundance of ritual practices and images and these ritual practices differentiate it from early Buddhism. In Sanskrit it is also known as *Vajrayana* and the concept travelled to Tibet in the ninth century (Child 2003: 58). Chanting of *mantras* and deity worship are common rituals of tantric Buddhism. Unlike other Buddhist traditions, in tantric Buddhism God is not worshipped as such but his existence is not denied. In tantric Buddhist traditions, God is not believed to be powerful enough to change human conditions. Everything is governed by the law of karma and this is illustrated by the descriptions of the forms into which beings can be re-born including as god. According to this tradition, a human enjoys a pleasurable state only till the merits of his good deeds exist (Ibid: 59-61).

Through pilgrimages to India, Tibetans learnt the Tantric tradition of Buddhism, and likewise the Buryats learnt the Tantric God tradition from pilgrimages to Tibet. Some of the zealous Buryat yogis came to Tibet and equipped themselves with *Vajrabhairava Tantra* and carried it to Buryatia. There is a famous story from oral tradition that in the nineteenth century, a Buryat yogi Nyamnaney who lived on the Alkhanai Mountain went to Lhasa to learn the secret teachings. After many ventures, he somehow settled near the Potala and managed to penetrate its library. There he found the most overwhelming explanation of *Vajrabhairava Tantra* written by the famous Lhundup Pandit. He learnt the 350 pages of the manuscript by heart and left Lhasa. The Tibetans chased in an attempt to capture him but he managed to cross the Russian border. Nyamnaney instructed the local peasants to bury him quickly and show the Tibetans his grave when they approached. He further instructed them to "dig me out when the Tibetans leave and sprinkle me with water, I will become alive"

(Terentyel 1996: 62-63). The peasants did as instructed and he was saved. The memorised text was engraved on wood and printed in the Aginsky Datsan. He also sent young Agwan Dorjiev (the future tutor to His Holiness the 13th Dalai Lama and most outstanding personality among Buryat lamas) to Mongolia and Tibet to study Buddhism (Ibid: 63).

Conclusion

Buddhism in Buryatia penetrated from Mongolia and Tibet and in particularly, the Tantric creed came from Tibet. The major impediment to Buddhism came from the Communist regime which brought about the actual destruction of the social, economic and cultural life with the announcement of the Collectivisation Programme in the 1920s-30s. However, the genuine revival began with the onset of the *Perestroika* which granted full religious freedom to various faiths.

There are instances when Buddhist identities were used to isolate Buryats from Russia by fostering the creation of a separate state during the Soviet period. In post-Soviet Russia, "Negedel", a non-governmental political organisation based on Pan-Mongolian identity, was blamed for attempting secession of Buryatia from Russia in 1992. So, these attempts are a reflection of the misuse of the Buddhist identity for political advantage. Though Buryat Buddhism does have Mongolic and Tibetan roots, , they however identify themselves separately. Thus, any outside penetration which attempts to seek political advantage should be restrained and the actual religious freedom granted under the Russian Constitution must be effectively implemented.

NOTES

1. Pan-Mongolian doctrine refers to the unification of Mongolia with Inner Mongolia, Buryatia, Kalmykia and Tyva Mongols which would led to the restoration of the historical region of Mongolian habitat and turn a new country into a truly independent and sovereign state (Baldano 2011: 327-328).

REFERENCES

Baldano, Marina N. (2011), "The Interaction of Ethnocultural and Ethnopolitical Processes in Russia during the 1990s", in Suchandana Chatterjee and Anita Sengupta (eds.) *Communities, Institutions and 'Transition' in Post- 1991 Eurasia*, New Delhi: Shipra Publication.

Buraeva, O.V. (2011), "Ethnic and Religious Identity in the Borderland of Cultures", in Suchandana Chatterjee and Anita Sengupta (eds.) *Communities, Institutions and 'Transition' in Post-1991 Eurasia*, New Delhi: Shipra Publication.

Child, Louise (2003), "Mantras and Spells: Durkheim and Mauss, Religious Speech and Tantric Buddhism", *Durkheimian Studies*, New Series, Vol. 9: 58-67.

Hamayon, Robert N. (1998), "Shamanism, Buddhism and Epic Heroism: Which Supports the Identity of the post-Soviet Buryats", *Central Asian Survey*, 17(1): 51-67.

Hurelbaatar, A. (2000), "An Introduction to the History and Religion of the Buryat Mongols of Shinehen in China", *Inner Asia*, 2(1): 73-116.

Krader, Lawrence (1954), "Buryat Religion and Society", *Southwestern Journal of Anthropology*, 10(3): 322-351.

Krader, Lawrence (1975), "The Shamanist Tradition of the Buryats (Siberia)", *Anthropos*, 70(1/2): 105-144.

Official Census of Russia (2010), "Official 2010 Census of the Russian Federation" 21(1), September, Russian Federation [Online: web] Accessed 21 January 2019, http://www.gks.ru/free_doc/new_site/perepis2010/croc/perepis_itogi1612.htm.

Terentyev, Andrey (1996), "Tibetan Buddhism in Russia", *The Tibet Journal*, 21(3): 60-70.

The Constitution of the Russian Federation (1993), "Chapter 2: Rights and Freedoms of Man and Citizen" 12(2), February, Russian Federation [Online web] Accessed 12 February 2019, http://www.constitution.ru/en/10003000-03.htm.

Verdu, Alfonso (1995), *"Early Buddhist Philosophy: In The Light Of Four Noble Truths"*, Delhi: Motilal Banarsidass Publishers Private Limited.

Zhukovskaia N.L. (2000), "The Revival of Buddhism in Buryatia: Problems and Prospects", *Anthropology and Archaeology of Eurasia*, 39(4): 23-47.

Index

*